D0407263

VICTORY FOR US IS TO SEE YOU SUFFER

VICTORY FOR US IS TO SEE YOU SUFFER

IN THE WEST BANK WITH THE PALESTINIANS AND THE ISRAELIS

PHILIP C. WINSLOW

BEACON PRESS
BOSTON

Beacon Press
25 Beacon Street
Boston, Massachusetts 02108-2892
www.beacon.org

Beacon Press books
are published under the auspices of
the Unitarian Universalist Association of Congregations.

Printed in the United States of America

10 09 08 07 8 7 6 5 4 3 2 1

This book is printed on acid-free paper that meets the uncoated paper ANSI/NISO specifications for permanence as revised in 1992.

Composition by Wilsted & Taylor Publishing Services

Library of Congress Cataloging-in-Publication Data

Winslow, Philip C.
Victory for us is to see you suffer : in the West Bank with the Palestinians and the Israelis / Philip C. Winslow.
p. cm.
Includes bibliographical references.
ISBN 978-0-8070-6906-6
1. West Bank—Social conditions—21st century. 2. West Bank—Politics and government—21st century. 3. Military occupation—Social aspects—West Bank. 4. Palestinian Arabs—West Bank—Social conditions—21st century. 5. Israelis—West Bank—Social conditions—21st century. 6. Jews—Colonization—Government policy—West Bank. 7. Arab-Israeli conflict 1993—Occupied territories. 8. West Bank—Ethnic relations. 9. United Nations Relief and Works Agency for Palestine Refugees in the Near East—Employees. I. Title.

DS110.W47W56 2007
956.95'3044—dc22 2007013411

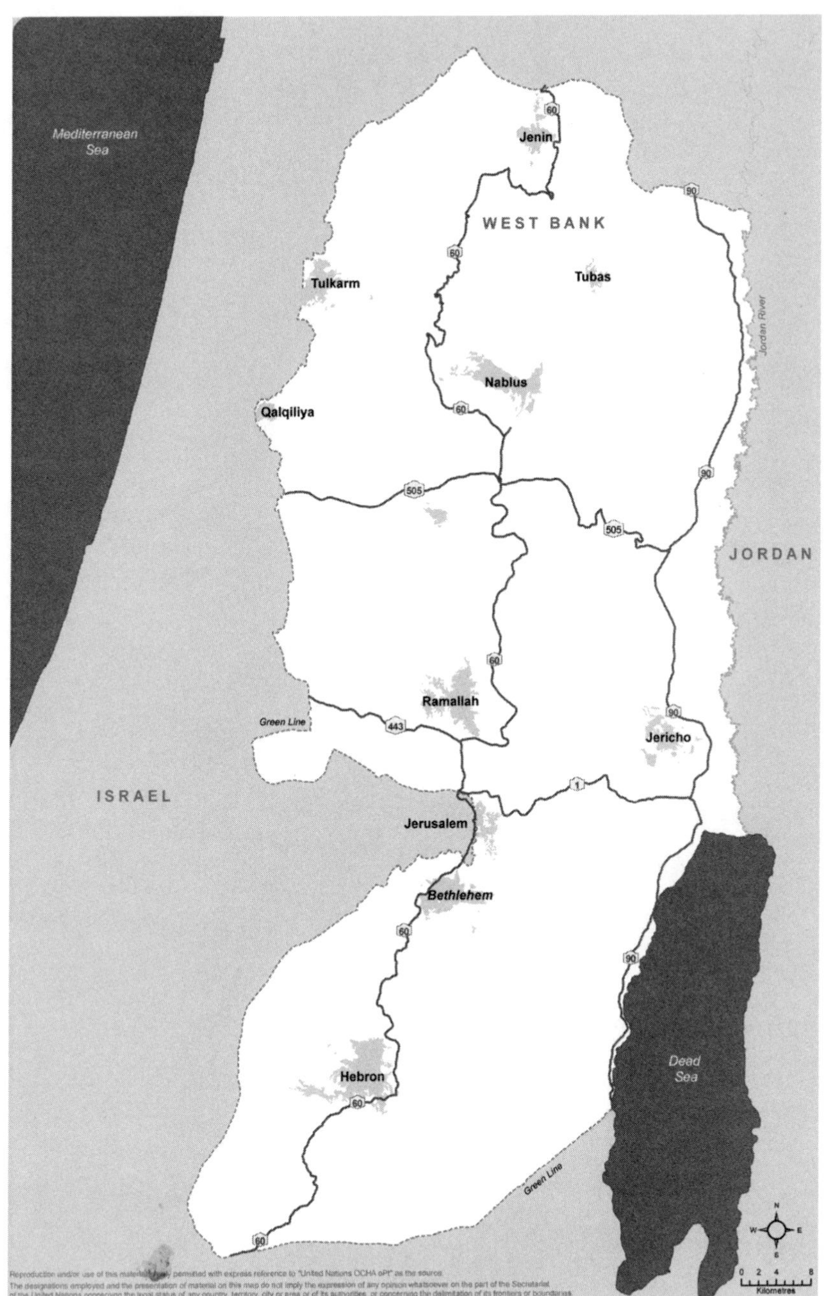

United Nations OCHA oPt

CONTENTS

INTRODUCTION

Some years ago, when reporting on the troubles in Northern Ireland, I was interviewing an Irish republican above a seedy bar in West Belfast. The man was describing in lurid detail the alleged torture of his grandfather by British security forces as though it had happened the week before. Something about people's ages and the time frame wasn't adding up. I asked him when the incident had occurred. "It was October 1916, so it was," he said. So it was and so it remains, the long memory and abiding sense of grievance in human conflicts.

More recently, I listened as a Palestinian in Jerusalem vented his anger over a letter that U.S. president George W. Bush wrote in April 2004 to then Israeli prime minister Ariel Sharon. The letter signaled tacit White House approval of "existing major population centers," Israel's controversial settlements in the West Bank, and Bush's view that a return to the 1949 armistice lines was unrealistic. "It's another Balfour Declaration!" the Palestinian raged, referring to British foreign secretary Arthur James Balfour's 1917 letter to Lord Rothschild declaring support for "the establishment in Palestine of a national home for the Jewish people." There certainly were similarities in the sentiments and intent of both documents.

The history of the Middle East is a long continuum, and to extract and view a segment it's helpful to understand something of what went before. Books and papers only about the struggle for Palestine could fill many library shelves. One could embark from a number of milestones, for instance the wave of Jewish migration to Palestine in the 1880s; that British declaration of favor in 1917; the increase in Zionist settlement in the 1920s and 1930s; or the 1936–39 Arab revolt against the immigrants and their British supporters during the turbulent chapter of the British Mandate.

Two dates that stand out in modern annals are the 1947 UN resolution for the partition of Palestine—accepted by the Jews and rejected by the Arabs—and the Arab-Israeli war and the creation of the state of Israel in 1948. For Jews, 1948 was the victory of the dream: a homeland and a state. It was achieved at the expense of Palestine's Arabs. For the Arabs, 1948 was the *Nakba*—the catastrophe—and the end of homeland. That year saw the wholesale loss of their land and the expulsion or flight of more than seven hundred thousand Arabs, who scattered as refugees. Today a Palestinian will display to visitors an iron key to an old stone home in Jerusalem or Jaffa, a yellowed property deed, or a vial of earth from a garden and will talk about a lemon tree as if it was still right outside the kitchen window. When a Palestinian, particularly an elderly one who lived through it, speaks the word *Nakba,* he does so with a sense of bottomless loss.

It's a complex and strenuously disputed history, but one in which the Palestinians consistently have emerged with less than they started. The Palestinians attribute that outcome entirely to Israel (and its principal ally, the United States), but they—and other Arab nations—also bear the blame for it, at least for the failure to recover significant parts of the land. Today the Palestinian territories—the West Bank and the Gaza Strip—comprise about 5,997 square kilometers (2,315 square miles). And they are not even contiguous. The West Bank, by far the bigger of the two territories, remains largely under Israel's direct military control, and Gaza is surrounded and tightly contained by Israel from both the sea and the land.

There are two more important notations on the political timeline. After Israel occupied the West Bank, the Gaza Strip, East Jerusalem, and the Golan Heights[1] following the stunning victory of the Six-Day War in 1967, Jews immediately began building settlements in the territories. The settlements expanded in number and population over the years, surging after Prime Minister Menachem Begin's Likud election victory in 1977. Several are now essentially small cities.

The post-1967 settlements in the Palestinian territories are regarded as illegal under international law. Israeli governments have dismissed that decision, claiming that the territories on which the settlements sit are, at most, "disputed" rather than "occupied." But the Jewish settlements, and Israel's control over the roads and lands that strategically connect them, have squeezed Palestinians into an awkward and shrinking patchwork in which normal life and travel are restricted and sometimes impossible.

The other historical occasion, and the one from which I begin this account, is the second Palestinian intifada, or uprising, which began in September 2000 after Ariel Sharon, then head of the Israeli opposition party, Likud, visited the large religious compound in Jerusalem's Old City known to Jews as Temple Mount and to Arabs as al-Haram al-Sharif. The compound was the site of the First and Second Jewish Temples, and today it houses the Islamic shrines of the Dome of the Rock and al-Aqsa Mosque. The site is a nucleus of faith to both peoples, as well as a hotly contested political symbol. Depending on which name you use in conversation, it can bring a sharp correction or an allegation of bias.

Although the news media always cite Sharon's visit as the start of the second intifada, that is not exactly accurate. Palestinians had long opposed the occupation, particularly during the first intifada, which began in Gaza in 1987 and lasted until 1992, and again afterward right until 2000. The two uprisings, with eight years between them, share some superficial similarities in the way they started and a single cause.

Sharon's provocative walkabout on September 28, 2000, detonated the unstable mixture of resentment and hopelessness Palestinians felt, fifty-two years after the *Nakba,* over the fact that Jewish occupation in the Palestinian territories was still expanding, and theirs decreasing. The optimism that the Oslo accords in 1995 generated had evaporated, and the promise of an independent Palestinian state was no closer. Tension had been brewing in the towns and refugee camps, particularly through 1999 and 2000, and required only a spark to ignite. The oversize Israeli politician, whose nickname was the Bulldozer, provided it. Whether by intent or due to insensitivity, Sharon, the old combat veteran and aggressive promoter of settlement, was adept at gestures that chafed Palestinian injuries over the unending occupation. Palestinians threw stones at Jews in Jerusalem the next day, and several were killed and wounded by police. Demonstrations and outrage spread like wildfire through the West Bank and Gaza Strip.

What followed was the second, or al-Aqsa, intifada, a years-long cycle of confrontations, repression, suicide bombs, assassinations, mass arrests, house demolitions, curfews and closures, and finally the building by Israel of a 703-kilometer (437-mile) wall and fence around and through the West Bank and East Jerusalem.

The precursor to all this was the 1987 uprising, triggered by a road accident in Gaza. Rumors about what lay behind the accident, in which four Palestinians were killed by an Israeli truck driver, took hold, and protests spontaneously flared up across Gaza and the West Bank. On the Palestinian side, the first intifada was more bare-knuckle disobedience and stone throwing than armed revolt, but its rapid spread across the territories took Israeli politicians by surprise. The army was ordered to use force at will and did so. Soldiers reportedly acting on instructions of Defense Minister Yitzhak Rabin broke protesters' bones with clubs, and video footage of the beatings flashed around the world.

Although hundreds were killed in those years, the human cost was eclipsed by the death toll and destruction of the second intifada. Between September 2000 and January 2007, more than five thousand Palestinians and Israelis died, and thousands more were wounded.[2] The majority of the casualties were Palestinian, and some Palestinians became homeless for the third time in their lives.

After years of unremitting bloodshed and extensive reporting by the international media, Israel unilaterally evacuated its settlements from the Gaza Strip and four more small ones in the northern West Bank in 2005. But the government continued to allow the enlargement of the major settlements in the West Bank, arguing—when queried under mild pressure from Washington—that the new construction was merely "thickening" the settlements to absorb natural growth.

Israelis worried about demographics, which were underscored by the high Palestinian birthrate, and politicians kept the trend in the public eye. If the uprising was not crushed and the territory permanently secured, they said, the majority-Jewish state itself would be at risk, with Jews eventually being outnumbered by Arabs.

Israelis may not have regarded the unilateral Gaza pullout and the wall or fence as a perfect solution, but they did see the moves as the beginning of a vital separation from the Palestinians, and "separation" was the word they used. The disengagement, however, did not bring peace; Palestinian suicide bombs and rocket attacks and Israeli incursions and assassinations continued to claim lives. Palestinians found their lives as marginal as before the intifada. Their daily movements—not only across the Green Line into Israel but between their own towns and on their own farmland—were as tightly controlled by Israeli security forces as before the 2005 pullout, and they were still losing land to the settlers. International peace plans and proposals hung in limbo, and the United States exerted no meaningful pressure on Israel.

In January 2006 the militant Islamist party Hamas swept to victory in Palestinian parliamentary elections, surprising most observers in Israel and in the West. Many Palestinians had hoped that Hamas, a movement that already had proved effective at delivering social services, mostly in Gaza, would be a new broom in the Palestinian political house, helping to sweep out corruption, and perhaps even the instrument for political stability within the Palestinian factions that Yasser Arafat's self-serving Fatah Party had not been.

The political earthquake, as everyone called it, brought additional turmoil. Within days of the election, Hamas, already on the West's list of terrorist organizations, came under intense pressure to recognize Israel's right to exist, forswear violence, and accept previous agreements. Both sides blundered. Hamas prime minister Ismail Haniyeh in Gaza—and Hamas political boss Khalid Meshaal, in exile in Damascus—had little room for maneuver; without the promise of reciprocal concessions from Israel, they would not meet the demand. But by responding with the usual inflammatory statements and standard pledge of indefinite armed resistance, Hamas missed an opportunity. Had the organization managed to break out of the ossified thinking of the old Palestinian national movement and boldly moved to recognize Israel, the equation might have changed. Such an extraordinary step (Arafat made one in 1988, after all) might have helped heal enmities with Fatah, brought the international community onboard, and even—eventually—brought Israel around. As it was, avenues to change stayed shut.

Hamas, and, more important the Palestinians of Gaza and the West Bank, got hammered hard. The United States, the European Union, and Israel tried to force the collapse of the government by imposing crippling sanctions on the Palestinian Authority (PA), making it impossible for the PA to pay the salaries of teachers, health workers, and other civil servants. The sanctions worsened poverty and exacerbated the internal political crisis. Hamas officials were reduced to trying to smuggle suitcases stuffed with millions of dollars in cash into Gaza from Egypt. Israel further tightened the screws, withholding hundreds of millions of dollars in tax receipts they collected for the Palestinians, jailing Hamas parliamentarians, and further restricting the movement of Palestinians in the West Bank.

The pressure was too much, and frustration and fury found another outlet. Fatah and Hamas leaders blamed each other for the fact that the "unity government" was broke and broken. The bitter power struggle—mainly over who controlled the well-armed security forces—escalated into gun battles on the streets of Gaza City and some West Bank towns. Palestine hovered on the edge of civil war. Desperate and depressed civilians, caught in the internecine violence, said things like this: A plague on Fatah *and* Hamas *and* the outside world. What about us, the people?

Beneath the destabilizing chaos of 2006 and 2007, however, fundamental facts had not changed. The years of the Palestinian intifada had been destructive but had not shaken off the Israeli occupation or stopped Jewish settlement in the West Bank and East Jerusalem. Nor had Israel's military response lessened Palestinians' insistence on their right to have an independent state. Many Israelis agreed with them, and thus there was a measure of common ground. For years opinion polls had shown—with variance in times of extreme violence—that a majority of Israelis and Palestinians wanted a peaceful two-state solution to this intractable conflict. Their voices were heard only faintly in the general hubbub.

Beneath it all, familiar rumblings continued. Extremist elements on both sides claimed title to the land between the Jordan River and the Mediterranean Sea. When the common and emotive phrase "between the river and the sea" was employed—by a Palestinian or an Israeli—its connotations were not those of a bucolic travel brochure but an indication that somebody was about to say "It's all ours."

■ ■ ■

One afternoon in April 2002 I walked into the emergency-room corridor of Government Hospital on the edge of the Jenin refugee camp in the northern West Bank and briefly wondered how things had gotten this bad.

Although the sights were familiar, they could still shock. Under sickly pale fluorescent lights that cast ghostly shadows on faces, Palestinians milled about in a long hallway greasy with a mixture of blood and general grime. They smoked cigarettes, wept, or just squatted, staring at nothing. Waiting, looking for someone, trying to process whatever they had just seen or learned. The institutional-green walls were also smeared with blood in places and at shoulder height were plastered with "martyr posters," photographs of young men—children, some of them—who had either blown themselves to pieces as suicide bombers or been killed by Israeli soldiers. The young men had been elevated by violent death to the status of *shahid*—martyr—and were revered in the camps.

The posters disturbed me, as usual. They were the indelible postscripts of the intifada that adorned walls everywhere in the West Bank and Gaza: boys puffing out scrawny adolescent chests in heroic poses against a background of al-Aqsa Mosque in Jerusalem. In these composite photos they held M-16 rifles or rocket-propelled grenade launchers and were draped with heavy bandoliers of ammunition. Actually, the posters were not indelible; over time, the portraits faded in the rain and wind of the camps until only tattered fragments remained. As the intifada dragged on, the scraps were replaced with new posters, cranked out by local print shops within hours of a killing and with the blessings of the families who had supplied the snapshots. I could never stomach this celebration of youthful violent death. To me, these kids should have been playing basketball and studying. But that's the way it was.

I can't remember now what took me to the Jenin hospital that day, but I was not keen to linger. The place stank of death and grief.

Through the height of the intifada, from October 2001 until the summer of 2004, I served as one of several West Bank field-operations officers (the official title was operations support officer) with the United Nations Relief and Works Agency for Palestine Refugees in the Near East (UNRWA), the agency that since 1950 has provided basic health and educational services and work programs for those Palestinians officially classified as refugees.

Palestinian suicide bombings were not a new phenomenon—they began long before this intifada—but as the uprising entered its second year, their frequency and scale of carnage were on the rise. The bombers, young Palestinians wearing shrapnel-packed explosive vests, were taking a horrific toll. Israeli teenagers, housewives, professional people, and off-duty soldiers were murdered in Jerusalem pizza parlors and Tel Aviv discos, at wedding and holiday parties, and on their way to work in green city buses.

Israel struck back with overwhelming force, using everything from undercover hit squads to infantry, armored, airborne, and naval units. The Israel Defense Forces (IDF) launched punishing forays into Palestinian areas, pounding densely packed towns and refugee camps with cannon fire, missiles, and aerial bombs and conducting "targeted killings" —the assassination of suspected militants. Palestinian orchards and agricultural lands were dug up (they provided cover for fighters, the IDF said), particularly in the Gaza Strip, and olive groves were damaged by settlers while the army watched passively. Palestinians, including noncombatants, were killed intentionally and by accident, wounded, or hauled off to jail, where they were sometimes kept indefinitely without charge or trial. Large numbers of Palestinians were collectively subjected to long periods of military quarantine in their villages and homes.

The night after I arrived in Jerusalem, Israel's extreme right-wing tourism minister, Rehavam Ze'evi, was shot dead by Palestinian gunmen in a Jerusalem hotel just up the road from the hotel in which I was staying. The army quickly assaulted and occupied six Palestinian towns and their refugee camps and curtailed the movement of Palestinians across the West Bank.

After a while it seemed irrelevant who had started it. They fought each other with a ferocity and retribution that seemed biblical. Israelis lived in fear and defiance as they waited for the next gruesome attack. Once-lovely Palestinian towns began to disintegrate under the punishment of modern weaponry. Gunfire, bombs, and funerals became a daily occurrence.

For thirty months I lived in Arab East Jerusalem and worked in the West Bank, driving up to one thousand kilometers (more than six hundred miles) a week between almost every Palestinian town, village, and refugee camp and every Israeli checkpoint from dusty Ramadin in the south to battle-scarred Jenin in the north. I and my colleagues worked daily to facilitate the movement of humanitarian aid through hundreds of Israeli checkpoints in the West Bank and the Gaza Strip.

Since I worked in the West Bank, I mention the perilous situation in the Gaza Strip only peripherally; UNRWA operations in Gaza were covered by a separate staff. I do not mean to slight the dire predicament and suffering of Gazans; it's just that I wasn't there. And although I use the personal pronoun, "I" does not always indicate that I functioned alone. My UNRWA colleagues and the officials of many other UN agencies and nongovernmental organizations performed similar functions in a broad international humanitarian effort in the occupied Palestinian territories. In the difficult winter and spring of 2002, many Jerusalem and Gaza UN office staff and other professionals volunteered their time and put themselves in harm's way to work alongside us in the West Bank. The events I describe are by no means a complete historical record of those years and represent only my cross section of a bigger picture.

Usually working in two-person teams—an international staff member with a Palestinian assistant—we negotiated with the Israeli army and the paramilitary Border Police to deliver aid to towns and refugee camps under military closure and during military operations. I led convoys and assessed security and checkpoint conditions, and I spent many hours trying to win the release of Palestinian UN staff members or the passage of emergency medical workers or food-distribution teams. Although there were many dramatic and dangerous days, sometimes the job was as simple as trying to cross a checkpoint in the course of a routine patrol. I brokered local cease-fires, on the fly and alone or with the assistance of UNRWA operations staff in Jerusalem. At various times I and others helped evacuate civilians caught in the fighting, delivered food and medicines to Palestinian families whose houses had been taken over by the Israeli army, and took Palestinians to hospitals. I conducted investigations into the death, wounding, and detention of UN staff members, incidents of damage to UN schools, health clinics, and offices, and the demolition of refugees' homes by the IDF; I also wrote reports on deteriorating economic conditions.

When the going got tough, the Israeli security forces were single-minded in disregarding the long-standing bilateral agreements that granted us freedom of movement. Many soldiers and most of the harder-line Border Police regarded UNRWA officials as the fellow travelers of suicide bombers. "So why are you feeding the terrorists?" was a common sneering query at a military checkpoint.

UNRWA also serves refugees in Gaza, Lebanon, Jordan, and Syria, and 99 percent of its employees are Palestinians. After more than half a century, the UN agency has become part of the regional furniture and was seen by many Israeli soldiers as purely Palestinian, rather than international. Some said they had no idea what our mandate was or professed not to know that UNRWA's humanitarian operations had the full agreement of their government.

Palestinians often didn't seem to like us any better than the Israelis did; they would grumble that we were foreign dilettantes who did nothing to improve their long-term situation: that is, end the occupation. The last part of that assessment was accurate; UNRWA's mandate was humanitarian and not political, and that's what we did.

In conversation, Palestinians and Israelis frequently referred to each other as "cousins." The reference could be sardonic, or it could be said with a laugh and a nod toward a grudging respect, or at least an acknowledgment that they were stuck with each other. Semitic peoples who have much in common despite different religions and cultures, Israelis and

Palestinians may not like each other, but they certainly understood—or thought they understood—some basics. Many were willing, if only the killing and seizure of land would stop, to work out a modus vivendi. But there was little evidence of that during my time there, nor much in the way of goodwill. Compromise was not in the vocabulary. The all-around sourness was not hard to comprehend, considering the daily battering of reciprocal violence and iron-fisted military control.

The sourness was compounded by growing isolation and occasional twinges of nostalgia. After all, Israelis used to shop for bargains in Qalqilya and Jenin, and thousands of Palestinians crossed the Green Line daily to work in Israel. Israel got the better of that arrangement with cheap labor, but Palestinians got a steady wage. A shaky coexistence had worked as an interim measure within the occupation. Now the Palestinians and Israelis were alone in their fight.

Sharon's 2001 election-campaign promise to bring "peace and security"—a well-worn phrase in Israeli politics—had brought the opposite. Israeli civilians, as well as soldiers and the armed settlers, were daily targets. For ordinary Palestinians, the intifada brought great daily suffering and precipitated the collapse of their economy, which was already on international life support as a result of corruption, cronyism, and malfeasance by the governing Palestinian Authority.

Six years after it began, the intifada had largely sputtered out, and so had the shaky peace process. The "road map" was still on the books as the official replacement for the failed Oslo accords, but the international political plan was producing no results. The once-robust Israeli peace movement was weakened, and international sympathy for the Palestinians vanished with the grisly suicide bombings. In a way, every Palestinian suicide attack in Jerusalem or Hadera was a gift to Sharon's governing Likud coalition: condemnation of Israel's disproportionate punishment was drowned out by outrage over Palestinian terrorism. Anyway, the Bush administration was largely hands-off except for military aid to Israel, financial aid to the Palestinians, and the tepid mantra about the "road map."

Such notions were distant from daily reality in the West Bank. For every IDF soldier who regarded himself as a moral person and felt bad for making a Palestinian woman and her children stand in the pelting rain at a checkpoint, another would see Palestinians as subhuman objects of hatred. For these, the hatred had been taught at home or in the army, and it ran deep. In a sleet storm one morning at an army checkpoint near Biddu, west of Jerusalem, a mixed group of people were equally cold, wet, and miserable: a dozen women teachers who were trying to get to their UNRWA school; the soldiers who had closed the checkpoint; and my assistant and I, who had been dispatched to try to sort it out. As a bit of an icebreaker, so to speak, someone produced cups of steaming sweet tea from one of the hardy Palestinian vendors who set up roadside stands near all such bottlenecks. *Great idea,* I thought; *hot tea all around, and maybe the negotiations will bear some fruit, and the shivering teachers can get to work, and we can get back in our heated jeep.* It was cold enough that the young, red-bearded checkpoint commander could barely grip his M-16 rifle. But when a plastic cup of tea was proffered, he glared at me and everyone else and growled: "I don't take tea from Arabs!" Negotiations—*sans* tea—remained deadlocked for another hour, until everybody had been sufficiently punished. It was a typical morning. There were many more such, and worse.

Yet, in this complicated land that so frequently provides refracted images of itself, there were acts of kindness that surprised me. Soldiers occasionally would disobey orders from senior officers in order to help a Palestinian. On more than one occasion, a soldier walked up to my jeep and said something like, "I want to let these old people through. Will you drive them across the checkpoint and to wherever they are going?"

Big deal, one might say. The elderly, the mentally handicapped, and small schoolgirls are forced to wait in the rain or turn back at a checkpoint, family homes are blown up, and Palestinians are jailed by the thousands, and I'm pleased by an isolated gesture? And yet through many months when no progress was measurable, I was glad for small acts of humanity, even when the gate slammed shut again. Like it or not, and despite what UN resolutions and the Geneva Conventions said, Israel for now occupied and controlled the Palestinian territories without fear of sanction. On-the-spot negotiations and reminders to the soldiers about international humanitarian law frequently succeeded. But I always hoped for some extra humanity, simple heroics on the personal level, to show up in a difficult and inequitable situation. When it did happen, I figured it must have leaked out of a reservoir that held more, which would prevail *ba'adain,* that useful Arabic word for "later," or "sometime in the future."

There were times when I thought that this conflict, which urgently required innovative diplomatic pressure and serious political concessions, would never end. But I remember thinking in the former Yugoslavia that Serbs, Croats, and Muslims would fight one another tooth and nail until only one of them was left standing, and, later, I thought much the same thing about warring forces in Angola.

Individual Israelis and Palestinians provided plenty of reasons for hope. There were the "refuseniks," the hundreds of Israeli soldiers, including officers and combat veterans, who refused to serve in the territories and went to prison or were ostracized for their refusal. In Israeli society army service is mandatory and deeply ingrained as honor and duty. It takes a powerful conscience to buck that, and many have mustered it proudly as far back as Israel's invasion of Lebanon in 1982. Former soldiers, whom I met two years after I left the UN, broke the IDF code of silence and spoke out publicly and forthrightly about what they and their units had done in the occupied territories.

When it comes to heroics, the Palestinians can be hard to beat. I repeatedly witnessed nurses, physiotherapists, doctors, social workers, ambulance drivers, and teachers refuse to leave an area under heavy fire; they simply ignored IDF threats and gunfire until the wounded or the students had been brought to safety. Warehouse workers, cargo handlers, and truck drivers insisted on delivering bread and medicines to the refugee camps under curfew as tanks shelled the places. Some of these low-paid workers were severely beaten by soldiers at checkpoints but carried on anyway.

In the same category I include Palestinians who simply got up and went to work every day. They stood at checkpoints for hours in wet clothing as they tried to get through to tend their crops or visit someone who lived on the wrong side of a barrier. Men were punched, kicked, and humiliated in front of their wives and children and often turned away. They persevered as the economy fell apart and family poverty deepened. No one will ever give them a medal.

▪ ▪ ▪

This is not a political book. It deals mainly with what I saw and was told by the Palestinians and Israeli soldiers with whom I spent my time. Mostly, it paints pictures of what armed conflict does to humanity, a fragile condition in the best of circumstances. Some readers may find the book unbalanced. The nature of the Palestinian-Israeli conflict is so disputatious that no personal observation or analysis is likely to go unchallenged. I try to show what happened to both peoples, how they acted and felt. However, I worked for an international agency tasked with aiding Palestine refugees, so most of my time was spent on the Palestinian side of the lines.

I saw plenty of suffering on that side, and I saw young Israelis in uniform doing things that were not only illegal but made no sense in terms of providing security and protecting the Israeli public. And I saw that some (but not all) of these soldiers were clearly uncomfortable with what they were doing and were becoming brutalized by their power over another people. More than one Israeli soldier on active duty told me plainly that he knew it was wrong and "I'm not like that."

I was curious about many things that I was unable to explore at the time: what made Palestinians tick and what the soldiers really thought, as well as whether there really was any common ground. To find out, I returned to Israel and the West Bank in the summer and fall of 2006 and spent a lot of time listening. I have omitted or changed the names of some people, on both sides, because they asked me to.

During my days of working with UNRWA, uncertainty about what lay around the next bend in the road and the high probability of violence were almost daily fare. Several UN staff members were killed during my tour, including Iain Hook, the fifty-four-year-old British manager of the Jenin refugee camp reconstruction project, who was shot dead inside a UN compound by an IDF sniper on a chaotic day in November 2002. There were days when others of us came close; many evenings, as I scraped the mud off my boots and tried to order my thoughts, I figured that my assistant and I had been lucky to have survived that day in Tulkarm, Jenin, Qalqilya, or Nablus.

But I could go home to a safe neighborhood at night. For the Palestinians and the Israelis there was less respite, and the way forward looked bleak.

That's the way it was. Sometimes things worked out all right, and the violence tailed off for a few days or even a week or two. The soldiers relaxed and allowed the Palestinians to travel between their own towns. On those days we got our convoys through and had a good hummus and falafel lunch.

Despite the widespread suffering of civilians and the intractability of the conflict, it was a rewarding and interesting place to have spent nearly three years. Occasionally people were nice to each other, and the almond trees always bloomed in the spring.

ONE
"GOD GAVE IT TO US"

At times the whole conflict seemed to boil down to this one case of attempted murder.

Driving through the hill country west of Nablus on a clear October day, in my first week on the job, we came up behind a yellow Mercedes Palestinian taxi with three female passengers in the back seat. A passenger car was approaching from the opposite direction.

As the oncoming car got closer, a hand reached out the driver's side window, fingers curled around a rock the size of a grapefruit. In one fluid movement the arm hauled back and fired, and the rock, seemingly in slow motion, crashed through the windshield of the taxi. The settler's arm withdrew into the car. As our vehicles flashed past each other, his bearded heavy face was a frozen snarl, lips pulled back over his teeth. He was gone in an instant.

The settler's aim and judgment of trajectory and combined vehicle speeds had been precise. The rock punched through the left center of the windshield and struck the driver squarely in the forehead. Amazingly, he managed to stop without plunging off the side of the hill. We slithered around and pulled up front of him. We were alone on a remote stretch of road. The Palestinian women, wearing fancy clothes and gold jewelry for the wedding they were about to attend, got out of the back seat. One wore a long green dress. My two colleagues quickly bandaged the head wound of the driver, who was now unconscious and lying on his back on the cold pavement, while I got on the radio.

A Palestinian ambulance was summoned, and eventually IDF and

Israeli police jeeps pulled up. The soldiers gave the situation a cursory glance and drove off, and the police officer unenthusiastically took my report, brushing off details of the attack. "I'm the one doing the investigation," he said. He drove away, an ambulance arrived, and we left. The freeze-frames hovered in front of me: the settler's outstretched arm, the rock leaving his hand, his contorted angry face, the taxi driver's blood-spattered shirt. And the finely dressed women in their gold earrings and bracelets standing on the lonely road, waiting for another taxi to pass.

The incident didn't make the newspapers. Soldiers across the West Bank were hunting for the assassins of Israel's tourism minister, and the country was in an uproar about other murderous attacks that month. In one, Hamas gunmen armed with rifles and grenades infiltrated a small Jewish settlement in the Gaza strip, killing 2 teenagers and wounding 14. Two days later, a Palestinian disguised as an Israeli soldier killed 2 and wounded 10 in the bus station in Afula, Israel. In response to the upsurge in such attacks, particularly the murder of a cabinet minister, IDF armored and infantry units had invaded several West Bank towns.

Settlers in the West Bank and Gaza were fearful and furious, and some took revenge on the open roads or wherever they could get at Palestinians. As far as the security forces were concerned, attacks like the one on the taxi driver counted as minor traffic accidents. Over the next thirty months I would have several encounters with West Bank settlers, some of them involving firearms or threats, some benign; but the images of the assault on the taxi driver and his passengers remained among the most disturbing.

The settlements have been the core issue of the conflict between Israel and the Palestinians since 1967. The UN and human rights groups keep track of the violent clashes and various other incidents involving settlers, but the attacks, whether by Israelis or Palestinians, are more than statistics on a spreadsheet. Stripped of politics, the blood on the pavement and the agony of destroyed families look much the same.

According to Peace Now, the Israeli advocacy and monitoring group, about 268,000 settlers live in 121 settlements in the West Bank, about double the number of a decade ago. Another 190,000 live in East Jerusalem, and 16,000 more in the Golan Heights. Peace Now says that through 2006 the population of the settlements was growing by more than 5 percent a year.[1]

And in a highly publicized November 2006 report, the group cited leaked government documents revealing that about one-third of the settlements' land area in the West Bank is privately owned by Palestinians; the report buttressed Palestinians' claims that Israel has simply seized their land for the settlements. (The government has maintained that only state land is used, or when Palestinian land is taken it is done so legally.)[2]

The settler movement and its relationship with Zionism go back to long before Israel was founded as a modern nation and has more twists and turns than a back-country West Bank road. It has been the subject of numerous books and interminable public debate. Since 1948 the settler enterprise has been a major tool—or obstacle, depending on one's view—for Israel's kaleidoscope of political parties: Likud, Labor, Herut, the National Religious Party, and others.

But for all the heated discussion among Jewish Israelis about the settlement enterprise, there are a few uncomfortable facts: a majority of Israeli citizens historically have supported settlement, as have their elected governments and the IDF, which is mandated to protect the settlers and has even encouraged them. A minority of Israelis, secular, left-wing, and vocal, have antisettlement convictions going back to 1967; they believe Israel should withdraw to the June 1967 borders, with some adjustments.

On the settlement spectrum, the basics of today's tangled debate go like this: Jewish settlement of biblical Israel is the foundation of Zionism, and the views about it range from secular to religious to ultrareligious. At one end of the scale are Israelis and many immigrants who may be more attracted by cheap or subsidized housing than by religious zeal. In the middle are secular, pragmatic Israelis who say they are Zionists and who believe in some settlement but maintain that Jews cannot hold all the land. It will have to be shared with Palestinians, they say, because that is the moral thing to do and because it is the only way to maintain a secure and internationally accepted Jewish state. At the other end of the spectrum are ultrareligious Jews, fundamentalist settler movements and powerful rabbis who hold that Jews are not only entitled but duty-bound to settle the Land of Israel, meaning all of it.

Two historians, the late Israel Shahak, an Israeli, and Norton Mezvinsky, an American, argue in their book *Jewish Fundamentalism in Israel* that Jewish messianic ideology in Israel poses a much underestimated danger, not only to Palestinians and other non-Jews but to a democratic Israeli state. The historians write that the subject, while widely discussed in the Israeli Hebrew press, goes virtually unreported and therefore is little understood outside Israel.

In addition, they write, even those who oppose the settlements are reluctant to be seen criticizing Jewish fundamentalism for fear of being accused of anti-Semitism. "The religious settlements should be viewed from three standpoints: their standing as citadels of messianic ideology, their present and potential influence upon Israeli society and their potential role as the nuclei of the new society that messianic leaders want to build," Shahak and Mezvinsky write.[3] And when it comes to the impact on the Palestinians, "It is insufficient, if not folly, to advocate Palestinian rights without understanding and referring to the principal cause of the denial of those rights: Jewish fundamentalism in general and the messianic variety in particular."[4]

One group has a long history in radical settlement activism. As a religious-political movement, Gush Emunim, or Bloc of the Faithful, has been, since 1967, the most aggressive and politically influential group of religious settlers. It has built and expanded Jewish settlements across the occupied territories both by creating "facts on the ground," in the old Israeli phrase, and by pressuring successive Israeli governments and the IDF—reportedly from within—to support and protect the settlements.

Despite its influence, there have been plenty of clashes between the settlement movement and the state, particularly when it came to giving up land for peace. When soldiers struggled, both physically and in their hearts, to drag Jewish settlers from their homes in Gaza in 2005, they were doused with paint and urine by men and women who wept and cursed their former protectors as traitors.

The phenomenon of protest against a government-ordered evacuation was not new. Gershom Gorenberg, an American Israeli who lives in Jerusalem, described in his book *The Accidental Empire: Israel and the Birth of the Settlements, 1967–1977* the final scene of Prime Minister Menachem Begin's evacuation of settlers from the Sinai in April 1982. The settlers had already accepted financial compensation and left, but Gush Emunim protesters invaded Yamit, a settlement just inside northern Sinai. As another generation of Israeli soldiers would do with settlers twenty-three years later in Gaza, soldiers dragged the Gush Emunim radicals from Sinai rooftops. The group's leaders might have gone further in their resistance against the government if another bolt of providence had not intervened.

> Prominent Gush Emunim activists had planned to stop the pullout [from Sinai] by far more extreme means: blowing up the Dome of the Rock, the Islamic shrine at the center of the Temple Mount in Jerusalem. Yehudah Etzion, the founder of Ofrah [a settlement north of Jerusalem], was a leader of the conspiracy. The withdrawal, he believed, was a sign that God was again chastising Israel for not pursuing redemption. Only the fact that the group's bomb expert came down with hepatitis just before the withdrawal scuttled the plan.[5]

Yet the majority of Jewish Israelis, even settlers, are by no means locked in ancient biblical thought; nor do most believe it is acceptable to murder innocent Palestinians or blow up mosques. Tolerant Israelis—most are secular, but some are religious—believe that the settlement enterprise is eating Israel alive from the inside like a cancer and contributing to regional instability.

The settlements often begin with isolated hilltop outposts (new ones are now illegal under Israeli law) where settlers plant a handful of caravans as connecting points between existing settlements and anchors for future ones. The seizure of the hilltops—once specifically advocated by Ariel Sharon—or other strategic locations is also meant to interrupt whatever contiguity exists between Palestinian lands. Outposts are often settled by ultraradical "hilltop youth" who tangle violently with police when the government responds to one of the periodic cycles of international pressure to curb the settlements.

Although the government occasionally dismantles an illegal outpost, I tended to view these exercises as something of a conjuring trick for international consumption. Hauling away a busload of defiant hilltop youth and flattening a few makeshift sheds is not the same as evacuating an established settlement. Besides, many of the outposts are rebuilt again. But it makes a good splash for the cameras. Television viewers in the United States are generally spared the distinction between an outpost and a settlement and are hardly ever shown the broader context. Some outposts, of course, have put down roots that stayed, which really was the settlers' intent if they could get away with it. The indefatigable tenacity and ingenuity of the religious settlers can be quite astonishing.

On the other end of the scale are the huge established settlement blocs such as Ariel, between Jerusalem and Nablus; Gush Etzion, in the Hebron hills near Bethlehem; Beitar Illit, west of Bethlehem; and Ma'ale Adumim, east of Jerusalem. With a population of thirty thousand, Ma'ale Adumim is the largest settlement in the West Bank and a city on its own. These blocs come complete with shopping centers, schools, sports facilities, and heavily guarded perimeters and entry points.

The cost of the settlements to Israeli taxpayers is either classified or unknown because their funding has been buried in various ministries or departments and is never discussed by the government. But after more than thirty years of encouraging settlement growth with generous financial incentives, grants, tax breaks, and construction, the government outlay is staggering. Peace Now figured that the cost to taxpayers is at least $556 million a year.[6] In 2002 one Israeli legislator estimated that since 1967 the country had spent $11 billion building the settlement infrastructure in the West Bank and Gaza Strip.[7] Critics say that financing the settlements has had a measurably deleterious effect on the economy by reducing funding available for social programs and education.

The settlements are everywhere, and their strategic importance is plain to any traveler in the West Bank. Drive on nearly any road from the Jordan Valley west across the mountain ridges to the Green Line, and from Jenin all the way south through Jerusalem and past the vineyards of Hebron, and keep an eye on the hilltops: most are sprinkled with caravans or huddles of neat frame homes with red tile roofs. The big blocs are impossible to miss and look like the cities they have become.

Whether settlers move there out of religious conviction, attraction to affordable housing, or a combination of both, few have an existence that could be called completely secure. Many homes in the smaller settlements have no windows on the side facing roads, and for good reason. Palestinian militants carry out what amount to suicide missions to attack the heavily armed communities with rifles or, if they can get close enough, with hand grenades. Many settlers have been killed in their beds or in ambushes on the roads. In response, Israeli security forces mount massive operations, in a much-repeated cycle of destruction and death.

The settlements consume considerable military resources, as they must be guarded and patrolled around the clock. The intensive military requirement has divided opinion within the army. Religious soldiers, or settler soldiers, regard guarding the settlements as obligatory. Others resent it. One officer in the reserves who refused to serve any longer in the Palestinian territories referred to the settlers as a "violent, unbridled cult."[8] Soldiers on active duty told me they hated having to defend the settlers and saw them as overprivileged and even as thugs or criminals. They say that guarding a quarter of a million settlers takes them away from their real duty of defending Israel from outside attack and dilutes the strength of the army. Civilians who oppose the settlements worry that they threaten national stability. As one journalist wrote, the return and settling of the Jewish homeland of Judea and Samaria, as Israelis call the West Bank, has become "a catastrophic parody."[9]

Although settlement growth can be viewed as an intersection of religious and secular forces, Israeli politics, some of it cynical and manipulative, has operated both openly and secretly behind the movement for decades. The persistent turmoil in Israel over covert government funding for the outposts, along with a nudge from Washington, forced then–prime minister Sharon to appoint a former government lawyer,

Talia Sasson, to investigate. Sasson's March 2005 report was a blistering criticism of the whole enterprise and could not have made comfortable reading for some government officials. Outposts, she wrote, had in some cases been illegally built on private Palestinian land with the knowledge of government ministries. Officials in some of those ministries offered Sasson less than full cooperation in her investigation, even though it had been ordered by the prime minister.

The outposts, Sasson concluded, had received

> massive financing by the State of Israel, with no appropriate transparency, no criteria. The establishment of unauthorized outposts violates standard procedure, good governing rules, and especially [amounts to] an ongoing bold law violation. Furthermore, the State authorities speak [with] two voices. Sometimes [they] grant, and sometimes [they] prevent. Rules have become flexible. One hand builds outposts, the other invests money and force to evacuate them. These actions were not done by individuals only. The problem is [that] . . . State authorities and public authorities broke the laws, regulations and rules made by the State. . . . The State of Israel is a democratic state. This is what the Declaration of Independence and the Basic Laws teach us. This is the glue that sticks all of its citizens together, allows them to live together in one political entity. Democracy and the rule of law are two inseparables. One cannot exist without the other. The reality drawn up in this opinion shows that all of these deeds seriously endanger the principal [*sic*] of the rule of law.[10]

Sasson recommended that the government take "urgent measures" to change the situation. But nearly two years later little had changed. There was much to-ing and fro-ing among cabinet ministers over whether the 102 illegal outposts in the West Bank would be dismantled and their two thousand settlers relocated. Earlier undertakings by Prime Minister Ehud Olmert to evacuate more settlements in the West Bank were put on indefinite hold after the Lebanon war in the summer of 2006. The settlement enterprise remained what it had been for decades—an unstable fault line under the democratic Jewish state and under prospects for reaching a just peace with the Palestinians.

...

Driving through the Golan Heights on a brief holiday, my partner, Zeina Mogharbel-Vallès, and I were intrigued by a notation on the map that read "paleo-magnetism," indicating a site not far from the Syrian border. In a howling gale on top of a hill, we experimented with a compass near some rocks, and the needle duly swung around, demonstrating a reversal in the earth's polarity.

A car pulled up, and a man, woman, and two teenage girls got out and joined us. The man, a tall, rangy, and relaxed Israeli who turned out to be a high school physics teacher, took out a collection of compasses and other instruments and began experimenting and explaining the natural phenomenon to his daughters. We were soon caught up in the discussion. He was a good explainer.

The discussion turned to other matters. He was a former paratrooper with combat service behind him, and they lived in a settlement between some Palestinian villages west of Jerusalem. The daughters were like teenage girls anywhere: curious, easygoing, animated, and, once they got talking, disinclined to stop. They were a lovely, engaging family.

The eldest girl, at eighteen, was in the army. When she said so, a security concern popped up like a red light. In Hebrew, her father cautioned her not to reveal where she was stationed. Continuing in English, she said she would do her service but not make the army a career because her overall duty as a religious woman was to have children and be with them.

Unlike many settlers, they were not put off by the fact that we worked for a UN agency helping Palestinians. After I pretended I understood paleomagnetism, the girls enthusiastically invited us to visit them in the settlement. "You must come and have dinner with us. Will you?" they asked. Their father, a gracious man, agreed with a trace of reluctance, or maybe it was just decorum activated by his daughters' keenness to befriend perfect strangers. He gave us their phone number.

The girls thought that my partner's half-Spanish family name derived from an old Jewish name, and they urged her to contact a Jewish heritage agency to research it. One girl volunteered to go with her.

Then, with a glance at the fading light and the coming snow, the parents apologized that they had to leave; it was Friday afternoon, and they had only an hour of daylight before the start of Shabbat.

As we headed for the cars, we commented on the beauty of the Golan Heights.

"Yes, it is lovely," the elder daughter replied with a smile that would have melted ice. "God gave it to us."

The compass needle spinning around near the ancient rocks felt an apt metaphor. Reality depended where you stood and who you talked to.

TWO
CHECKPOINT

If you were a Palestinian at a checkpoint, it didn't make much difference where you stood, and you were usually talking to the same person. One who looked the same, anyway, in battle dress and behind a weapon. It usually meant that you weren't going anywhere anytime soon.

During curfews or closures or when the IDF declared an area a closed military zone, there was no knowing how long you'd wait. It depended on the soldiers' orders, their personal antagonism, or their frustration at doing an impossible job. How long the Palestinians waited could depend on how long their patience or inner rage held or on something going badly wrong, either at this checkpoint or a hundred kilometers away; they had no say in the matter. Checkpoints are as much a part of West Bank life and landscape as the olive trees. If a Palestinian had a dollar for every hour spent waiting to cross a checkpoint, he would be able to pay the family grocery bill for months.

In practice, Palestinians who worked for UNRWA and other UN agencies were subject to the same IDF-imposed movement restrictions; a UN ID card did not ensure special consideration. As international UN officers, we frequently were sent to help Palestinian UN staff members stuck at the checkpoints and drive them across. Having an international driver did not guarantee a speedy crossing, but it often helped.

Depending on the level of security, which fluctuated with the violence in the region, Palestinian office workers, teachers, and health professionals lost many weeks of work when they were forbidden to cross West Bank checkpoints or were turned back at entrances to Jerusalem. The regular denial of access interrupted and slowed the delivery of humanitarian aid and the quality of education and health care.

Just after sunup one day, when all checkpoints were tight, I drove from Jerusalem to Ramallah to pick up an administrative secretary so that she could get to work on time. On the way back, Qalandiya checkpoint, the main crossing between Ramallah and Jerusalem, had been closed to all traffic, so I decided to leave Ramallah through a checkpoint known as Military Court near the Beit Il army base.

As we cleared the barrier, I noticed a Palestinian woman in her late thirties wearing a white *hijab* and the standard long brown overcoat having an animated conversation with a soldier, who would not let her pass. She was unlucky enough to live behind Military Court and was trying to get home. As her tirade gathered steam, I stopped nearby. My passenger rolled down the window to listen.

The woman was eyeball to eyeball with the soldier, a handsome man in his early twenties. She was shaking her index finger in his face and shouting in Arabic. The soldier held his rifle loosely, pointed at the ground. He looked at her and listened. And kept listening.

The secretary and I were transfixed, she because she understood what the other woman was saying and I by the controlled display of rage and the realization that this could get worse. I had never seen anyone simultaneously so enraged and focused. Her anger built until she resembled a Roman candle, and her words popped out in small explosions. Her eyes never left his, and her finger wagged back and forth in front of his nose. I didn't understand Arabic, but every syllable was clear and fierce.

The soldier was not overtly hostile or abusive, and seemed relaxed. "You cannot go. The checkpoint is closed," he said with a shrug. The woman spun on her heel and went back the way she had come, throwing one final burst over her shoulder as the soldier walked back to his protective concrete blocks.

My passenger had gone pale. "What did she say?" I asked as we drove off. The secretary, a demure woman and a veteran daily crosser of checkpoints herself, replied in a whisper: "She used very, very bad language." I wished I could have gone back to hear what the soldier had to say.

This incident, one of hundreds of confrontations in the West Bank on any given day, ended unhappily enough, with a woman forced to take yet another detour to reach her home. Many ended worse, with death, injury, or arrest, when the dam holding back the resentment or hatred—a Palestinian's or a soldier's—burst.

The checkpoints and roadblocks were the biggest source of anxiety and hardship for Palestinians of all ages and physical or mental conditions. Deir Sharaf was one of two difficult army checkpoints on the west side of Nablus, the bustling historic city nestled between Mount Ebal and Mount Gerizim and famous for its sweet cheese *knefeh* pastry and well-made furniture. Before the intifada, Palestinians and Israelis would make special trips to Nablus to buy both; when I was there, the *knefeh* was seldom consumed outside the city limits, and many of the furniture shops were closed. Fourteen Israeli settlements and a number of illegal outposts are scattered through the hills around Nablus. Inside the town are three Palestinian refugee camps with a combined population of more than forty-three thousand. The camps, particularly Balata, and much of the rest of the city have long been a stronghold for the militant factions. Although Jenin gained more attention in the outside world, Nablus was the scene of the heaviest fighting and some of the highest casualties of the intifada.

Deir Sharaf, near two massive stone quarries, was a three-way junction that connected to the north on Route 60 and to other routes north and south. Vehicle and pedestrian queues here were long, and the checkpoint frequently was closed altogether.

One day, at midmorning, dozens of Palestinians were lined up waiting on two sides of the broad checkpoint. A woman said they had been there since daylight. In the weeds to one side, several men sat on their haunches, blindfolded and with hands cuffed behind their backs. I wanted to negotiate the release of three ambulances, which sat in the middle of the checkpoint with all the doors open. Two of them had patients inside on stretchers.

"Go home! Just get out of here! You are completely useless, and we do not want you here!" a well-dressed Palestinian man exploded as I walked past him up the long queue. I explained what I was doing and said I would speak to the soldiers about the pedestrians as well.

"You are doing nothing! You accomplish nothing, and I don't care whether you speak to the soldiers or not. We have been here since early morning, and I am trying to get to work. If I ever get there, then I have to do this again at night. We don't need you here, we don't need the UN here. We need an end to this occupation!"

I walked up the line and approached two paratroopers, one of whom was talking into his radio. The other one told me to mind my own business and leave. The ambulances were Palestinian rather than UN, but I said it was my business anyway because it was a humanitarian matter.

"We'll check the ambulances when we feel like it, and them too," he said, nodding toward the Palestinians. "You can go now." I went back to the jeep and got on the phone to an IDF liaison officer, who was polite but noncommittal. Nil score all around.

When checkpoints were particularly difficult, soldiers would say it was because of a bombing or other incident up the road or because of a "terror alert" in Israel. Or, as Palestinians said over and over, it was "just up to the mood of the soldiers."

Many soldiers would tell you that checkpoint duty is more stressful than combat. Thousands of Palestinians attempt to cross a major checkpoint on any given day, and they are persistent and not necessarily meek in the face of constant refusal. To the soldier, every Palestinian is a potential human bomb or at best just another headache-inducing hassle in a long and uncomfortable day. Soldiers with the most experience or equanimity treat it as an unpleasant job and hope to get through the shift without an incident. But they know they are targets, and standing behind the blocks in body armor, ammunition pouches, and helmet for nine hours in the rain or sun is tough on the most composed person.

It was tough in another sense. Soldiers had almost unlimited power over a vast civilian population. How they used that power, under pressure in a fluid situation, varied. "We are occupying their land and—I hate to say it—we are their masters," one reservist told me over coffee when I met him again in 2006. "We tell them when to go to sleep, we tell them when to get up. We tell them whether they can go through the checkpoint and what they can carry with them."

The power can be confusing and corrupting. "The guys who stand day and night at the checkpoint... their job is to distinguish between ordinary civilians and the ones who have come to hurt you," he said. "To the simple soldier at the checkpoint the next guy is the one who is going to kill him. We are not tyrants," he told me, in a variation of a common statement.

Throughout my tour and again two years later, I observed how soldiers behaved in a process that sucked the humanity out of everyone it touched. I watched their eyes and gestures and listened to how they spoke to one another and to Palestinians. A woman would explain that she was trying to get to a drugstore to fill a prescription for a sick relative, and the soldier would say no. She would plead her case and show the prescription; the soldier would say no again. IDF command maintained that humanitarian-aid cases were to be allowed through. But soldiers had a lot of latitude to decide. When a checkpoint was closed, soldiers' minds were closed too.

"I heard this story," the reservist told me. "Special Forces brought a suspected Palestinian militant to an army checkpoint at five in the morning. He was blindfolded and handcuffed, and he lay there on the ground from five in the morning until three in the afternoon. It was a very hot day in July."

What happened next was that the soldiers forgot about their prisoner: he became invisible. "An officer passed by and asked a soldier for the story. The officer asked, 'Has he got food and water?' The soldier said no. The officer told him to give him food and water." Determined to find out why a prisoner had been made to lie on the ground handcuffed and blindfolded for ten hours, he tracked down the Special Forces squad that had brought him in.

"'Oh, I forgot to tell you,' the Special Forces man said. 'We don't need him anymore.'" The prisoner, no longer a suspected militant, was uncuffed and released.

"The nineteen-year-old [soldier]... he's the god at the checkpoint, and he has no qualifications to be God," the reservist told me, still bothered by the incident four years later.

During my UN tour, there were about seventy-five manned military checkpoints in the West Bank, some run by the army, others by the Border Police. In addition, roughly an equal number of mobile, or "flying," checkpoints operated on most roads; their number changed daily. Settlers occasionally would throw up an illegal roadblock and beat or harass Palestinians who blundered into it; on one occasion south of Nablus they fired a few shots in our direction as we approached. When notified, the army forced the settlers to dismantle such barricades and get off the road.

In addition to the manned checkpoints, Palestinian villages and towns were ringed by deep bulldozed trenches or steep earth mounds. Unmanned entry points were blocked by torn-up pavement, meter-high concrete cubes, cubes on top of earth mounds, earth on top of cubes, or sometimes a simple coil of razor wire. Israeli security forces intended to keep terrorists penned up. In reality, quarantining towns for weeks collectively punished an entire population, and the Israelis knew it.

The trenches and other unmanned barriers carried lethal uncertainties. Was anyone watching from a hidden observation post? A Palestinian who was observed evading a blockade risked getting arrested or shot.

All of these obstacles would come to look rather primitive in the shadow of the barrier that during the intifada introduced industrial-strength movement control: the West Bank wall, a winding composite structure of hundreds of kilometers of nine-meter-high interlocking concrete slabs or parallel strips of intricate electric fence fitted with alarms, movement sensors, gates, and watchtowers. The fenced areas, with the earth carefully raked in the no-man's-land in between, looked like stretches of the old Berlin Wall in rural Eastern Germany.

Apart from the wall, the number of manned fixed checkpoints had declined to fifty-two in February 2005, but there still were more than six hundred temporary barriers or other general closure points; the number continues to fluctuate. All this in an area smaller than the American state of Delaware. I sometimes imagined that you could drive around the West Bank all day without getting out of second gear.

This did not apply to Israeli settlers, who would whiz through checkpoints at speed, bawling out a soldier for any delay. "*You* do not tell *us* to slow down!" they would shout. In theory, it did not apply to us, as UNRWA had general freedom to travel under protocols known as UN Privileges and Immunities. But the IDF ignored Privileges and Immunities at will, and we were often stopped and searched, under protest, along with everyone else. We resisted search demands, and when we did, we spent hours waiting for the situation to be resolved. Sometimes it depended on who blinked first or who got tired of the game. We spent so much time at the barriers that when I was waved through without a stop, I was surprised.

As if the physical obstacles weren't sufficient to deter free movement, there were also the permits, a bewildering and multilayered system of documentation that resembled the old pass system in apartheid South Africa and to which UNRWA unfortunately had agreed for its own Palestinian staff. All Palestinians carried color-coded ID cards in plastic wallets and an Israeli-issued permit of some type. The documents were kept close at hand because they were thoroughly checked several times a day. A soldier's verdict determined whether a Palestinian passed, went home, or was detained.

Some permits were valid for only thirty days, others for ninety days. Renewing them was no quick task, and Palestinians spent many hours in queues at military district offices.

Palestinians who held Jerusalem residence permits generally had more leeway than did West Bankers, who were treated almost as an alien species and couldn't travel far. West Bankers trying to enter Jerusalem, even as medical patients, could count on a long wait for a computer check or, usually, outright denial unless the trip and the reason for it had been vetted in advance by the IDF.

West Bank Palestinians would be barred from entering Jerusalem because their driving licenses said they were "not allowed to drive in Israel." Or soldiers would not let a Palestinian with a Jerusalem ID cross a checkpoint "because you've been in a Palestinian area." Or, even more bizarrely, a Palestinian from Jerusalem would not be allowed to cross into a Palestinian town such as Nablus "because you're an Israeli." An argument between a soldier who insisted that a Palestinian was Israeli and the Palestinian who insisted he wasn't could be hard to follow. (None of these scenarios included Arab Israelis, Palestinians who after 1948 chose to stay in Israel and became Israeli citizens.)

Sometimes no document, however preferential in theory, was acceptable. "Your ID means nothing to me" was a common response, particularly from the Border Police and some new arrivals to Israel, who would curse and throw an ID card back in someone's face or on the ground.

Vehicles were subject to their own restrictions. Cars with green-and-white Palestinian number plates were never allowed into Jerusalem and sometimes not allowed to move from one Palestinian area to another. The military's interpretation of the permit system seemed to change frequently; soldiers candidly admitted to me that they were given plenty of slack.

A checkpoint commander, whether officer or other rank, had complete discretionary authority on that patch. More than once I watched a junior noncommissioned officer (NCO) disobey a direct order from a superior officer about who could cross. The checkpoint was "his," as the NCO frequently reminded Palestinian supplicants. If I protested when UN staff were stopped and searched, or said that a particular issue had been sorted out at a higher level, the reply was likely to be "I can do whatever I want."

"Whatever" had broad scope. Palestinians who mouthed off (or ones who didn't) faced a variety of punishments, including being handcuffed, taken behind a tent, and beaten. Or made to squat blindfolded for several hours as a reminder of who really owned the place.

Ein Arik was a small and notorious checkpoint on a major artery into Ramallah that had been closed to all vehicle traffic since shortly after the beginning of the intifada. Pedestrians were allowed to cross, but on an irregular basis and usually after long waits. Taxi drivers, area residents, and Birzeit University students told me repeatedly that they had experienced or witnessed harassment, beatings, and shootings. These are a few stories that were related to me on a single day:

- Soldiers ordered passengers out of a minibus taxi and tossed a stun grenade inside, shattering the windshield and burning the seats.
- A pregnant woman said to have been hemorrhaging as she tried to get to hospital in a taxi was kept waiting for more than an hour.
- A soldier opened a woman's handbag, dumped the contents on the ground, and said, "Now collect your things and go back."
- Soldiers demanded bribes of cigarettes—even specifying the brand—for passage.
- Soldiers routinely fired tear gas and plastic-coated steel balls into waiting crowds (spent tear-gas canisters littered the ground and ditches).
- A man was shot in both legs and dragged into a tent, where he is said to have died.

Following a long series of such incidents, Palestinian fighters staged a deadly assault on the checkpoint in late February 2002, killing six soldiers. Sixteen Palestinians were killed elsewhere in Israeli reprisals for the ambush. The IDF post at Ein Arik was later dismantled.

▪▪▪

As checkpoints go, Huwwara, near the village with the same name just south of Nablus, was one of the busiest and had a reputation as one of the worst. It accounted for much of my waiting and negotiating time, as it did for my colleagues and for nongovernmental organizations and even foreign diplomats.

IDF units rotated through the various operational areas, so Huwwara occasionally was manned by reserve troops, recognizable by their faded fatigues and slightly advanced years. These soldiers had finished their regular service and been out in the world for a while before being called up. They tended to be more mature than troops on first service, and their presence could signal an easier crossing.

But Huwwara was frequently tense and hostile. As I was about to cross into Nablus one day, I noticed a group of six children, between eight and twelve years old, and two elderly people all standing oddly motionless near the barrier. Two soldiers were looking in their direction but ignoring them. As I got out, I realized that all the children were blind, as was the elderly woman, who was the grandmother of one of them. Her husband, leaning on a bent stick, was the only one of the group who could see. Two of the children clutched half-empty water bottles. After a day in Jerusalem at a school for the blind, they were returning home to Nablus and had gotten this far in a taxi. They stood there in the sun with cracked lips, silent and waiting.

I approached the soldiers, both Russian émigrés, and explained what they already knew: that the children were blind and had been waiting for more than an hour. I asked that they be allowed to cross. "They have to wait," the older man said, contempt for the Palestinians and for me clear in his blue eyes. I reminded him that keeping a group of blind children and elderly adults standing in the sun was a violation of humanitarian law. He wouldn't budge. I persisted.

"They will wait, and I will check and pass them one at a time. Now fuck off. Leave the checkpoint." He squared his stance and adjusted his rifle sling.

I phoned the International Committee of the Red Cross (ICRC), which had a more specific mandate in such matters. The ICRC told me later that eventually they had gotten the group through.

Huwwara had a sister checkpoint called Awarta, on a single-track dirt road a few kilometers to the east and near Itamar settlement, whose residents had been implicated in attacks on Palestinian farmers. Awarta was behind an IDF base that contained half a dozen converted shipping containers used to hold Palestinians who awaited transfer to Israeli jails. It was on the edge of a natural bog that was often ankle-deep in mud, with a piney wood on one side and a rocky field on the other. Fat francolins, a type of partridge, scurried about the rocks on fast, stubby legs; when they stopped moving, they disappeared into the pattern of the stones and clay.

During a long wait one day while I tried to clear some UN vehicles, I remarked to a soldier that he could put his rifle to good use for a change and shoot one of the francolins and cook it for lunch. "Tasty meat," I said. "But you'd have to be careful how you shot it with that rifle, or you'll just get a pile of feathers."

"Shoot the bird?" he said, narrowing his eyes and regarding me as though I had said something deeply stupid. It had been stupid, and I was sorry I said it, as useful as small talk could be sometimes.

In December 2001 the IDF had reconfigured Huwwara and Awarta into a circular one-way system into and out of Nablus, mainly because Huwwara got too choked with commercial traffic. On bad days as many as a hundred tractor trailers, flatbed trucks, vans, ambulances, donkey carts, and pedestrians solidified into an impossible jam that could take a whole afternoon to clear. Tempers flared in the dust and the heat, and there were fatal shootings.

The idea was that most traffic, including all commercial vehicles, would enter Nablus through Awarta and leave by Huwwara. This IDF decision split up the traffic and took some of the pressure off Huwwara, but impatient lorry drivers thundering along the narrow back road turned tiny Awarta village into a dust-coated and dangerous place. For Palestinians, even the sick and elderly, the circular arrangement made little difference; one checkpoint was as bad as the other.

I was sent to Awarta one morning to negotiate the passage of a UN van carrying refrigerated medicines to a Nablus clinic. The driver had been turned away from Huwwara and sent around to Awarta, where he was stuck well back in a stationary queue of about thirty heavy-goods vehicles. The checkpoint was closed, and he did not have enough maneuvering room to turn around. After two hours of arguing with soldiers and calling IDF liaison, the UN van was allowed to go through. The other trucks were not, and they were still there the next day.

When I related this tale to a veteran ambulance driver for the Palestinian Red Crescent Society (PRCS), he told his own story, one of a type that would become increasingly frequent in coming weeks. The day after a Palestinian had stabbed a settler to death, the ambulance driver and his medic were trying to go through Awarta with a cargo of medicines for a local hospital.

"Surrender your weapon!" the soldier barked.

"We have no weapons," the driver replied. "It's an ambulance. All we have on board are medicines."

In a downpour, the soldier ordered the driver and two Palestinians who had been waiting nearby to unload the ambulance onto the muddy road. When the driver protested, he was punched, kicked, and frisked. The soldier searched the boxes and then allowed the driver and his erstwhile helpers to put the soggy cardboard containers back in the van.

"I spent two hours in the rain," the driver said with a shrug and a smile. So did the soldier, he pointed out. It didn't have to be this hard.

Israeli authorities repeatedly charged that Palestinian ambulances (and UN vehicles) were used to smuggle weapons and explosives. The ICRC confirmed that an explosive device was taken from a PRCS ambulance near Ramallah in March 2002 and detonated by security forces. (The ICRC did not object to the IDF searching ambulances as long as it did not cause undue delay. It appealed to both sides to respect the transparency and unobstructed movement of emergency medical services.) Additional Israeli accusations that Palestinian ambulances carried explosives were not independently corroborated as far as I know. During my time in the West Bank, UN ambulances were never found to have transported weapons or explosives.

However, Palestinian gunmen did sometimes commandeer ambulances—in one case a clearly marked UN vehicle—to transport themselves and their wounded comrades. Ambulance drivers were hard-pressed to refuse such commands at gunpoint. When one UN driver in Gaza protested, he was threatened with being shot and complied under protest. UNRWA promptly condemned this incident.

The IDF continued to obstruct ambulances, medical teams, and medical-supply trucks even when security concerns had been addressed or were not an issue. I witnessed and investigated numerous cases of soldiers refusing to let Palestinians in ambulances, private cars, and on foot cross a checkpoint to seek medical care. Women in labor and other patients reportedly died at the checkpoints. Several Palestinian emergency workers were shot inside their ambulances, including some from the UN. The head of the PRCS Emergency Medical Service in Jenin, Dr. Khalil Suleiman, was killed while evacuating a girl from the refugee camp.

▪▪▪

The roadblocks and other obstacles seriously disrupted all levels of the Palestinian health-care system, from clinic visits and routine procedures to emergency treatment. UN agencies and other humanitarian-aid organizations issued formal reports about the problem.

One hot morning I had a ferocious and absurd argument with a young soldier at Qalandiya, the busy crossing point just north of Jerusalem, where a UN ambulance had been turned back as it tried to take an elderly woman into Ramallah for what I had been told was a surgical procedure. The inside of the ambulance was like an oven. I checked the woman's pulse: it was 108. After an hour and a quarter of arguing with the soldier and intermittent phone calls to IDF liaison and my own office, the soldier opened the barrier and waved the ambulance through. I figured the woman might live to see the inside of an operating room.

The episode wasn't over. As I turned the jeep around, my assistant yelled, "They're coming back!" and we saw the ambulance reversing through the lane toward us. I assumed that they had been stopped on the other side, as larger checkpoints had two sets of soldiers. When I asked the driver what had happened, he said soldiers told him they could enter Ramallah but would not be let out again after delivering the patient. So rather than risk getting stuck in Ramallah, they aborted the mission. Our discussion grew heated, and I reminded him that he had a sick elderly patient in the back. He relented and drove the unfortunate woman through the checkpoint for the third time.

That still wasn't the end of it. The soldier called me over to the blocks and angrily told me he had just learned that the woman had been scheduled not for surgery but for dialysis. "See, that's why we don't trust the UN. You always lie to us," he said.

I knew only what the ambulance driver had told me, but the nature of the medical procedure was irrelevant. "So it's okay to refuse access to a dialysis patient?" I asked sarcastically. He tried to tell me that dialysis was not an emergency procedure. There was no point in talking to this man and nothing to do other than to file a report about him—and about the conduct of the ambulance crew. My own heart rate was well elevated, and I left Qalandiya thinking about seeing a doctor myself. The woman finally got her dialysis.

Toward the end of 2001 violence increased dramatically in the West Bank and the Gaza Strip. In the first two days of December, Palestinian suicide bombs in Jerusalem and Haifa killed twenty-five and wounded scores of others. Israel bombed Palestinian Authority targets in retaliation, closed roads and checkpoints, and sealed off towns and villages. Movement was difficult everywhere. UN convoys of food and medicines continued, but were slowed or postponed.

One afternoon, as we were returning to Jerusalem, fifty or so pedestrians stood in a knot on the Nablus side of Huwwara. A few said they were registered refugees, which put them within my mandate.[1] I said I would try to get them through but was not optimistic, considering the level of tension that week. I asked them to stay put while I walked to the checkpoint.

I yelled up to the soldiers concealed behind camouflage netting in an elevated steel tower and asked that they let the people cross. "I would like to, but we have strict orders today that no Palestinians cross except critically ill patients in ambulances," one replied from behind the net. He agreed to phone his headquarters and inquire, and soon he came back with the same answer: no one passes. When I pressed the matter, he said, "These are my orders. What do you think I am, a monster?"

As I was about to abandon the effort, I heard another soldier shout and the metallic clack-chunk of a light machine gun being locked and loaded as the muzzle of the weapon jabbed through the netting. I turned around and saw that about twenty Palestinians were right behind me and still coming. They assumed that the UN could help and were tired of waiting.

"Go back, go back, make them go back or I will open fire!" the soldier behind the machine gun bellowed, sounding close to panic. I was in the uncomfortable position of having to get Palestinians back from a checkpoint, not through it, and right away. They refused to retreat, but my Arabic-speaking assistant convinced them there was no choice.

An identical situation occurred at Awarta a few days later, and again a soldier threatened to open fire at Palestinians who had followed me up to the blocks. I don't know whether either man would have fired into the crowd. But my attempt to broker freedom of movement may have risked lives, and I modified my techniques to avoid such close calls in the future.

After soldiers checked our cards, they usually allowed us to cross in the white UN jeeps. It was never a pleasant feeling to drive away from a checkpoint leaving Palestinian pedestrians and drivers behind in the dust. When we jumped the vehicle queue, as we usually did to get the day's mission done, we frequently got told off by those who had to wait. On other occasions, it was our turn to wait, as soldiers "punished" us for jumping the line. We could stay and work the phones or seek other routes through less hostile roadblocks.

And when UN international and Palestinian staff were forcibly searched or abused at checkpoints, or when the IDF took over UNRWA schools during military operations, meetings were called and memos flew from UNRWA legal offices to IDF high command. Over the years so many protest letters were sent that they could have wallpapered army headquarters. Replies from the army or the Ministry of Defense usually contained the same central point, such as the following sentence in a letter sent to humanitarian organizations in 2002: "The closures imposed on Palestinian cities arise directly and solely from the need to prevent terror attacks emanating from these cities against innocent citizens."

That was the official and unshakable message. Israel could have done more to live up to international agreements and ease the passage of humanitarian aid, but the general attitude resembled that of Israel's first prime minister, David Ben-Gurion, who brushed off the UN with the remark "Um shmum." The phrase, using the Hebrew acronym for the UN, translated roughly as "UN, so what?" Settlers and some soldiers continued to play with the acronym to show their scorn; one favorite was to tell us we were "Unwanted Nobodies."

The mood changed frequently, and even in tense times some soldiers would try to strike a balance. One summer afternoon, at Zatara junction, south of Huwwara on the way to Nablus, a young commander approached one of our field teams and told the female UNRWA officer that he had a problem. He pointed to a veiled Palestinian woman and her husband, a sheikh, who stood to one side.

"She has shown me her ID card, but I have to confirm that her face matches the photo on the card," the soldier said. "Her husband is religious, and he will not let her lift the veil for me to see her face. As you are a woman, could you help here? It's either that or we wait for the Red Cross, and I have no idea how long it would take for them to get here." The temperature was over thirty degrees Celsius (eighty-six degrees Fahrenheit), and there was no shade.

The UNRWA officer, an Arabic speaker, talked to the couple, who agreed to the compromise. The woman lifted her veil, the UN officer compared her face with the photo, and told the soldier waiting a discreet distance away. There was a triple round of thanks, and the couple crossed the checkpoint. Such improvised solutions, irregular or not, reminded us that humanity lurked somewhere beneath the hard surface.

But on more occasions than I can remember, a soldier would be goaded into a fury by whatever personal demons he carried around. While waiting to cross the Tunnels checkpoint on the Hebron road into Jerusalem just before the Eid al-Adha holiday during my last spring in the West Bank, I watched a relaxed soldier playing with a Palestinian baby through the window of a car much as he might have with a child in a supermarket queue. He spoke Arabic to the baby and patted his hand, and the parents smiled.

No problem crossing this afternoon, I thought, greeting the soldier when it was our turn. In the blink of an eye, Dr. Jekyll turned into Mr. Hyde.

"Passport!" he shouted, addressing me but glaring at my assistant.

"We don't carry our passports," I said, showing him my UN ID and then the card issued to us by Israel's Ministry of Foreign Affairs (MFA) with the agreement of UNRWA.

"Passport!" he screamed, refusing to look at the MFA card. "Turn off the engine!"

"We do not turn off the engine," I said.

Beads of sweat broke out on his forehead, and he backed up a step to give himself room to raise his rifle if that was going to be the next move. He demanded that my assistant speak Hebrew and that we drive into a far corner of the checkpoint; I refused. My assistant that day, a cool-headed young man who knew that this soldier was dangerous, kept his hands on the wheel and stared straight ahead.

The soldier kept shouting at me but staring at my colleague. Even though it was a cool day, he was sweating heavily under his steel helmet. Now seriously concerned, I called loudly for an officer. I wanted someone else there before this one pulled the trigger.

A captain walked over and said quietly to the soldier, "It's okay." The soldier flung my colleague's ID back into the car and walked off with a final remark: "Next time speak Hebrew!"

At a notoriously unfriendly checkpoint east of Nablus and not far from where Route 505 meets the Jordan Valley, a soldier refused to let me drive up to the blocks or even leave the jeep. When I tried to get out, he leveled his rifle. Another soldier kept a light machine gun trained on me, its bipod resting on a concrete cube. I kept the conversation going over a distance of 50 meters (164 feet) and slowly walked up to him. Five minutes of testy remarks followed. Then he abruptly relented.

"Okay, go back and get your vehicle and drive up."

The soldier was nineteen or twenty and had collar-length hair covered with a red bandanna instead of the regulation helmet. The afternoon was lung-searing Jordan Valley hot, and he was sunburned and looked as though he would rather be anywhere else on earth. After checking our IDs, he motioned us through. Then he told me to stop again.

"Wait. I want you to do something."

"Yes?" I said. *Now what?*

"HELP US FIX OUR SHITTY COUNTRY!" he yelled in general exasperation, throwing both hands in the air.

We all broke into smiles, and I drove off. My assistant hadn't looked so pleased all day. You just never knew how it was going to work out.

THREE
LONG WAY AROUND

The shortest distance between two points no longer existed. Palestinians trying to get anywhere for any reason required reserves of stamina and the patience of Job, qualities they had in abundance.

One morning, after clearing Awarta for Nablus, I paused. The checkpoint was packed and tense, as most were that month, and soldiers had started firing over people's heads. A soldier saw me watching and ordered me to get going. I thought a rear tire looked a bit low, so I got the spare tire out and started to jack up the jeep. The soldier yelled again, louder, and I held out my hands and pointed. "Flat tire," I yelled back.

When things calmed down and we prepared to leave, I noticed a woman carrying a baby in her arms walking out of the checkpoint. She was unsteady on her feet and said she felt faint. Iman Rayan had taken a taxi that morning from her home village of Zeita, seven kilometers (four miles) east, to Huwwara, where she planned to cross into Nablus to see a doctor. After an hour's wait, the IDF turned her away. "Go to Awarta," they said. Low on money for another taxi, she walked, carrying the baby in her arms, the three kilometers (about two miles) around to Awarta. Forty-five minutes later she was allowed to cross. Driving her to a health clinic in Balata refugee camp, I asked about her half-day journey. "It's normal," was all she said, slumped in the back seat. After more than thirty-five years of occupation and two uprisings against it, the abnormal had become normal.

The ambulance drivers, who logged more kilometers than anyone else, didn't bother with dialectics; they just tried to find roads or navigable tracks across hillsides and through orchards and olive groves. The white vans with the Red Crescent logo were seldom idle. Their repair bills must have been huge.

Above the wide vistas of the Sanur Valley north of Nablus, the dirt road from Qabatiya west to Route 60 was so rutted and beat up that it rattled the teeth. As an ambulance lurched toward us on the washboard track one afternoon, the driver flagged us down. It wasn't clear how far he'd come or what route he might have taken before the road closures, but even with an acquired tolerance for the long way around it was a detour too far.

"This road is just impossible," he shouted as the dust clouds settled. "I have a patient in the back with a broken leg, and you can hear him crying from this rough road. Listen to him." The moans were clearly audible through the hull of the ambulance.

"This is common now," the driver said. "The road increases their suffering." He knew that I couldn't help but hoped that I would tell someone so that the road could be fixed.

Road repairs by Palestinian municipalities had largely stopped, and there was no one who could offer more than sympathy. By blocking main roads between towns with earth mounds, the army had compelled heavy-goods vehicles to use back roads such as this one. The constant pounding by the lorries and the steady winter rains turned the roads to primitive tracks. The holes just got deeper.

When he got out to Route 60, once a decent hard road between Jenin and Nablus, the patient was not going to feel more comfortable and would be lucky to get to hospital at all. For lack of patching, the highway had become a breath-holding gamble. Taxi drivers blithely swerved around deep, jagged-edged holes, choosing the wrong side of the road if the surface looked better. Two taxis approaching each other at high speeds competed for smooth pavement in what resembled a game of chicken.

Violence had reached extreme levels in early 2002, and Nablus was isolated. In January a Palestinian gunman shot dead six Israelis and wounded thirty at a girl's bat mitzvah in Hadera, Israel. In response, Israeli fighter jets destroyed the old Palestinian police station in Tulkarm and occupied the town. Shootings, suicide bombings—including the first by a Palestinian woman—and reprisals continued. In the first week of February, gunmen attacked an Israeli settlement called Khamra near an IDF base east of Nablus, killing three Israeli settlers and wounding four others. The IDF were frantically hunting for the attackers and for suicide bombers who, according to intelligence warnings, were trying to get out of Tammun. Palestinians caught on the roads were arrested.

At Wadi Bidan, on the northeast approach to Nablus, a formidable barrier awaited ambulances heading south out of the Far'a refugee camp and villages such as Tammun and Tubas. Palestinians used to travel this road, with its pine forests, gorges, and springs, to a small amusement park on the outskirts of town; now its Ferris wheel sat motionless and rusted amid a litter of machine parts and clown paintings.

With a ravine on one side and steep hills on the other, all the IDF had to do to close Wadi Bidan was rip up the road. Armored bulldozers did a thorough job, leaving craters that were impassable to any vehicle, and the weather kept them that way. Then they stationed tanks or armored personnel carriers (APCs) on the hills to keep watch. Depending on the level of closure, pedestrians were allowed through if they were agile enough to manage the eroded ditches. Elderly women and men sometimes crawled across the steepest parts on their hands and knees.

After an urgent personal request from a PRCS medic, I was assigned to escort his ambulance to Nablus, to negotiate at any flying checkpoints on the way. The driver assured me that his three patients were unarmed and had been wounded in a firefight we had just witnessed in Tammun. The ambulance was driving faster than I cared to on the twisting road above the gorge. There were no checkpoints, and when I caught up at Wadi Bidan, the driver and medic were unloading their stretcher cases for what was called a back-to-back transfer.

Another PRCS ambulance had been summoned from inside Nablus and was waiting on the other side of the gully with its back door open. Carrying their patients on stretchers, the ambulance men were picking their way one step at a time across 200 meters (650 feet) of a treacherous, winding footpath. A soldier watched their every move through binoculars from the open turret of his tank on the hillside. As harrowing as such transfers were for the patients and their caregivers, they had become routine and were borne stoically; by this time, no one expected anything different.

Back on Route 57, the road where the Israelis had been killed two days earlier, soldiers were in a black temper. Nothing was moving except jeeps, APCs, and infantry patrols scouring the hills. Palestinians trying to find a way out went in circles and wound up back at Khamra checkpoint near the settlement. People waiting in a line of about seventy cars, trucks, and taxis told me they had been there for more than twenty-four hours, forbidden to leave their vehicles to collect drinking water from a spring or even to urinate. At the rear of the queue and out of view of the soldiers, people slipped out and drank water from windshield-washer tanks. Mothers pointed to their children, dehydrated and listless inside the cars, and pleaded with me to talk to the soldiers. The soldiers weren't listening to anyone, and for the Palestinians there was no going forward or back. I left, with regret, to continue my day's mission farther north. There was nothing to do other than file a report about the blockade.

▪ ▪ ▪

Travel was difficult the length of the West Bank. Down south in the Hebron area, Palestinians' shoes told the story of long and tiresome journeys.

Smartly dressed women in *hijab* and long overcoats and men in sport coats or work clothes climbed over the earth mounds that blocked vehicles from entering or leaving Fawwar refugee camp. Once past the slippery mounds, which were a couple of meters (six feet) high, the women stopped on level ground, carefully wiped the mud off their shoes, and headed up Route 60 toward Hebron and Jerusalem. The army was keeping taxis off the roads, and they were prepared to walk.

Some found a way to avoid the mounds. Walking in a line and holding the hands of children, they squished their way through a low field that was as green and wet as a rice paddy. Out on the highway, a soldier rested his rifle barrel on the hood of his jeep and took potshots in their direction. The shots were not aimed to hit the women but to scare them into going back or just to harass them. Without breaking stride, the women and children clambered up on the road, cleaned their soggy wrecked shoes, and started walking north. For good measure another soldier fired a few plastic-coated steel balls into the crowd gathered at the edge of the camp, and they ricocheted harmlessly off a boy's shoes. The fact that my assistant and I, in fluorescent yellow UN vests, were watching from the front did not serve as a deterrent. The steel balls, which weigh seventeen grams (half an ounce) each and are intended as crowd-control rounds, can cause serious injury or death if they hit a vulnerable part of the body. Nobody on either side of this minor incident seemed upset, and a boy picked up one of the balls and handed it to me.

The southern third of the West Bank, particularly the twenty-plus kilometers (twelve miles) between Bethlehem and Hebron, revealed some of Israel's strictest attempts to keep Palestinians and Jews apart. The closures were meant to protect the settlers, who are allowed to use the road, and to keep the suicide bombers out of Jerusalem. Whether Israel said so or not, the measures were meant to keep as many Palestinians as possible completely off the roads. The impact on the residents of Bethlehem and a dozen villages and five refugee camps along this section of Route 60 was devastating.

When the highway was open, traffic was mixed: settlers, Palestinians, humanitarian vehicles, army, and police. It's a busy road, carrying thousands of private and commercial vehicles and taxis daily through the undulating vineyards and orchards of the Hebron hills, past the Palestinian villages and the settlements of Kiryat Arba and the massive Etzion bloc, and up through the Gilo tunnels to Jerusalem. But even when traffic flowed, peace was not assured. Settlers rolled down their windows to hurl insults or garbage at Palestinians on foot; young Palestinians waited in ambush on the low bluffs and bombarded settler cars with rocks. When the stones flew, the roads were closed again.

My assistant and I were caught in a hail of baseball-size rocks near Arroub refugee camp. We were not the target, but the settler's car in front of us was. As the settler slammed on the brakes, I swerved to keep from rear-ending him. He was out of the car with his M-16 in an instant, a man in his forties with a trimmed salt-and-pepper beard and wearing jeans and a black V-neck sweater. Before I had gotten around his car, he had snapped off five shots at the stone throwers, who quickly ducked and disappeared out of sight. It lasted less than fifteen seconds. As we drove north, army jeeps roared south to pursue the Palestinians through the orchards on the bluff.

Everybody was used to these violent confrontations on the roads, but that didn't make life any easier. Whenever there was a serious Palestinian attack, as soon as the army determined the location of an attacker's village, long stretches of highway would be shut down. The sight of a jeep escorting an army-green bulldozer on a flatbed transporter signaled the start of such an operation. Grinding along the verges, the giant earthmovers gouged drainage ditches into major trenches, field after field, sealing off the tiny farm villages such as Sa'ir and Shuykh and larger towns like Bani Na'im and Halhul, for example, for weeks at a time with a jumble of earth mounds and smashed cars.

Halhul had experienced punishment in an earlier era. Toward the end of the Arab revolt in 1939, the British Army, as part of its counterterrorism campaign, kept villagers in outdoor pens without food and water in extremely hot weather during a raid. Several villagers died.[1] The behavior of British troops (and Arab rebels) in parts of Mandate Palestine would have sounded familiar to today's residents of Halhul.

When the IDF bulldozers had done their work and gone, Palestinians came out with tractors and shovels, or used their bare hands to dig away at the mounds and pour earth into the ditches. At first the IDF underestimated their determination. We were obliged to check on refugees and UN schools and clinics off this road, and we would find that overnight someone had scraped a narrow opening in a hedgerow or berm. The bulldozer didn't bother with some places because a metal guardrail was not crossable anyway, or it wasn't until a Palestinian unbolted the rail at its joints; a car could just fit between the remaining posts. The bulldozer returned and flattened the section of guardrail and dug the ditch deeper, or it built up the earth mound that villagers had breached under cover of darkness.

The deeper and higher the obstacles grew the more the Palestinians were determined to cross them. It became the clandestine war of the

Subaru sedan against the Caterpillar D-9. This back and forth had consequences on a pretty landscape. As the months passed, the ditches were littered with the squashed carcasses of Palestinian cars, apple trees from eroded hillsides, huge boulders, twisted guardrails, and anything else the bulldozer drivers found handy. Once-neat country roadsides became kilometers-long junkyards.

The hardier Palestinians kept trying, often in places where I would not risk the UN four-wheel drive. More than once I saw a battered Subaru perched like a seesaw on the fulcrum of an earth mound, with the driver and passengers trying to pry it loose. On a lucky day a passing Palestinian truck would offer a winch cable.

Although Palestinians took any road closure as a challenge to be met, it was not a friendly match. Passing soldiers would interrupt such attempted breaches by arresting the driver or confiscating his car keys. The driver would have to walk to the local IDF office and apply to get his keys back; this was not a quick operation. The confiscation of keys was a particularly unhappy feature of this duel. Sometimes a soldier would take a Palestinian's residence permit as well as his keys and leave him stranded on the road; when the next jeep stopped, the Palestinian would be unable to identify himself and was likely to be arrested for having no permit. The IDF held all the cards, or in this case, the keys.

One summer morning on Route 60 in the northern West Bank, I was surprised to see a yellow Mercedes taxi astride a dry wadi in the middle of a field. The only way the driver could have gotten there was by driving over the mountain, a task I would not have thought possible for any vehicle. He was sitting behind the wheel of his taxi, and we drove out to him. Soldiers in a jeep had spotted him coming down the rough mountain track the evening before and took away his car keys. He didn't want to abandon the vehicle and spent the night there. Now he didn't know what to do, had no plans to do anything, and was plainly dejected. When I passed the place a day later, I half expected to see him still sitting in his yellow taxi in the dry creek bed. But he and the taxi were gone.

Those who had no car and therefore no keys that could be confiscated had only their Palestinian Authority–issued ID cards, Israeli permits, or cards identifying them as an employee of the UN or a nongovernmental organization. Without documents, a Palestinian was truly vulnerable.

Ali Idris Ali Hamdan may have had one of the shortest commutes to work, but he ended up confined to a very small area. He lived in Fawwar refugee camp and worked as doorkeeper at the UNRWA health clinic in Dura, four kilometers (two and a half miles) away across Route 60. In November 2002 soldiers stopped him as he was crossing the highway and confiscated his ID card. Having no other useful identification, he was repeatedly picked up by the army every time he tried to leave the refugee camp. The Palestinian Authority, for reasons no one would explain, would not issue him a new card, and his case kept disappearing in the UNRWA bureaucracy. He spent the next year and a half living in fear of arrest as he tried to cross the road to his humble job at the health clinic.

Salah Abu Joudi drove the UN rubbish truck in the Hebron area and was a valued worker in the Arroub refugee camp. He was also the most cheerful and resolute man I had ever met. Nothing seemed to bother him, or at least not his long-distance hauls on hot summer days and his continual tangles with the army. His job was to collect the rubbish in the camp and elsewhere in the area and take it to a dump near Yatta, a good-size town below Hebron. He undertook his daily mission with enthusiasm, even when the IDF said the roads were closed and UNRWA told him to wait.

We were frequently sent to extract him from his latest encounter. Soldiers regularly harassed Abu Joudi, but not as badly as they could have. They seemed to realize, and one told me so almost apologetically, that he was just collecting the rubbish. However, Abu Joudi's trash compactor was not low profile, and the IDF pursued him with orders passed down from regional army headquarters. When they caught him, they announced that the Yatta pit had been declared "an illegal dump," even though it was well inside Palestinian territory. Long and surreal discussions between the IDF and UNRWA followed about what constituted an illegal Palestinian dump; the IDF were wrong.

Although I wasn't keen to get these unglamorous calls, I admired Abu Joudi. He was a nice guy devoted to his solitary task. "You were told to stay put today; things are really tight," I'd tell him. "Well, just thought I'd try. Have to get this load to the dump!" he would say with a smile, driving off to find another route. He should have gotten a commendation for hitting the road every morning in the clapped-out blue UN garbage truck.

I appreciated the importance of rubbish collection even more as the roadside ditches and gorges filled up. One lay-by near Tulkarm became the final resting place for thousands of decomposing chicken corpses from a local poultry farm, and the heap kept growing. People simply couldn't get out of their towns to authorized dumps, and once an unofficial site got started and inevitably caught fire, it was hard to stop. Two villages near Tulkarm were under virtual siege from one of these dumps; a nurse told me that residents suffered a dramatic increase in respiratory complaints from the clouds of evil-smelling smoke carried on the prevailing winds. Soldiers stationed at a checkpoint on the highway complained about it too and told me that when the wind changed direction, they ended a shift with sore throats and headaches. The nurse had a further story about this dump and said that a relative of hers had gained infamy because of it. Some years back, the relative had profitably leased the land to local Palestinian government officials, who allowed the dump to get started. Her relative pocketed his money, slipped out of town, and hadn't been seen since. "Everyone in the village curses his name every day," she told me.

Driving on Route 60 south of Bethlehem, I noticed an empty flatbed truck typically used to haul massive stone blocks from local quarries barreling across a rutted field on the inside of the earth mounds. The truck driver was being pursued by three Palestinian passenger cars whose drivers were hooting their horns and shaking their fists out of the windows. I couldn't see how any of these vehicles had gotten there in the first place. The highway ditch was firmly sealed with large stones, but inexplicably—as in a cartoon—there were fresh tire tracks on both sides. A group of men were watching the chase from the roadside, a few smiling nervously, the rest looking worried. They told me what had happened.

Local boys had spent the previous day ducking IDF jeeps while furtively digging out a new opening in the berm. The field beyond led to tiny Palestinian villages that had no other exit to the outside world. The opening became a small overnight sensation. Spotting the slot, as motorists were quick to do, the truck driver decided to squeeze through with his cargo of a single huge stone. This meant a plunge and a climb, feasible for passenger cars but a challenge for a long-wheelbase lorry. The driver made it over the top with a mighty jolt that snapped the stone's restraining chains. The stone block, weighing several tons, slid off and tumbled back into the berm opening as neatly as if it had been cut to fit. The hole was closed tighter than the IDF had managed, and drivers of the cars wanted to have a few words with the truck driver.

"What will happen when they catch him?" I asked the men watching the pursuit. Eyebrows shot up, mustaches twitched, and someone let out a short whistle. I felt for the hapless truck driver.

▪ ▪ ▪

The seclusion deepened, and the countryside seemed to slip back into preindustrial time. The highway south and north of Jerusalem was often deserted except for an elderly *hajjeh* in embroidered Palestinian dress, walking along the road with a bundle of kindling on her head as she followed her husband and their donkey. They would hold their palms up, imploring us for a ride.

On the more remote roads, you could drive for hours during curfew periods without seeing a Palestinian car or anyone other than a farmer stealthily hoeing his garden and glancing up in case the approaching vehicle was an army jeep. From the highway it seemed a depopulated land.

But if you looked up at any hillside in the West Bank, you could see tiny dots snaking down the rocky slope, and as the dots grew closer they took on human form—men and women, even the elderly balancing on canes, making their way to the road. Villages were under curfew, but people still had to get to work or the doctor or to grocery stores, and this meant sneaking out of villages to evade the jeeps at the entrances. The soldiers knew this, of course, and watched people walking over the hills. When the Palestinians got down to the highway, they found an army jeep waiting for them; they would be told to go back home, the way they'd come; younger ones would be detained for an ID check and sometimes arrested.

Men slipped out of the closed towns and took work wherever they could find it, traveling long distances in the process. I met groups who said they had been sleeping rough for days as they hid from army patrols.

Ten men made it from Jenin down the Jordan Valley and found jobs on a large farm near a spot in the road called Al'Auja. They pooled their money, rented an unfurnished house, and started working and saving their shekels. But Israeli authorities had introduced new rules: if you did not have a permit proving that you were a legal resident of a particular place, you could not stay there overnight. Tipped off that "illegals" were sleeping in Al'Auja, Border Police rousted the men from their beds in the middle of the night and "deported" them back to Jenin and the other villages they had come from. Everyone paid the price: ten men lost their jobs and savings, and the farmer lost his laborers.

The same draconian law was applied to teachers who shared funds and rented rooms closer to their schools to avoid being stranded at a checkpoint after dark. When police caught the teachers during an area-wide sweep, they moved them on. In the northern village of Ya'bad, UN teachers faced morning journeys whose outcome was never certain. Instead of taking minibus taxis, which were sure to be stopped, they cut through fields and olive groves on foot. The resourceful teachers got to know what time soldiers packed up the tire spikes at flying checkpoints and timed their afternoon trip home accordingly, when taxis were moving again. Still, with the road network fragmented, we often would come across a taxi or private car full of exhausted teachers on remote up-country tracks who had spent hours trying to get to or from school. A good part of their salaries was consumed by taxi fares.

Palestinians came up with novel ways to move their goods. The price of donkeys, the standard beast of burden that could go where cars could not, skyrocketed. But donkeys were not a foolproof means of transport. The owner of a small construction company told me with cheerful fatalism that the IDF had stymied his efforts to move an air conditioner by truck to a building site. Seeking less conspicuous transportation, he strapped the unit to the back of a donkey, figuring it would be easier to negotiate an animal than a truck. Soldiers, who kept a pocketful of prohibitive excuses, told him that he and the donkey could not cross together.

Well, the man thought, *that's a start. I'll catch up when I get across.* The donkey and air conditioner were cleared to go and disappeared down the road. They were never seen again. "*Inshallah bukra maalesh,*" the man said. (God willing, it'll be better tomorrow.) But even donkeys, which reportedly had been used to transport bombs, became as suspect as their Palestinian owners. In 2004 a road near Ramallah was closed for some hours because a donkey was suspected of wearing an explosive belt. Suspect donkeys, usually strays that had broken their tethers, were shot by suspicious soldiers.

▪▪▪

Palestinians applied ingenuity and guile in roughly equal measures as they tried to maintain a semblance of normal life. Ambulances, which had some leeway to move, occasionally were employed in ways that had negative consequences for everyone. In a plummeting economy, ambulance drivers, as dedicated as they were to saving lives, could find it hard to turn down a cash bribe. One man who could afford the ruse told me that to attend his daughter's wedding in another town he hired an ambulance and acted the sick patient, moaning and groaning, to pass the checkpoints. He got to the wedding on time. One morning when I stopped to assist an ambulance stuck on the Hizma road outside Jerusalem, the medic told me he was trying to get some children through to a city hospital. To gather verbal ammunition for negotiations with the Border Police, I opened the ambulance door. An entire family were sitting on the stretchers eating potato chips. No one was sick, and the mother was a bit sheepish. I had plenty of other tasks that morning and drove off.

UN ambulances were sometimes used as passenger taxis, but not for smuggling weapons or explosives. The army and Border Police quickly caught on to the scam and said—correctly—that it was an improper use of an emergency vehicle. Such ploys contributed to hindering all ambulance runs and remained one of the most contentious points between humanitarian organizations and Israeli authorities.

"They say all Palestinians lie to them, and they do!" an Israeli woman who belongs to the monitoring group Machsom Watch (Checkpoint Watch) told me in 2006 as the group tried to persuade soldiers to stop blockading Palestinians in their own areas. "If a Palestinian at a checkpoint says 'I want to go to Ramallah to buy a pair of shoes,' that's unacceptable [to the soldier]," she said. "So they lie—they say they're ill."

My field notebooks are full of cases of everyday activities being canceled. One of the most wrenching occurred in the winter of 2002 at the Ramallah Women's Training Center, a UN facility that was a kind of employment finishing school. Efficiently operated and immaculately maintained, it was home during the school year to several hundred teenage girls, who returned to their family homes throughout the West Bank at holidays.

There was no holiday pause in the fighting, however. In the middle of February, the IDF was badly shaken when Palestinian guerrillas blew up a Merkava tank in Gaza, killing three of its crew; it was the first time Palestinians had destroyed one of the massive war machines. This was followed in quick succession by a suicide bombing that killed two Israelis in a settlement shopping center and the guerrilla-style attack on the Ein Arik checkpoint outside Ramallah.

On February 20, the same day as the Ein Arik ambush, the Ramallah training center prepared to let the girls out for the Eid al-Adha holiday. Ordinarily they would have ridden buses and taxis on their own, but these were not ordinary days. I organized the final stages of a four-bus convoy that would take the girls to their homes in Bethlehem and Hebron. If all went according to plan, I would lead the buses out of Ramallah and down to Jerusalem and beyond. The IDF were told of the timing and the routes, and 140 chattering girls were herded onto the buses, their holiday thoughts already home.

We got as far as the razor-wire barricades at a main checkpoint out of Ramallah. The soldier was apologetic but firm. "No Palestinians on the roads," he said. "A new military order has just come down." When I got IDF liaison on the phone, it was clear that something had changed and the coordinated plans had been scrapped. "This is from very high up," he said. "You'll have to go back."

I boarded the lead bus and explained to the girls that there would be a delay. Smiles faded, but they were used to waiting. I got on the phone again to a liaison officer I knew to be particularly helpful and skilled when it came to breaking such logjams. No way, she said, it cannot happen. I broke the news that the trip was off, and fifty girls on the bus burst into tears. "I want you to listen to this," I said, holding my phone out in the aisle. The sound of the sobbing could have cracked a stone.

"Yes, Philip, I can hear them, and yes, it is sad," the soldier said down the phone line, dropping her matter-of-fact military voice. "I am truly sorry, but this cannot be fixed." She meant it, and I could hear the catch in her voice. It was a dismal drive back into Ramallah.

Ordinary Palestinians were caught in the tightening vise of war. The Israeli government was under intense political pressure, and on the day the girls' holiday trip was canceled, Sharon vowed "a new course of action" against the ever more deadly Palestinian attacks.

A week later helicopter gunships shelled Balata refugee camp in Nablus, and infantry and tanks poured into the narrow streets of Balata and Jenin camps, home to more than thirty-seven thousand refugees. It was the biggest assault on the camps to date and the most drastic attempt to smash the insurrection. For Palestinians, freedom of movement was beginning to seem less important than simply surviving in one place.

FOUR

CLAMPDOWN

It was true—as Israel claimed—that Palestinian fighters lived among the civilian population in the towns and refugee camps, and planned and launched attacks against Israelis. Palestinians were broadly united against the occupation, and it was now open warfare. Although Israel was aggressively pursuing its enemy in the territories, it had ratified the Fourth Geneva Convention on the protection of civilians during war. I assumed that the IDF would always allow medical supplies and food through to noncombatants. The assumption did not hold.

Kafr Qalil, on the southern edge of Nablus, was nearly a suburb of the city. Parts of the village were on the lowest slopes of Mount Gerizim and offered a panoramic view of Balata and Askar camps to the northeast. Employing a common tactic, the IDF took over three multifamily Palestinian houses and set up observation posts and firing points on kitchen balconies, terraces, and rooftops. The families in each house were compressed into one of the lower apartments and kept under strict guard. Soldiers told them that they would be confined as long as the military operation lasted.

Two of the houses on Kafr Qalil's upper road were home to twenty-five Palestinians. Lacking outbuildings for their animals, they kept nineteen goats in one unfinished second floor, from where the goats were let out to graze on the mountain slopes or vacant lots. Our teams had been sent in to assess the families' needs. Talking my way past a tank at an outer post, I got as far as the inner cordon and found a battalion commander, who said that everyone inside was all right and that the IDF would provide any medical help and food the occupants required. As far as he was concerned, that was the end of the conversation. But in another of the surprises encountered when dealing with this army, a young sergeant was eager to cooperate, and the officer agreed and walked away. The sergeant led us into the house past alert gunners with weapons trained on the camp below. The balconies and windows were draped with camouflage netting, and the family rooms were festooned with sleeping bags and assorted military gear.

Tzahi, the eldest son, said that no one was critically ill, but several adults had chronic ailments. One man was disabled and needed to see a doctor. A woman suffered from a nervous condition and high blood pressure and had run out of medicine. An infant and two children under the age of five seemed healthy but could not eat what little food remained in the house. Tzahi opened the refrigerator. It was empty, as were most shelves in the pantry. We organized supplies by telephone and made another trip in, this time a somewhat easier passage through the double cordon.

The IDF commander announced that starting that afternoon the curfew in Kafr Qalil would be lifted for two hours to allow people to shop. The gesture would provide residents with little more than fresh air: most shops were still closed, as were roads into town, and shelves were likely to be as bare as their customers' home cupboards. The ICRC sorted out the rest of the medical cases, evacuated two children sick with flu, and arranged for the delivery of emergency food parcels. We opened negotiations for a longer lifting of the curfew.

Down the hill, Kafr Qalil's main street was littered with stones and burned tires from earlier protests and was blocked at each end by APCs and infantry. The third multifamily house was in the middle of this desolate zone and, like the others with a good view, had been taken over by the army. Troopers escorted us up to a third-floor apartment, where several families were crammed into a darkened living room. I was concerned about a young woman with a head injury from an earlier accident; she told me that she had been examined by an army doctor but preferred to see her own doctor in Nablus. A pregnant woman needed a regular checkup, and a man was ill with what he said was "stomach nerves." That was not hard to understand. I spoke to the army doctor, a polite young officer who was familiar with their medical conditions.

"Yes, I do understand that they want to see their own doctors, but I assure you that while the situation lasts, I will check them daily and see that they get what they need," he said. I passed the information on to the ICRC, which after long negotiations was allowed to take people to their own clinics.

The Kafr Qalil chapter had an unhappy postscript. On a quiet day a couple of months later, I went to see how the families had got on, but couldn't immediately find the third house, even though it was on the main street. At a collection of tents that had been erected by the ICRC and an Islamic charity, I found one of the family members, and when I asked about her house, she pointed at a small mountain of concrete rubble and twisted steel reinforcing rods. She said that when the IDF no longer needed the house, they ordered the quarantined Palestinians to leave and blew it up. Soldiers would have known the background of every person who lived in the building; there was no military reason for the demolition.

The job of delivering relief supplies to refugees, who lived in scattered villages as well as the nineteen West Bank camps, became more difficult. The first week of March 2002 was one of murder and mayhem across the West Bank, Gaza, and Israel and the bloodiest period since the start of the intifada. On March 2 a Palestinian blew himself up in an ultra-Orthodox neighborhood of Jerusalem at the end of Shabbat, killing eleven people and wounding dozens more. Five of the dead were children. Among other attacks that week:

- A Palestinian sniper shot dead 7 soldiers and 3 civilians at the entrance to Ofra settlement on Route 60 north of Jerusalem; he might have killed more if his weapon had not jammed. He was tracked down and killed by soldiers.
- Three Israelis were killed and more than 30 wounded when a Gaza refugee shot up a prewedding party in a Tel Aviv restaurant; the gun-

man left behind a video message saying, "Don't cry for me, Mother; be happy because I am a martyr, a hero, like the others."

- A Palestinian suicide bomber detonated his explosives on a bus in Afula, Israel, killing 1 and injuring 11.
- Palestinian gunmen ambushed cars in the West Bank. At least 1 Israeli died.

Israeli warplanes bombed targets in Ramallah and Bethlehem. Dozens of Palestinians, including at least five children, died during the invasions of Jenin and Balata camps and elsewhere in the West Bank and Gaza. Ambulance crews and hospitals were stretched to their limits.

The IDF tended to treat Palestinians on the roads as though they all were in league with the fighters. The thousands of Palestinians who worked for UNRWA rarely got immunity from the clampdown. Sharon had promised to hit the Palestinians hard, and IDF blood was boiling following the string of suicide attacks. Our local drivers faced extraordinary risks.

After escorting senior UNRWA officials to Jenin, we got caught in a running two-hour battle between Palestinian gunmen and IDF tanks and took shelter in a disused factory. The lopsided and noisy battle gradually shifted down the street, providing the opening I needed: we had received an urgent call to meet a UN truck crew in trouble on the outskirts of town. We found them, and they were not in good shape. The driver, Jalak, and two cargo handlers, Amer and Mohammed, were in pain and badly shaken. They told an excruciating story.

Having volunteered to drive a load of urgently needed medical supplies from Nablus to Jenin, they had been stopped at a checkpoint outside a remote settlement. Soldiers demanded that the men unload the hundreds of boxes onto the pavement. In an act of astonishing bravery, the driver refused, saying that the truck flew the United Nations flag and carried humanitarian supplies.

Enraged, the soldiers punched one man in the face, another in the abdomen, and grabbed and twisted the genitals of two of them. They ripped open medicine boxes and scattered the contents on the road while other soldiers continued to beat the men. It might have gone further if an officer hadn't driven up. He stopped the beatings and ordered the truck released. The battered and bruised workers loaded what they could of the medicines and continued their journey, passing more checkpoints without incident. Two of the three were what the UN called "daily paid," meaning that they worked on an as-needed basis for low wages and without a contract. They had volunteered for the mission knowing what the IDF mood was likely to be and that armored units had invaded Jenin Camp that morning.

While I took down the details, a UN ambulance screeched to a stop and the agitated driver jumped out. The army had just prevented him from evacuating a patient with gunshot wounds from Jenin Camp to the hospital. When the driver insisted that he was transporting an injured man, a soldier fired one shot into the clearly marked vehicle. The bullet missed the patient and the medic inside. I took a photograph of the bullet hole, and the ambulance raced off.

As the battle raged, I looked up a side street and saw a veteran ICRC delegate standing outside his jeep waving his arms in front of a tank. The ICRC man was insistently pointing to the Red Cross symbol on his cloth vest (ICRC delegates did not wear body armor). The one-man argument with the tank did not succeed; he was not allowed to pass. He told me that Jenin Camp, where he had spent the morning, was "huge chaos."

West Bank towns spent much of that winter and spring under curfew. In early March army bulldozers dug up strategic sections of the main streets in historic Bethlehem, and on most nights army units poured heavy machine-gun fire into the town's Deheisheh refugee camp, from where they often took sniper fire. Twelve thousand terrified refugees, including many of our staff members and their families, were confined to their homes. Several called our radio room to update us on the shooting.

One morning's assignment was to deliver food to the refugees in Deheisheh, medical supplies to a local hospital, and to arrange to rotate UN medical teams in the camp. The operation had been meticulously coordinated with the IDF.

As we began delivering bread and milk through the twisting streets, we came under small-arms fire from an army observation post on high ground across the main road. There had been no outgoing fire from the camp. We were sitting ducks, as was anyone who opened a front door to take the bread. We pulled back and waited for the IDF command to get the shooting stopped.

The night before, a Hamas suicide bomber had blown up the Moment Café, a coffee bar popular with liberal Israelis near the prime minister's residence in West Jerusalem; thirteen people were killed and more than fifty maimed by the nail-packed bomb. Was the shooting at our distribution team in Deheisheh Camp an angry finger in the eye following the Jerusalem bombing? Or did coordination just fall apart as details of our movements were passed down—or not passed down—the chain of command? The go-stop-go relief missions had become routine.

The IDF conducted mass sweeps of the towns and camps for wanted militants, using a bullhorn to order all adult males to report to a local school or other large fenced-in area, such as the large stone quarry in Bethlehem. Palestinians hid if they could; they could face indefinite detention if they showed up.

The army was rounding up and arresting so many Palestinians that month that it had a hard time keeping track of them. When news broke that soldiers had used blue marking pens to write identifying numbers on the arms and foreheads of Palestinians in Tulkarm refugee camp, there was an uproar. Yasser Arafat pounced on the issue and compared it to what Nazis did to Jews in the concentration camps. B'Tselem, Israel's main human rights group, in a March 12, 2002, press release, called it "a symbol of the IDF's loss of any moral compass in its treatment of the Palestinian population."

Soldiers, rather overwhelmed by the number of Palestinians they had swept up, were defensive and bristled at suggestions that they were behaving like Nazis. Later on, when I asked an officer I dealt with regularly what he thought about inking numbers on prisoners' arms, he sounded both exasperated and bemused. "Look, it washes right off," he said.

The debate got serious. Israeli parliamentarian and Holocaust survivor Tommy Lapid, speaking in the Knesset, called it "intolerable." The

West Bank IDF commander conceded that it hadn't been such a good idea. And Ra'anan Gissan, one of the prime minister's spokesmen not known for making concessionary statements, admitted that numbering Palestinians' arms didn't convey a good "public relations image." In the end the army chief of staff, Lieutenant General Shaul Mofaz, ordered the practice stopped.

The Tulkarm episode had a historical footnote dating back to the Arab revolt in the 1930s. Just down the road from Tulkarm, British troops rounded up and jailed Palestine Arabs en masse during a clampdown.

> In Nablus in August 1938 close to five thousand men were held in a cage for two days and interrogated one after another. When they were finally released, each man was marked with a rubber stamp. While they had been held, the city was searched. Some wanted men were discovered, as was a workshop for producing bombs and two pairs of khaki pants that were considered army property.[1]

As we entered Qalqilya on March 12, city streets were deserted except for APCs and tanks; we drove slowly, with emergency flashers on, windows open, and the large UN flag flying from a rear fender. The city was under general curfew, and soldiers were rounding up Palestinian men and confining them in a school playground.

We had arrived with a truckload of bread for the UN hospital but soon were diverted to other duties. In the citywide confusion, the hospital's pediatrician, Dr. Imad Hassan Kiwan, had disappeared. My assistant and I went to find him.

An estimated six hundred Palestinian men under the age of forty stood or sat in the school playground, some blindfolded and most with hands tied behind their backs with flexible plastic cuffs. They were held for most of the day and released one by one after computer checks determined that they were not on a wanted list. As the men left, their cuffs were clipped off, and they walked into the street rubbing badly swollen wrists. A cheerful IDF captain said the doctor was not among the detainees.

The UNRWA hospital's administrator, a feisty, slightly built woman called Arwa, was having her own tussle with soldiers who had entered the hospital courtyard. She managed to talk them out of entering the main building and told us that other soldiers had broken into a nearby apartment shared by eight doctors. As we walked toward the apartment hoping to find the doctor, we blundered into an army foot patrol warily searching the narrow streets and alleys. It was a tense moment that could have gone badly wrong. The platoon commander angrily ordered me and my assistant to leave, and I explained that we were looking for a UN doctor, who was urgently needed at the hospital. "Okay, we have some men detained over there; go look," the soldier said. "If you find him, take him and get out fast. If not, get out. You can see what is happening here, and you are likely to be shot."

Eight blindfolded men squatted against a wall under guard, and I called the doctor's name. To my surprise, considering how many Palestinians had been picked up that day, one answered, "Yes. Here." A soldier removed the blindfold and cut Dr. Imad loose. He had been held for four hours. His hands were red, swollen, and deeply marked by the handcuffs.

I wanted to get the doctor out before the soldiers changed their minds but was brought up short by another random vignette. As more Palestinians were marched into the alley and ordered to squat against the wall, one young soldier took over guard duty. Sweating heavily in helmet, body armor, and ammunition pouches, he had a string of plastic handcuffs and was restraining the new prisoners as they arrived. Unaware that I was watching, he put the cuffs on each man, loosely at first while he ripped a strip from a bundle of blindfold fabric. He carefully tucked the cloth strip under the plastic on each wrist before drawing the cuff snug, and checked again that the cloth kept the restraint off the skin. I had never seen this done before and wondered what the soldier and his Palestinian captives were thinking.

The following year, it was commonplace to see cut plastic cuffs scattered around outside IDF district offices and near checkpoints where detainees had been released. Or we'd see half a dozen men walking down the road, each holding the broken halves of the restraints. Because the area was still under curfew, the men faced the dilemma of having been freed but still having to walk home. The broken cuffs were meant to be a "get-out-of-jail-free" card when they were stopped again.

Many thousands of Palestinians were arrested and jailed without a formal charge or trial. Some were held for a long time in this process, which was known as "administrative detention." One of those caught up in the indiscriminate dragnet was Farid, a Palestinian UN staff member and assistant of mine who had become a good friend. A soft-spoken man with a wife and two children, Farid had joined UNRWA not long before.

A few days after the IDF launched Operation Defensive Shield at the end of March 2002, armored units and infantry were conducting offensive operations in most West Bank camps and towns, except for Jericho and Hebron. After one violent night in Ramallah, Farid was working with another UNRWA team leading an aid convoy into town when they were stopped by a foot patrol. Soldiers ordered my friend out of a UN jeep at gunpoint, forced him to remove his UN-blue flak jacket and helmet, and took him first to a local house and later to an outdoor detention camp outside Ramallah. He and hundreds of other men were kept, handcuffed behind their backs and blindfolded for most of the time, under a large shed that had a metal roof but no walls to protect them from the wind and cold rain. On the second day Farid fainted and was seen, twice, by an army doctor. Afterward, he was cuffed with his hands in front. Farid told me later that after two days in captivity without food or water, he and a hundred other prisoners were given a half-rotten melon and twenty-five unleavened crackers to share. It was the end of Passover.

Intensive efforts by senior UN officials brought no useful response from regional army headquarters at Beit Il, a stone's throw away, or from headquarters in Tel Aviv. For more than two days the army would not acknowledge that he was a prisoner or, if he was in detention, alive. Farid's wife, who was pregnant with their third child, phoned me and other UN staff through two long nights. I dreaded having to tell her each time that we had no information about her husband.

Then, in a brusque late-night phone call, an army officer announced that Farid would be freed. Fifty-six hours after he was taken out of a humanitarian-aid convoy, I went to pick him up where an army jeep dropped him and several others off just before midnight: on a main highway in front of a settlement. A more dangerous place and time to leave a Palestinian would have been hard to imagine. Soldiers told him that he had been arrested because his name and ID number had gotten mixed up in a computer search. There was no apology. Farid had visibly lost weight, and other than the basics didn't have much to say on the ride home. Feeling thoroughly rotten, neither did I.

The daily situation reports that our Jerusalem office sent to UNRWA headquarters and to embassies, consulates, and NGOs made grim reading. The death toll on both sides in Gaza, the West Bank, and Israel was rising alarmingly.

FIVE
TERROR

The blast came as a deep, concussive roar, a dull thud that was palpable kilometers away, even if the pressure wave couldn't have carried that far. It was followed by an instant of total silence. Maybe the silence wasn't real but a trick of the mind. At the bomb scene there was no silence, just carnage and chaos. But a safe distance away, dead quiet first and then that familiar, awful dread in the pit of the stomach. You knew what was happening there, what it looked like, what it smelled like. Then the sirens. A single one. Then another, and more, until the night seemed an unbroken electronic wail that rose and fell for an hour or longer as ambulances rushed in empty and left full. One night, after a bomb exploded at a settlement near my home, the red lights of ambulances streamed like tracer rounds up the highway in numbers I could not count.

The night seemed to draw in. Friends called friends. Even at midnight and when there was nothing to be done. "Did you hear it?" "Yes, it's just down the street from me. Sirens everywhere." "Yes, I can hear them up here too." "Details?" "Haven't heard yet." Later, helicopter rotors beat through the cool dawn air as the Apache gunships streaked north, noses down.

Most of the bombs went off during morning rush hour, at lunchtime, at evening rush hour, or at night when cafés and restaurants were bustling. The militiamen who planned the operations and fitted the bombers with their explosive vests and wires and detonators calculated targets and time of day for maximum slaughter.

Pagers shrilled, cell phones rang and security forces and emergency workers responded with the precision of long practice. Streets were cordoned off, access roads sealed, ambulances and forensics teams sped in and the dead and wounded were taken out of the rubble and blood and broken glass. Teams from ZAKA, the religious volunteers who identify disaster victims, got in as soon as investigators let them and set about their work in yellow vests, rubber gloves, and boots, carefully collecting body parts, even the smallest, for burial. They would be the last to leave. Police and intelligence agents searched for clues to the bomber's identity and where he came from. Blood was hosed off the streets, the melted bus skeletons were taken away on trailers, and the gaping holes in the restaurants were boarded up. A few hours after the explosion, traffic was moving again. Café business dropped off, but not for long. Israelis returned to the restaurants and chose tables away from the door but facing it, and they tied flowers and cards to railings at the bus stops. Bravado and anger reigned but were shot through with fear and disgust.

The dead were buried within a day according to Jewish law and families grieved while doctors and nurses tended to the wounded. The struggles in the hospital wards mostly went on away from the gaze of the news organizations, which tallied the numbers and waited for the next bomb. The maimed survivors slipped out of public view.

If the Palestinian refugee camps were not under Israeli bombardment or curfew the next morning, satisfaction might be on display in some West Bank and Gaza streets. Women ululated and handed out sweets, teenagers pasted up martyr posters, and children swaggered about with toy assault rifles. Adults tended to be more circumspect around foreigners but did not criticize the bombing. A unified hard line was expected in the camps and was usually present.

"How many?" they asked when told a bomb had gone off in an Israeli restaurant or bus. If one or two had been killed, the reply would be something like: "Oh." If the death toll was ten or twelve, the response might be: "Ahh . . ."

One particularly chilling attack was carried out in June 2002 by a bomber who rammed a bus carrying soldiers at Megiddo Junction in northern Israel—close to Megiddo Prison and to what is said to be the site of Armageddon. The explosion, which killed seventeen people, was so loud that Palestinians in their cells at Megiddo heard it and erupted in cheers. Islamic Jihad said the bomb was to mark the thirty-fifth anniversary of the start of the occupation.

The camps and West Bank towns were uneasy. After such bombings, they knew what was coming.

The bombers' identities were not secret, and prerecorded video messages were broadcast on television: a young man or woman in a green headband printed with a verse from the Qur'an sitting at a table reading a statement, assault rifle propped against the wall. If members of the bomber's family heard about the bombing in time, they would scramble to save what they could from the house, which the IDF would blow up; when they didn't have time, their gold jewelry and cash would be buried in the rubble along with clothing, pots and pans, and toys. The family moved in with relatives. It happened like a clockwork script.

Opinion polls conducted by respected Palestinian monitoring groups showed public support for the attacks. Seventy-six percent of people questioned in a 2001 survey supported suicide bombings.[1] After a Palestinian woman blew herself up and killed twenty-seven people in Maxim Restaurant in Haifa in October 2003, 75 percent of those polled said they approved of the action.[2] At other times, support for such operations hovered around the 50 percent mark, and then dropped after the intifada.

"It's the Palestinians' F-16," they'd say, seeing an equivalence between their human bombs and Israel's fighter jets and other heavy weapons.

Was there equivalence? If the nonnumerical components of terror could be calculated, there was a degree of sameness, a comparable satisfaction in the ability to inflict punishment and suffering. If some Palestinians celebrated the murder of Jews on a city bus, some Jews cheered when the army killed Palestinians in a refugee camp.

At times the hand of retribution seemed to reach out even to the dead. After Palestinians killed a woman settler and two soldiers in Gaza in February 2002, residents of Gush Katif settlement decided to wrap the corpses of any Palestinian attackers who had been killed in pigskin and lard. "That way we block their passage to heaven," said the Sephardic rabbi of the Katif bloc, Josef Elnekaveh. It was hoped that the extreme act of burying the bodies in the skin of an animal considered unclean by Muslims (and, coincidentally, by Jews) would deter future suicide bombers expecting heavenly rewards for their acts.[3]

Israel vowed that its military actions would continue as long as Palestinian terrorism continued. Palestinians retorted that their suicide bombings were driven by Israel's unyielding grip on stolen land and by a lack of other means to pry it loose.

All these arguments held elements of truth, which rattled around like stones in a tin can. Israel was deploying a mighty modern arsenal against the Palestinians' rifles, rocket-propelled grenades, and plastic explosives. Israelis didn't flinch at demolishing the home of a dead bomber's mother, and Palestinian youngsters were signing up to strap on a vest and walk into Israeli restaurants.

"Look, they kill our civilians too, our children," Palestinians told me. This was true. The Israeli military did kill innocent civilians while saying that it made every effort not to. (The statement at times seemed disingenuous considering the degree of blunt force applied.)

"They make us do it," Palestinians also said about the attacks on Israeli civilians. This was not true. When people looked for me to agree, I said that no one made them blow up people in restaurants. My reply, particularly if I added that the laws of war forbid harming civilians—any civilians—usually was met with silence. For good measure, Palestinians might add that their children were being killed by American-supplied weapons, implying that I, as an American, was complicit. Although I could mentally connect the dots each time I watched a soldier fire an M-16 or a helicopter shell a camp, the topic, which wasn't relevant to my work with the UN, was circular in nature and best avoided.

Palestinians took for granted nighttime gunfire and tanks tearing through their streets, and Israelis came to expect the explosions or suicidal gun attacks in their own neighborhoods. People paused before deciding whether to go out for the evening, and even debated which West Jerusalem night spots might be safest; lightning never strikes twice, went that line of thinking. A slight tightening in the stomach accompanied a meal from starters to dessert, and anyone who walked through the door was eyed with profound suspicion.

As UN staff members operating under heightened security rules those days, we were barred from West Jerusalem (although we continued to work in the West Bank every day, which probably was more dangerous). Many people went anyway. When I pulled up next to a green Israeli bus at a traffic light or added up the number of roadblocks we crossed daily, I began to calculate the odds. Thirty minutes after I passed a checkpoint near Ma'ale Adumim settlement in the winter of 2002, a suicide car bomber drove into the barricade, killing himself and one other and wounding several; I reflected on our decision not to stop for coffee on the way out of Jenin. Michael Contet, a colleague whose apartment was on the Green Line between West and East Jerusalem, was halfway across his parking lot one night when a bomb exploded down the street. The fireball lit up the sky, hot shrapnel clattered down around him, and he pulled his coat over his head and sprinted for the door.

Periodic attempts to secure a cease-fire fizzled out, and there was no significant international diplomacy. The Israeli political process would not budge while bombs were exploding in the streets, and on the other side there seemed to be no new ideas coming out of Yasser Arafat's Palestinian Authority or political debate within it.

The Palestinians' isolation deepened after public ceremonies were held in Tulkarm, and later in Gaza, to hand out payment checks from Iraqi dictator Saddam Hussein to the families of suicide bombers. Each bomber's family got $25,000, and the relatives of those who were killed by Israelis got $10,000. Gestures of pan-Arab solidarity from Saddam's Ba'ath Party didn't do the Palestinian cause any more good than had Yasser Arafat's championing of Saddam during the Gulf War of 1991. With the Bush administration adamant that Saddam Hussein possessed weapons of mass destruction, Washington hard-liners linked Saddam's gifts to the glorification of Palestinian terrorism. No one was talking about lights at the end of tunnels.

▪ ▪ ▪

After a suicide attack, the news spread up the West Bank checkpoint by checkpoint.

In Nablus I got a radio call saying that a bomb had exploded in central Jerusalem and that many were dead. I decided to pull out earlier than usual. The temperature had dropped in the last hour, and it was starting to snow. The checkpoints would be tight.

Vehicles were already stacking up on both sides of Huwwara. A young soldier with a red beard and wearing a kippa beckoned our jeep forward to the blocks.

"You've heard the news?" he asked.

"Yes, and I'm sorry," I said. In my position I was not sure that it was appropriate to say sorry, but I was. I said the same to Palestinians when their friends and relatives were killed.

"You are not sorry," he said. "You hate Jews. You hate Jews, don't you?"

"No, of course not. Of course I don't hate Jews," I said.

His eyes watered and his face reddened, either from the cold or from anger. He wanted to talk, and I would have listened, but protocol and practicality did not allow it.

"I know you hate Jews. Go." Without checking our ID and without a word to my Palestinian assistant, he turned his back and walked away.

Neither my assistant nor I said anything for a long time. Flying checkpoints with strips of tire spikes had been set up every few kilometers, and there were long delays on the drive back to Jerusalem. By the time we got there, it was dark and snowing hard.

SIX

OPERATION DEFENSIVE SHIELD

Just before 7:30 on the first night of Passover 2002, 250 guests were starting the Seder in the dining room of the Park Hotel in Netanya when Abdel-Basset Odeh walked in and pressed the button that detonated his bag of explosives. Thirty people were killed and 140 were wounded. "Suddenly it was hell," a fifty-two-year-old survivor said later. Odeh, the twenty-five-year-old Palestinian who had unleashed the hell, was from Tulkarm, eighteen kilometers (eleven miles) away across the Green Line. Hamas claimed responsibility for the attack.

Air assaults and armored invasions of West Bank towns and refugee camps in the previous months had not stopped the Palestinian terror attacks in Israel. Nor had the peace talks in Washington, Taba, and Beirut or the efforts of shuttling American envoys. In this vicious atmosphere, both sides called for punishment and revenge.

The murder of Jews—including the elderly—at a Passover Seder was more than the society and its government could stand. Two days later Israel bombed and bulldozed most of Yasser Arafat's sprawling Ramallah compound into a pile of rocks, leaving the Palestinian leader and his aides huddled in the basement. Tanks and infantry stormed back into Tulkarm, Qalqilya, Nablus, and Jenin, and Israel's military machine moved into high gear. Sharon called up thirty thousand reservists and promised that the battle would be "long and complicated." Over the next few days three suicide bombings took nineteen more lives in Jerusalem, Tel Aviv, and Haifa. On March 31 Sharon declared that Israel was at war. Although many would have thought the war had been under way for some time, worse was yet to come: it was code-named Operation Defensive Shield.

▪ ▪ ▪

The idea of negotiating with a tank had never occurred to me. I had gotten used to APCs and tanks blocking roads and entrances to the camps, but usually was able to find an infantry platoon dug in nearby and a soldier with a radio on his back who would either sort things out with the tank driver or force us to leave.

Now I was standing in the middle of a main street in Nablus looking straight down the barrel of a Merkava's 120-mm cannon 50 meters (55 yards) away. The hatches were closed, and there was no one around to talk to. Nothing was moving, not even a dog.

I yelled up the side alleys, hoping that someone would hear me over the gunfire in a parallel street and that a soldier would stick his head out. I yelled in the direction of the tank, gesturing at the four UN trucks behind me loaded with medicines, powdered milk, and flour. I signaled, sort of like airport ground staff do to a pilot, indicating that I wanted to take the convoy through. The tanker's reply was clear: when I stepped to one side and pointed to show where I wanted to lead the trucks, the cannon barrel followed me.

Resupplying UNRWA warehouses such as the regional one in Nablus was essential to getting food to the camps and medicines to the clinics and hospitals. Agriculture and the normal transport of food had been sharply curtailed, and UNRWA supplies were a main resource for the poor.

For more than a month, the IDF had insisted that we coordinate the convoys in advance. UNRWA resisted, pointing out that UN Privileges and Immunities gave us free movement on the roads. Then UNRWA management decided there was little choice but to give the IDF the plate numbers of the trucks and information about the drivers the day before. Unless we heard something to the contrary, the convoy moved out in the morning.

The trip seldom went without a hitch. We would clear the checkpoints after lengthy unexplained waits and then enter a town if it looked—and sounded—safe enough. But nothing was really safe in those days, and we took it block by block, monitoring the level of the fighting. Forward infantry and armored units, even if they had been told we were coming, put us through the same procedure several times, searching the trucks and sometimes the drivers. Under UN rules we were supposed to refuse to allow the search, or at least protest it; if we did refuse, we went nowhere. Routine two-hour trips were taking half a day or longer.

Now I was getting nowhere making hand signals to a tank with its crew buttoned down inside. I got on the phone to an IDF colonel outside Nablus. He assured me that he knew about our convoy and agreed to contact the tank commander by radio.

"Tell him to elevate his cannon barrel as a signal that we can pass," I said. This had worked on another occasion, and I had rather enjoyed sailing a convoy past the tank's raised barrel. "In any case, ask him to get the cannon out of my face. It's making me nervous." Down the line I heard radio chatter in Hebrew. The gun did not move.

Visibility was terrible. It was a bright sunny day, but you could chew the air, which was thick with smoke from the shooting and concrete dust churned up by the tanks as they ground their way through town crushing curbs and median strips and knocking down electric poles.

Now I had another problem, or several of them, and they cropped up all at once. A heavy machine gun was banging away on my right, and another tank, somewhere out of sight, was firing its main cannon; the blasts echoed off the stone-front buildings. A noisy exchange of fire between Palestinians and the IDF was going on in the Casbah, the Old City, to my left. The Casbah and its market had seen much fighting already and was a refuge for the fighters. The historic old city was a prime target.

While I talked to the IDF colonel, the tank suddenly rotated its turret forty-five degrees, but not to let the convoy through. An elderly couple had left their shuttered house and were walking across the main street. Others who had been watching from windows, all of them elderly, started coming out. They had been under curfew inside their homes for many days and had decided to risk the streets. The UN was there, after all.

A loudspeaker on the tank bellowed something in Hebrew. I couldn't understand it, but it was clear the people were being ordered back. A white-robed old man, tiny against the bulk of the tank, made a dismissive gesture, said something, and kept going, his wife right behind him. Machine-gun fire one street away was growing steadier, and a couple of rounds skipped off the pavement nearby and banged off the metal doors of a store. The city block was turning into chaos. Local people, who had envisioned safety in our presence, now were in imminent danger on the streets. The old man and his wife had disappeared up a side street in the smoke and the dust, but I saw only one choice: get out before someone got hurt. On the phone I told the colonel that I was aborting the mission. My assistant began organizing the trucks to turn around. "No, no, wait; you will be able to go in a minute," the colonel insisted. This was insane. He couldn't see what was happening but surely must hear it down the phone. "We're out of here," I said. "People are going to be killed if we stay another minute."

The army had cut several of the east-west streets in Nablus with earth berms or deep trenches, and movement everywhere was difficult, particularly on the main road past the bombed-out PA police station. Eventually we found another way to the warehouse, and this too was blocked by armor. Here, though, infantry were protecting the tanks, and it was possible to have a conversation with a soldier who had direct local control. UNRWA cargo handlers offloaded the convoy in record time.

That afternoon we left the Balata warehouse with empty trucks and drove slowly through silent, rubble-strewn streets. A cow lowed mournfully behind the steel doors of a long-closed pen.

Although I had become accustomed to the way the IDF conducted operations and managed its priorities, I always believed that the shooting would stop long enough for us to assist noncombatants. But when the plans consistently fell apart, I started to feel like Charlie Brown running for the kick while Lucy held the football. Still, we went out every morning convinced it would work.

One morning's mission, to two destinations in Nablus, was carefully planned. A convoy of UNRWA, United Nations Development Programme (UNDP), and United Nations Children's Fund (UNICEF) trucks would deliver generators, oxygen canisters, medicines, rice, sugar, and vegetable oil to the warehouse and to Rafidia Hospital.[1] Past Huwwara checkpoint, we inched our way into the city listening to the battles in Balata and Askar camps. The convoy was pinned down by nearby heavy fire on several occasions, and it took hours to unload food and medicines at the hospital because laborers had not been able to reach us. The supplies would last the hospital no more than a few days.

A week later we had become concerned for the welfare of eight families who were confined to part of their house that had been taken over, just outside Nablus. We had extra supplies in the jeep after a convoy run and could easily drop them off at the occupied house. IDF command, however, said it was a no-go. I decided to bypass official liaison and try the local approach. I flagged down an APC coming toward us and waited until a senior NCO opened the hatch.

"I want to take some food and water to the families in that house over there," I said. "Your headquarters will not allow it. The families have been in the house for several days. I would like you, personally, to help me do this."

The soldier, a rumpled older reservist whose fatigues didn't fit as well as they once might have, looked at me for a minute and said, "Okay, I will help you. What do you want to do?"

"I want you to lead the way in, in your APC, with only my car behind you, to the house, and I want you to talk to your colleagues and explain what we are doing and make sure we don't get shot doing it."

"Okay, follow me," he said. He set off in his battered Vietnam-era personnel carrier, and I followed. A volunteer from another UN office who was with me in the jeep fastened the chin strap on her helmet.

The house, in a low field on the east side of Balata Camp, was a typical white-tiled multifamily dwelling with wrought-iron balconies and window grilles. The yard, knee deep in dried mud, was surrounded by APCs, two tanks, and a good number of soldiers, who looked surprised to see a UN jeep following an army vehicle. The NCO emerged from his hatch and explained to an officer. Some shouting in Hebrew followed, and we waited. He walked back looking chastened but resolved.

"Okay," he said. "After we have looked at the boxes, the two of you will carry them to the front door, and one Palestinian man will come out and take the boxes inside. You may not enter the house or speak to the man at all."

"But I need to ask about the health of the people inside, whether anyone is sick or needs medicine."

"You cannot and you will not."

Envisioning the whole thing going down the drain, I reluctantly agreed. We carried the food and bottled water across the ruts to the door while the soldiers watched. *You guys could get some honest exercise and give us a hand,* I thought to myself. The Palestinian man came out and started carrying the boxes inside. He would not make eye contact.

"You okay?" I chanced. He already had the supplies. "Okay," he murmured and disappeared back inside. I thanked the NCO and we shook hands. He smiled, and we all left.

When the army took over inhabited dwellings, the occupants had no choice but to wait it out and hope for the best. Residents, particularly children, described the experience as a terrifying and humiliating ordeal. Occasionally, they said, soldiers apologized and even cleaned up after themselves. Such acts of civility were outweighed by the fear and disruption and sometimes by gratuitous damage.

We, along with other UN agencies and various NGOs, visited dozens of occupied homes to check on families' needs during military operations. The visits likely brought slim comfort, as we could do little other than deliver emergency rations or arrange for the evacuation of medical cases. But sometimes a friendly face was better than nothing.

Dozens died and hundreds were wounded as fighting raged through the Casbah and the Nablus streets and camps that winter and spring. Old stone homes, businesses, and the historic soap factory in the Casbah lay in ruins, and the rest of Nablus, disintegrating into a dusty and battered outpost, bore no resemblance to the town I had first driven through five months before.

▪▪▪

If asked about the high proportion of suicide bombers who came from Jenin during the intifada, Palestinians might have said they were carrying on a tradition of militant protest dating back to the Arab revolt, when the town was a base for rebel leaders. The militancy had not diminished.

The status of Palestine refugees remained unchanged after 1948, and over decades the tent camps of the 1950s grew into small villages of three- and four-story concrete-block houses, shops, and small businesses all jammed into narrow streets. Legally they are still refugee camps, although Israelis chafe at the phraseology.

At 373 dunams, the usual local unit of land measurement, or 92 acres, Jenin Camp is just inside the western limits of Jenin city. Packed with shoppers on most days, the city market and bazaar are a commotion of overflowing fruit and vegetable stalls, pungent sidewalk falafel and hummus stands, clothing stores, and numerous tea shops where men smoke hookahs and exchange news. The fresh produce is as good as in Jerusalem and cheaper. If you wanted to please the restaurant cook, you might say his hummus was the best in the West Bank. But you could say the same thing in Bethlehem and get the same nod of appreciation.

From the higher points in the camp, the Israeli cities of Hadera and Netanya are visible, and on a clear day the Mediterranean beyond. It's only about three kilometers (two miles) to the Green Line, which Jenin workers once crossed to reach the farms in Israel's lush fields and valleys. The refugee camp, which opened in 1953, is legally governed by the Palestinian Authority, but its schools, health clinic, and social welfare programs are administered by UNRWA.

By now IDF missile strikes, armored and infantry raids, house searches, and mass arrests were regular events in Jenin. Militants opposed the incursions, and the town and camp became urban battlegrounds; casualties on one or both sides occurred almost daily. The IDF gradually encircled the town with a double steel ring. Approaches from Nablus and other points south were closed with trenches or earth mounds, or they were blocked by armored vehicles. The approach from the northwest was for practical purposes off-limits to all except the IDF, which used it as a straight shot into Jenin from its base at Salem on the Green Line.

The other entrance was past tiny Jalame village, south of Afula and just inside the West Bank, which meant crossing two cordons. The outer one was a standard, heavily manned checkpoint. The inner ring came to be known as Jalame gate, which also served as a giant parking lot for tanks and APCs. Sometimes our convoys would be quickly cleared through the outer checkpoint and then stopped and refused entry at Jalame gate. I couldn't see the logic of it, but the reception was always different.

After crossing Jalame gate one morning, we stopped the convoy because of an ongoing assault on Jenin. I watched from a hill as a helicopter gunship poured rockets and machine-gun fire into the refugee camp. I knew those narrow streets, where a block of houses could be home to more than a hundred people and where in the alleys you could reach out and almost touch the house across the way. Under those dense urban conditions, talk of precision fire was not reassuring.

The IDF launched its full-scale armored and infantry invasion on April 3 and closed access to the outside world. For Israel, Jenin Camp was a fight to the finish with terrorists; the suicide bombers were going to be flushed out and killed, and everything else could wait.

Palestinian fighters in the apartments were well prepared and stocked with small-arms ammunition and explosive charges. In the end they were no match for IDF numbers and firepower, but house-to-house warfare raged for ten days in the cramped alleys and concrete-block houses. Israeli officers conceded later that they had not expected the resistance to be so fierce.

Fighting street to street, the army would enter a home and sledgehammer or blast "mouse holes" between the connected thin-walled buildings to avoid sniper fire, searching bottom to top as they went. On the sixth day Palestinian fighters spotted troops entering a house and detonated a sophisticated booby trap that killed thirteen soldiers. The IDF said later that they had been attacked by Palestinian gunmen wearing suicide bomb vests, and that stockpiles of hundreds of explosive charges were found after the battle.

Infantry squads forced Palestinians to walk in front of them as they approached buildings that were to be searched. The IDF later strenuously denied charges that they had used human shields, but in media reports soldiers allowed that they had made Palestinians knock on doors of homes.[2]

Palestinians had experienced the tactic more than sixty years earlier, during the Arab revolt. British troops were said not to "have any problems forcing Arab civilians to drive at the head of their convoys to prevent terrorists from mining the roads or railway tracks; they would even seat them in special cars attached to the train engines."[3]

During Defensive Shield, days of bombardment and constant activity by tanks and bulldozers destroyed water mains, and bullets punctured the rooftop water tanks that supplied the apartments. There was no electricity and no way to get food. Residents who begged to be allowed out were told they would be shot if they tried. Ambulance crews and Palestinians whose mobile phones still worked made desperate calls for help for the wounded and others trapped in their homes without water in the hot weather. Help did not come.

Medical teams from France, Canada, and Italy and supply trucks and water tankers were lined up on the edge of the camp a few hundred meters from the center. ICRC delegates, long based in Jenin town, slept on the floor of the hospital and, along with the UN, kept requesting access. Repeated insistence that international law stipulated care for noncombatants and the wounded did not change any army minds. The answer was always the same: military operations are ongoing. Aid workers were assured of access when the fighting subsided. But when it did subside, we were still prohibited from entering for critical days.

UNRWA's five operations teams rotated daily between Jenin, Nablus, and other Palestinian cities that were under siege or encircled. We ran into the same difficulties everywhere. Particularly during Defensive Shield, combat troops had fingers on triggers and safeties off. More than once as I sought to navigate a cratered road or find a safer route, I would round a corner and come face to face with a wide-eyed soldier, his face blackened with camouflage paint and rifle leveled.

"Leave the area immediately or we will open fire!" a battle-hardened Special Forces officer screamed at me one afternoon as his soldiers, hidden behind hedges on both sides of the street, kept weapons trained on us. IDF command had known we were in the area, but it made no difference. The inside of my mouth tasted like tarnished metal as we turned the trucks around.

Jenin was not unique during Defensive Shield. All our field teams had close calls and nearly every day in some part of the West Bank. After a long delay behind an armored position in Jenin town on April 11, the army announced that we could drop a cargo of water and powdered milk at a school just inside the camp on the condition that we leave immediately afterward. Machine-gun and small-arms fire rattled, and explosions from tank rounds, grenades, and demolition charges boomed through the streets. It was quiet compared with the previous days and nights.

Four days later and after a seven-hour wait, the IDF told me that I could take a supply convoy all the way into the camp. We had wasted the better part of the day, and I kept looking at my watch. Troops were so edgy and the streets so obstructed with battle debris that we moved cautiously, and it took agonizing minutes to reach the bullet-scarred UNRWA health clinic, which a UN security officer and I had chosen as a distribution point. Tanks surrounded us immediately, and the commander refused to let us unload. More time went by in a series of phone calls. IDF command eventually overruled the ground commander, and the tanks backed off. But again we had lost valuable time. By then, it was late afternoon.

There were too many uncertainties. As soon as we opened the truck, we would be swamped by frantic refugees. How would the jumpy and exhausted soldiers watching from hidden sniper positions react when they saw Palestinians running into the street? IDF command had assured me that no one would open fire. Had the order been passed down the chain? Would it reach soldiers on this street? Would they obey? I had already heard too many conflicting assurances and orders. I could not take the chance that something would go wrong and cause more casualties. I decided to take the trucks out of town and try again in the morning when I was satisfied with the chain of communications. Was it the right decision or not? The supplies were critically needed that afternoon. I would never know the answer.

As we headed out, we unloaded cases of rations on a quiet street to about a hundred people who had seen us and crept out of their homes. Seemingly out of nowhere, three international peace activists who had been in the camp through the battle appeared and helped us hand out the water and food. These activists seemed to know no caution. Strictly partisan on the side of the Palestinians, they were—and remained for another two years—a major irritant for the Israelis in the West Bank and Gaza Strip. Several became casualties.

The next day we got a better idea of the devastation. The camp was strewn with the wreckage of buildings, cars that had been crushed by tanks, downed power lines, scattered household goods and clothing, and a variety of metal trash. Streets were a vile brew of sewage and mud churned up by the armored vehicles. The stench of death hung heavy.

There was an unfamiliar, open expanse in the middle of the camp, revealing houses I had never seen from that angle. What had been the camp's noisy, active heart was a rough, bald scab running up the hillside. Dozens of multifamily houses were simply gone, their location marked only by jagged chunks of concrete and steel sticking out of the earth. Around the edge of the scab, parts of houses and shops that had been repeatedly holed by shells or had entire walls sheared off leaned at crazy angles, and furniture and curtains dangled out of the gaps. In some of the exposed apartments family pictures still hung on the walls. A few children dug with their hands in the debris.

An area later estimated at 40,000 square meters (about 431,000 square feet) had been flattened or heavily damaged. The center of it, the bald patch, was quickly dubbed "ground zero" by the residents. More than 140 buildings were destroyed, and an estimated 4,000 people were homeless.[4] Under the wrecked houses and inside standing ones lay an unknown number of bodies. Even if recovery teams had been immediately available, no one knew which buildings the Palestinian fighters had booby-trapped. It would be a long search.

I wondered if anyone was alive in the row of houses facing me or if residents had managed to flee. We called out in Arabic and English. A few shutters cautiously opened, faces appeared behind curtains. The IDF was still in the camp, and survivors were taking no chances. When they saw the trucks and our blue helmets, about two hundred people came out into the street and quickly grabbed whatever they could, mainly water. On one truck, workers retreated from the crush for their own safety. The head of our social services unit, a slender, dedicated man trying to direct the distribution, was roughed up and nearly trampled underfoot.

My radio squawked. It was a senior IDF liaison officer. "You have two hours to unload, and you will have to get out due to planned military operations," he said. Our trucks had been delayed for many hours or missions postponed on each of three previous attempts, and I had been made to hold this convoy for an hour and a half. I had a good foothold and no intention of pulling out.

"We are already working, and we have people in the streets," I radioed back. "We're sticking to the earlier arrangements and will be distributing food and water all day." As we continued, another officer informed me that we would not be allowed to distribute provisions the following day because it was Israel's Independence Day. The order was obscene. The distribution went ahead as scheduled.

People slipped out of their homes with the utmost care and with a look in their eyes I had seen only in besieged and battered cities in Angola. "You cannot imagine what the last ten days have been like," said one UN camp official who had been trapped with his family since the beginning of the battle. "Shelling and shooting and bombing day and night. No food. No water. No electricity. We had to drink water out of the toilet tank. We lay on the floor and dared not move."

Others told stories of utter desperation and terror. An elderly woman covered her nose and mouth and pointed to the ground-floor doors of her neighbor's shop. I already knew about it. We did not know how many were dead or where the wounded were, but most of them were on streets up the hill nearer the camp center. Other than occasional bursts of automatic weapons fire, the fighting had stopped. But ambulances still were not allowed in. People feared that their neighbors had been buried alive.

Most of the destruction had been done late in the battle by armored bulldozers. Much of it seemed to have been done personally by one unhinged and whiskey-fueled football fanatic who called himself Kurdi Bear and spent seventy-five hours driving his sixty-ton armored D-9L bulldozer through the camp knocking down houses, ostensibly to open paths for other IDF vehicles but mainly just to "erase" homes. Palestinians who had been in the camp throughout told me and others that they saw a bulldozer crushing houses before people could escape.

Kurdi Bear, whose real name was Moshe Nissim, had had, by his own account, a less than illustrious military career and a disastrous, debt-ridden personal life. He saw Operation Defensive Shield as his chance for personal redemption, not to mention the opportunity to liberate some of his ferocious personal devils.

"For three days, I just destroyed and destroyed," he said later in a lengthy detailed statement to the *Yediot Aharanot* newspaper, admitting that he had never driven a bulldozer before, apart from two hours of training before the mission.

> Do you know how I held out for 75 hours? I didn't get off the bulldozer. I had no problem of fatigue, because I drank whisky all the time. I had a bottle in the bulldozer at all times. I had put them in my bag in advance. Everybody else took clothes, but I knew what was waiting for me there, so I took whisky and something to munch on.
>
> Clothes? Didn't need any. A towel was enough. Anyhow I could not leave the bulldozer. You open the door, and get a bullet. For 75 hours I didn't think about my life at home, about all the problems. Everything was erased....
>
> Difficult? No way. You must be kidding. I wanted to destroy everything. I begged the officers, over the radio, to let me knock it all down; from top to bottom. To level everything. It's not as if I wanted to kill. Just the houses. We didn't harm those who came out of the houses we had started to demolish, waving white flags. We screwed just those who wanted to fight....
>
> I didn't see, with my own eyes, people dying under the blade of the D-9. And I didn't see house[s] falling down on live people. But if there were any, I wouldn't care at all. I am sure people died inside these houses, but it was difficult to see, there was lots of dust everywhere, and we worked a lot at night. I found joy with every house that came down, because I knew they didn't mind dying, but they cared for their homes. If you knocked down a house, you buried 40 or 50 people for generations. If I am sorry for anything, it is for not tearing the whole camp down.[5]

Looking at the camp center, I thought that the rubble appeared dense in places, as though it had rained for a month or something else had happened after the houses had collapsed or been blown up. Amnesty International delegates said later that "the IDF had used bulldozers not just to destroy the houses but to drive backwards and forwards over them, impacting the rubble and rendering it very difficult for residents to dig in search of their possessions, valuables, or missing family members."[6]

Unexploded Israeli ordnance and Palestinian munitions and booby traps posed a threat of an unknown scale. One day a Palestinian boy of about nine casually handed me a crude unexploded pipe bomb, warm to the touch from lying in the sun. I gingerly put it on a sand bed with Israeli grenades and other Palestinian explosives that residents brought into a temporary UN operations room in a girls' school. International demolition teams were on their way, but for now the explosives were a major hazard for everyone.

In the middle of the camp I found myself alone in front of a burning house. Its window shutters were open, but the front doors were closed. No one answered my calls. I thought of searching the house floor by floor and remembered the booby traps.

As the military curtain gradually lifted, survivors picked through the compacted mud and slabs of concrete, hoping to find someone alive in a protected pocket or their life's savings. Their efforts were futile, but they had nothing else to do. The streets ran with sewage and water from broken mains and pipes. Buildings and parts of buildings were unstable, and if unexploded shells or trip wires were inside, they were hard to spot. It was dangerous to walk anywhere.

There were no young men about. Fighters had either been killed or escaped. Children and the elderly tugged at my sleeve and pointed to a building, begging me to remove a body or a live grenade. Or they asked me to escort them into a partly collapsed house to collect personal possessions. I could only note the location and report it to the experts.

The propaganda war began even before the IDF assault ended. Journalists had begun to arrive in numbers and were hungry for sensational details. They didn't have to look far: every square meter was awful. As I went about my job, television and print reporters seemed to have only one question: Had there been a massacre? The word carried enormous political and psychological weight.

A senior Palestinian Authority official had declared that the IDF had committed a massacre, killing as many as five hundred Palestinians. The charge, which was put about as fact rather than as a possibility, acquired a life of its own and was repeated for days in the world's news media. Considering the extent of the army's operation and the denial of humanitarian access for so many days, it was not unreasonable to at least ask the question.

In interviews with reporters, I described the destruction as staggering in scale and confirmed that a number of people had been killed. But I kept pointing out to reporters that nearly three-quarters of the camp was still off-limits to aid workers, and it was too early to say how many had died.

"But have you seen evidence of a massacre?" the journalists insisted, pursuing the body count.

"Numbers of people have been killed, and many more have been wounded, but no, I have not seen evidence of a massacre," I said. The journalists seemed disappointed. The truth in the middle of April was that no one had any accurate idea. I just kept describing Jenin Camp as a major international disaster zone.

Journalists descended on one house up a side street that contained five bodies. A television reporter collapsed with some type of seizure and thrashed about on the ground. Someone summoned an IDF squad, which set up a defensive perimeter and nearly shot a Palestinian who was watching from an upstairs window. A medic gave the journalist water and helped him walk out. I recorded the location of the bodies, which the IDF insisted on seeing as well.

Technical experts began planning for the camp's reconstruction, a project of vast dimensions that would be aided by $27 million from the United Arab Emirates. But first the remains of the camp's center had to be cleared away. Three months later, when most of the dangerous explosives had been collected and the unstable buildings knocked down, someone calculated that sixty-five thousand cubic meters (about 3 million cubic feet) of rubble from the destroyed houses would have to be hauled to a dump site and that it would take eighty trucks a day one month to do the job. Finding a suitable site outside Jenin and then negotiating with the IDF over which roads the trucks could travel was a laborious process. They controlled even the removal of debris.

The propaganda and political skirmishes over casualty figures continued for some time afterward. Once the massacre claims had been dismissed (although some still use the term today), the final toll, generally agreed, was that fifty-nine Palestinians and twenty-three Israelis had been killed in the battle for Jenin.

At the time, the agony in that ruined camp was not measurable in numbers, volume, or weight. When the soldiers, tanks, and bulldozers left, residents came out and searched for the bodies of missing relatives or sat in front of their houses in shocked silence, surveying the devastation. Nobody had much to say except about drinking water and food. When access to the camp became easier, the refugees told their stories many times and in detail to the hundreds of journalists, aid workers, engineers, urban planners, and foreign government representatives who passed through the camp.

That summer the IDF began to withdraw armor and infantry from the Palestinian cities, but they didn't pull back far. They could—and over the next two years frequently did—reenter to conduct search-and-arrest campaigns and other military operations against Palestinian fighters and suicide bombers. Some of the repeat incursions lasted for weeks and continued to claim lives.

Driving down the Jordan Valley after one long day in Jenin, I had to stop for a road accident as I rounded a bend. A truck in a military convoy had overturned, and soldiers and officers were sitting and smoking in a field while heavy equipment righted the truck. A balding captain in the reserves walked out to explain that it would take some time to clear the accident. Seeing the mud on our jeep, the officer, who was in his early thirties, asked where we'd been.

"Jenin," I said.

"Jenin. I was there through it all. It was terrible," he began. "I lost several friends." The officer was one of the thousands of reservists called up for Defensive Shield, and now he was being stood down or redeployed. As he started to tell his story, his face crumpled and he began to cry. A major saw him talking to us, and although he could see only the captain's back and could not have overheard, he strode over and firmly led him away by the arm.

SEVEN

REFLECTIONS: ISRAELIS AND PALESTINIANS

The lieutenant took his M-16 rifle off the desktop and leaned it against the wall behind him. It was not a gesture of courtesy but a reflexive action: his weapon had been within my reach. It was a slow day, and he was glad to have someone to talk to other than his fellow soldiers or Palestinians. His office contained the standard army-issue gray steel desk, two chairs, his unit flag, and a white board with Palestinian ID numbers on it. Grenade-proof steel grates covered the two windows. The army officer, not yet twenty-one, had been transferred to the West Bank after eighteen months in the Gaza Strip. Rafah, Khan Yunis... he had seen the worst of it there and saw himself as a link in an unbroken historical narrative. The lieutenant regarded me cordially, but as if from a distance. During the time it took him to tell this short story, he never took his eyes off me. Once he started talking, he found it easy to continue, but with long pauses. Some things he was not ready to talk about at all.

How many kids in your country... and I am still a kid although I'm a soldier, I'm only twenty, how many kids there could say they have seen what I have seen, have done what I have done?

When I get home to my parents' house, that's where I live, I don't even want to take my pack off, don't even want to take my uniform off. I just sit in a chair. I just want to sit there. I don't want to do anything. I just want to sleep. I want to sleep, want some peace and quiet in my head. There is no peace. Imagine: you survive two weeks here, one of the most high-risk places on earth, you survive it. Then you go home to Tel Aviv, you go out with your girlfriend, to a restaurant, a discotheque, you're in a suit. And you get blown up there. I can never remove it. It's like the uniform. You can never take it off.

When I was a kid, my father was in the reserves, and he came home always with a weapon, and I loved it. I thought it was great. I wanted to play with it. Then my older brother was in the army, and he came home with a weapon. And now I come home with a weapon. What am I doing, what kind of life is this? Now I am arranging for a pistol to carry as an off-duty weapon because it is not safe to travel here. I mean, what am I doing here? I know. I'm a soldier, and I'm protecting my country and my family and my girlfriend. And I like the action. I love the action. Adrenaline is like a drug. I love it. But what am I doing?

One friend of mine was killed in January 2004 at Erez crossing [the main crossing point from the Gaza Strip to Israel] in a bombing by a female Palestinian. He was my good friend. I would still be in Gaza with him if I hadn't gone to officer school. He didn't go, and he was blown up there. Maybe he would be here now. I have one good friend still there; he's been there two and a half years, and he's this close [he holds a finger and thumb half a centimeter apart] from being off the edge, completely crazy. There was another bombing at a checkpoint where we were. I saved my friend's life. His head was open, and I put two fingers inside his head, and it saved his life. I could see his brain and his skull. I had never seen that before.

Do you know how it is at a checkpoint? Everyone who comes up... how do you know he hasn't got a bomb under his shirt? You're there. You're in a bad mood. Your girlfriend calls up and breaks up with you right on the spot, right there, on the phone. What do you do? You make 'em wait. You say, "They can wait all day." Internationals, the ones with the aid groups, they phone me here for help when they can't cross a checkpoint. They're frustrated because they can't go. When they shout, or give you a hard time, and they do that, you say to yourself, "You can wait. You can wait all day. I've got all day. I've got a lot of time."

▪▪▪

Hidaya is a Palestinian architect who lives with her husband, a doctor, and their three children just outside Jenin refugee camp. She, like the IDF officer, sees herself as a point on a long historical narrative. Her parents fled into the West Bank in 1948. She was born the year before the Six-Day War of 1967 and learned what violence meant before she reached her teens. I met Hidaya for the first time in Jenin in 2001 and again, with her family, when I went back in 2006. She writes to me periodically about life in Jenin and about experiences that have shaped her and her family.

Let me tell you about my family. My mother's relatives and my father's relatives all came from Jaffa, from different parts of what is now Tel Aviv. Both families lived there for generations, and Palestine is the only homeland we know.

My parents married young in 1938, so when the war came in 1948, they had five boys. I have five brothers and six sisters, and I'm the youngest. Before the war my father built a house. It had two floors, and he planted all kinds of trees around it. Mother used to tell us how she picked the oranges right from the window because they were so close. My grandparents also had a garden at their house, and Dad used to tell us that it was very big and full of trees, especially oranges. He said whenever my grandfather saw oranges in the market in later years he always cried.

When the war began, my parents had just moved into our new house. News spread that Jews were killing Arabs, and many people were running away. My family was afraid, and my father decided that they would leave for a few days until things calmed down. My mother tidied the house and watered the plants, and they left everything except for a few things they took for the road, hoping that in a few days they would be back. Those days lasted for fifty years, and they both died without moving back.

After 1948 my parents moved from place to place and finally settled in Nablus. We found the chance to go back to Jaffa once, when I was nine years old. It was almost thirty years after they had fled. We took a taxi to the house of my dreams, the house that my parents had told me so many wonderful things about.

We got to an intersection of two wide streets, and my mother wondered where we were and asked my father if this was the right neighborhood. My father was amazed at how everything had changed, but then he began to recognize the place. The taxi stopped, and my mother said, "Yes, this is our house, but the street was not so wide." My father pointed to the traffic lights and said, "Yes, we had our water well just there."

I looked at the house, and now I am an architect, but my memory can't help me draw it. I was only nine years old. I thought, *So this is the paradise my parents told me about?* It seemed to be a big house, and I remember a large window on the second floor with something painted yellow around it. Inside the wall the garden was full of trees, big trees.

My parents tried to talk with the Jewish lady who was living in our house. My father tried to tell her that he owns it . . . he planted those trees . . . and he has the keys and the documents to prove it. The lady said that if we didn't leave immediately, she would call the police. My cousin told my father that it would be better if we left before something bad happened to us. Until then I had never seen my father so sad. He took a small branch from the olive tree outside the gate that he had planted thirty years ago, and he looked at the house for the last time with tears in his eyes, and we left.

We put the branch from our tree in a vase in our living room, and we all watched it for months lose a leaf at a time. My father was badly ill for almost three months after that visit. He died a few years later still dreaming that one day we would go back and live in our house.

▪ ▪ ▪

The 1970s were a decade of stunning violence. They saw a wave of airline hijackings and deadly bombings by Palestinians, and the massacre of Israeli Olympic athletes in Munich. In 1975, the year after Yitzhak Rabin succeeded Golda Meir as prime minister, Palestinians stormed a seafront hotel in Tel Aviv with guns and grenades and set off bombs elsewhere in Israel. One, placed in a refrigerator in West Jerusalem's crowded Ben Yehuda Street, killed fourteen and wounded more than seventy. Afterward, Rabin said: "We must continue to firmly adhere to Israel's policy of not entering into any negotiations with the terrorist organizations. The only language they understand is that of the sword—and it is in that language that we shall talk to them." As a child growing up in Nablus, Hidaya heard the language, long before the word intifada entered the international political lexicon. It was 1976.

Let me tell you about another incident in my childhood which changed me from the inside. It was the death of our friend Leena.

I was ten, and it was the year after we visited the house in Jaffa. Demonstrations were taking place in Nablus, and I was at home and heard that the IDF was shooting students. There was so much noise, and then we heard that some girls were injured. I was afraid because I knew that my older sister would be there. When I went down to the street, I saw two young men carrying a girl and heard my sister Fadwa shouting "Leena, Leena" and the street was full of people all going to our neighbor's house. There were a hundred people inside shouting and crying, and I went into Leena's bedroom and was shocked. Leena was lying on her bed in her school uniform covered with blood.

Leena was sixteen years old. She was beautiful, very bright, and full of energy. She was my sister Fadwa's best friend, and our families were also friends. She used to spend so much time with us, and we all loved her. I sat beside her staring at her. She had three bullets in her body, one in her neck and two in the left side of her chest; any one of them would have been enough to kill her. I'm now forty, and I still see this when I close my eyes. I always asked myself, "What did Leena do to deserve this? She was only marching in a peaceful demonstration against humiliation and oppression, and what did she get? Three bullets from an Israeli soldier who now doesn't even remember that he killed an angel who was full of life and dreams for the future."

My sister and I used to visit her grave. I collected jasmine from the garden, and my sister made her a necklace, and we put it on her grave. There was a third friend who witnessed Leena's killing, and whenever we visited the grave we saw her sitting there. She could not wait anymore and died a few months later.[1]

▪▪▪

When Israel launched Operation Defensive Shield after the wave of suicide bombings in 2002, the army took over Hidaya's apartment building because the roof offered a clear view and field of fire into Jenin Camp. Confined to the apartment with their neighbors, Hidaya and her husband and children listened to the battle rage for more than a week. Afterward, Hidaya continued her work as an architect for UNRWA and helped design new homes to replace those destroyed during the battle.

I could not sleep that night. I knew something would happen. It was dark and cold and I stood by the window listening to noises from far away. We were all waiting. The Israelis said they would hit us hard and I could feel the tension in the air.

I slept for a few minutes on the couch, and the sound of tanks woke me up. I looked out the window, and the Israeli soldiers were everywhere around our building. My building has eight apartments, and we live on the ground floor. Apache helicopters were in the sky and there was shooting everywhere. The soldiers ordered everyone in the upper apartments to leave within minutes but not us. I didn't know what to do and went out and tried to talk to the soldiers. One soldier ordered all the people from upstairs into my apartment. I let everyone in. We were five families; everyone was carrying bread or milk for the kids, and others were holding blankets. We were twenty-two people—ten adults and twelve kids. Everything was happening fast and the soldiers occupied the eastern four apartments in our building, the tanks were filling the town and we were under curfew with no electricity and no water, just the supply of food and water I had in the house.

We spent seven days together not daring to go near a window because all my windows were smashed from the shooting. The soldiers set up a machine gun on the third floor and that machine gun did not stop day or night, targeting the camp a few hundred meters behind my house.

I hated the night and I hated the candles because when night came the soldiers were more active and the tanks came and parked by our building, making the earth shiver underneath and with it all our hearts shivered and the rockets from the helicopters did not stop all night, and most of the time I was praying to God to let us all die together and not leave any one of us to suffer.

Each morning I would sneak out to see if there was anything left of the camp, and in my heart I was always praying for them. In the middle of that I had twenty-two people to feed and the house to clean and manage with very little. When I let the kids use the bathroom one after another, they didn't use water and I cleaned afterward. We had so little water and it was precious.

Even remembering those days makes me shiver because at that time I did not think we would make it. But then I thought, *We will survive, and we will stand against the brutality of the Israelis, and what we went through will make us even stronger.*

▪ ▪ ▪

The conflict is about many things, and for Jews one of them, going back to 1948 and beyond, is overwhelming strength and the willingness to use it. The sergeant, now out of uniform, is a humane man who spent a good part of his service, including Operation Defensive Shield, seeking approval for Palestinians' humanitarian-travel permits. Fellow soldiers teased him for being a "social worker." The sergeant has thoughts about the complex connection between Israeli and Palestinian societies that are sometimes at odds with each other. He opposes the occupation and the way Palestinians are controlled and humiliated; but in 2002, he said, Israel did what was necessary. When we met again, four years later, he talked about his army service and the occupation.

Defensive Shield had to be done like that. Right then. We could not wait any longer. The bombings were intolerable, and if we had waited any longer, we would have looked weak. Mistakes were made, yes, but we had to strike. We cannot ever afford to appear weak.

It is very hard to see these people suffer. To go to a hospital in Israel they needed an invitation [an authorization saying that the treatment is not available in the West Bank]. Much advance documentation was needed. Most of the responses were negative if the cases were not urgent. I always tried, even if I knew it would fail. At least you tried, you didn't just say no to them. You had to hear their stories, and they were very sad. They brought their sick children. One man held his child up like a bag of potatoes: "Look—my sick child." These elegant people were just standing there in front of the filthy gate and the soldier in his filthy uniform. You just had to help them. But sometimes you got fed up and couldn't listen to their stories anymore. Of course, you do see them as people. But they were different because at the end of the day, you finish your duty and go back to your base, or go home and leave it behind, and I always tried to have a clean conscience. We go home, and if we want to go to the mall, we get in the car and go. They cannot. For them it's never over. I don't care about the religion or the culture. They have the same basic needs as we do. A soldier was killed, and the next day I went to his funeral. It's basically, "The enemy shot my friend, and now I'm helping them through my checkpoint." You have a hostile population and armed soldiers on the other side. We haven't yet got to the point where we realize the occupation is bad for us.

▪▪▪

Hidaya wrote me a postscript to her recollections of Defensive Shield. After days of shooting and shelling, her youngest child, a year-old girl, was vomiting and listless. In his depleted medical bag, her husband found some medicine that eased the baby's stomach; but she was barely moving. When soldiers left the house to occupy one closer to the camp, Hidaya weighed the risks of taking the baby to hospital, a few streets away. Then the family encountered a bulldozer driver on a mission. It may have been Kurdi Bear.

I called the hospital, the Red Cross, . . . anyone I could think of for help, but the answer was the same: "We cannot move under any circumstances; the soldiers will shoot anything moving." I saw people holding a white flag and walking, and I told my husband I will do the same and take my baby to hospital because we were losing her. . . . But he said, "Are you crazy?" We heard that a woman had been shot while walking with a white flag. We were still under curfew and still didn't know what was going on outside. We only heard the explosions and saw the tanks and the bulldozers eating the roads and everything in front of them.

That night we were sleeping in the living room in the middle of the house and the baby was sleeping on my chest, holding me. . . . I heard loud noises, tanks and bulldozers and more. The phone still worked, so I called my upstairs neighbor to ask her what was going on, and she said the bulldozers are knocking things down very close to us and coming our way. It was cold and dark, and with my baby very sick we did not know what to do and. . . . Then the phone went dead so I knew they were just outside our building. We wrapped the kids and tried to leave from the kitchen door, and there it was, a huge D-9 bulldozer almost as big as a two-story house. The bulldozer hit the gate, and there was a car near it and he took his time smashing it to pieces. Then the boundary walls went down and we were watching from behind the door . . . seeing our house as a game in the hands of a crazy guy. He hit the corner of the building and then something fell on him. We were lucky, because he stopped and went to the other side of the road, still hitting everything in front of him. This was one of the most frightful nights I ever had, not just for me but for the kids. Afterward we spent more than three months sleeping in the same room, the five of us, [because of] the nightmares, which until now my son still has.

▪ ▪ ▪

In my years with UNRWA in the West Bank, the few times I saw Palestinians and Israelis together in any numbers were at checkpoints or during confrontations in the towns and camps. The only other time was a day when everybody's radiator boiled over at once.

Returning from the northern West Bank one summer afternoon, I turned onto the final leg of Route 60 leading to Pisgat Ze'ev checkpoint, the last Border Police barrier before entering Jerusalem. As far as the eye could see around the curves, the road was a shimmering steel ribbon of motionless vehicles. I called our radio room and was told that the IDF had declared a major alert after warnings of an impending bomb attack.

I checked my canteen and the jeep's exterior thermometer. It was 37 degrees Celsius (98.6 degrees Fahrenheit)—body temperature—outside and hotter than that inside, as the air conditioner was broken. The water in my canteen was as hot as coffee, and heat radiated off the pavement in sheets. The five kilometers (three miles) to Pisgat Ze'ev would take the next three hours.

Cars and trucks crept forward a meter and stopped again. Many had given up the ghost and were abandoned by the roadside, hoods up and hissing. The traffic jam and the heat were egalitarian. As people abandoned cars and vans, they took to the highway. Orthodox Jews in broad-brimmed black hats and white shirts, women in long skirts, settlers in kippas, and Palestinians of all ages and professions were inching toward Jerusalem like lava. Jackets over shoulders, they mopped their brows and outpaced the cars. As the numbers grew, the temperature rose a degree and personal radiators boiled over too. People weren't speaking to each other—it was too hot to hold a conversation—but some found the energy to speak to me.

"Nazi!" was a frequent epithet from some Israelis. (I was used to unpleasant gestures from settlers, but I had never been able to make the mental leap of associating the UN with Nazis. UN cars parked in parts of West Jerusalem would occasionally have a swastika carved into a door panel.) I ignored those comments, but when someone spat at the jeep, it left me an uncomfortable choice. I could leave the windows open and take my chances, or close them and roast. I left them open and kept smiling.

Passing Palestinians also had a go, making spirited remarks in Arabic, which I regretted I could not understand. Since they were making fists or waving their arms at the same time, I figured they were not wishing me a nice afternoon.

My canteen was running low, but so far the jeep's radiator was steady. I didn't fancy joining the great trek, and besides, I was not allowed to leave a disabled UN vehicle. I sat and sweated and watched the parade and the temperature gauge, my shirt glued to the seat. The traffic jam was not improved by what must have been the singularly most unattractive view in the West Bank. On one side was a barren hill where a few bony goats wandered around, and on the other side a rocky field strewn with plastic bags and bits of trash. There were no trees to look at, and not a breath of air was moving. The pace never increased, but we were getting there one car length at a time, and the "Nazi" comments had stopped.

Two and a half hours into the jam there was movement from the car in front of me. The passenger-side door of the faded blue Subaru sedan opened, and a uniformed girl soldier, a corporal, got out with her M-16. She scanned the long line of barely moving cars and put the rifle back in the car, muzzle down on the floorboards. Still watching the traffic, she pulled her uniform blouse out of her trousers, reached inside, and somehow managed to extricate her bra without removing her blouse. She flung the bra back in the car, tucked in her blouse, and gave a long, luxuriant stretch. Then, presumably cooler and happier, she flashed me a grin. The young corporal had perfect teeth.

The last half hour before the checkpoint passed quickly. Palestinians and Israelis were still walking. No one had been shot or gotten into a fistfight, and the bomb rumor had been a false alarm.

EIGHT
"CLOUDS RAINING STONES"

The Islamic festival of Eid al-Fitr celebrates the end of the holy fasting month of Ramadan and falls at a slightly different time each year, depending on the phases of the moon. Families wear their best clothes to pray, visit friends and family, and exchange gifts of clothing and food. A few months later and ten days after the annual hajj, Muslims celebrate Eid al-Adha, which observes the prophet Ibrahim's readiness to sacrifice his son to Allah. Families who can afford it sacrifice a sheep or goat for a feast and perform charitable acts such as giving food to the poor and new clothing to other family members. Children are usually given new clothes or a toy.

In recent years the Eid gifts most desired by boys have been guns: scaled-down plastic M-16 or AK-47 rifles and black matte-finish 9-mm handguns with a removable magazine. From any distance the toys cannot be distinguished from real guns, and boys playing intifada games carry them everywhere and point them at passersby. Once in a while an Israeli soldier mistakenly kills a child brandishing one.

In 2005 a twelve-year-old boy holding a toy gun was shot in the head by soldiers in Jenin Camp during Eid al-Fitr. The IDF apologized right away. Then the parents of the dead boy made a stunning gesture: They donated their son's organs to six people in the hospital where he died; all six recipients were Israelis, and four were Jews. Senior Israeli government officials and the head of Jenin's most powerful Palestinian militia praised the gesture. The goodwill that grew out of the tragedy didn't last long.

Some parents say they try to discourage the toy-gun fad, but like parents in other countries they tend to succumb to persuasive childish pleas at holiday time. Alternatively, they see no reason why their children should not carry toy weapons in the streets. Guns, whether imitation or real, are as much a part of life as bread.

Just before I left the West Bank in the summer of 2004, I stopped in Tulkarm Camp to take a picture of a little boy holding a toy gun made of bits of pine planks and tied around his neck with a string. It wouldn't have fooled anyone. Uday was five years old and was standing outside his house with his eleven-year-old sister. He wore thick glasses and an oversize baseball cap that sat crookedly on his head. When I approached with a camera, he bolted into the house crying. His mother came out to investigate, wiping her hands on her apron. "Oh," she said. "Uday ran in and said the Jews were coming." She served us orange soda, and Uday eventually posed for a picture, still clutching his gun but not quite sure that we weren't dangerous. A group of older boys, between eight and ten, gathered around until their attention was diverted by the powerful engine of an army Humvee roaring up the next street. The older boys took off to stone the jeep, but I caught two of the smaller ones. "I want you guys to be careful," I said through my translator. In shocked tones, she told me what they said in reply. "We hope the Hummer comes back and runs over you both, and we hope you die!" they had said cheerfully. The translator, a woman with grown children of her own, leaned over and gently asked why they would say such a thing. "Because we all want to die! We want to be martyrs and go to heaven!" they said as they ran off to chase the Humvee. It was not an idle boast by children too young to know what violent death looked like. And it wasn't that they wanted anything bad to happen to us; they just figured that if we were crushed under the wheels of the Hummer, we got a special pass. Life on earth—theirs or ours—was nothing special, and paradise awaited.

Some months earlier, in a village not far from there, I was visiting a Palestinian banker at his home during Eid al-Adha. As we chatted over coffee, the ten-year-old child of a relative came in wearing a new designer-logo baseball cap and new shirt, trousers, and shoes, his Eid presents. He also carried one of the toy 9-mm handguns that were so hot that year, and he kept taking the magazine out of the handle and ramming it back in. It made a satisfying, solid click. He repeatedly stuck the gun in my face, which I found slightly unnerving.

The banker had been describing the routine difficulty of travel. His bank was in Nablus, and he often spent five hours getting there, a trip that without checkpoints would have taken half an hour. Then he told me this story:

> I was on a bus going to work, and I saw the guy next to me shot to death. By a soldier. They shot the bus. Five others were wounded. The soldier cried. He was crying. An officer came up to him and said, "You shouldn't cry, this is your job, you are a soldier and you killed a man. This is part of your job." They are human. They are just young boys. This is not right for them.

It wasn't right for any of these young people. In the weeks after Operation Defensive Shield, Palestinian boys roamed the ruined streets of Jenin Camp with murder and confusion in their eyes. They patrolled their alleys clutching scrap-wood guns and were hostile to foreign aid workers and adults in general. It could be startling to meet them rounding a corner. Conversations were predictably grim.

There were days when I thought I was observing a war between rival gangs of boys, except that one gang was slightly older and packed lethal power. The Arabic word *shabab* means boys, older boys, or male youth. Although the word is used literally, during the intifada it acquired a slightly militant or conspiratorial shade. The greeting "Hi, *shabab*," brought grins from kids who relish fighting tanks and do not fear death.

The clashes of rocks against steel made good television and were filmed by crews from around the world. On one of my first trips to Ramallah, I watched the pageant unfold after Friday prayers, the traditional time for a confrontation in most West Bank towns.

As jeeps drove at speed over a rocky field, boys came out of hiding and let loose with slingshots from corner getaway positions and the windows of an unfinished apartment building. Stones pinged off the armored jeeps' grated windows with impressive accuracy. Some of the olive-drab jeeps wore splotches of red, white, black, or green paint, the colors of the Palestinian flag, from earlier clashes. Paint bombs became increasingly popular and particularly goaded the soldiers: paint exploding on a windshield was hazardous and left a graphic and annoying reminder.

More jeeps arrived, followed by more boys and more rocks, which rained down on the squat armored vehicles. A pair of APCs took positions on the edge of the field and, farther outside, a tank. With their flanks protected, a jeep stopped and a soldier got out and knelt behind the open door to fire a tear-gas canister or a cluster of plastic-coated steel balls, each projectile the size of a child's marble.

Spectators from NGOs and various monitoring groups gathered on the hillside as they did every Friday afternoon in Ramallah. From a cynical point of view, the ritual combat had become an episode of weekend entertainment. Clouds of tear gas wafted over the battle zone and drifted up over the spectators, who retreated coughing and with stinging eyes.

Above the churning melee of a dozen jeeps and a hundred *shabab*, a fleet of Palestinian Red Crescent Society (PRCS) ambulances stood ready, engines idling and medics watching as they leaned against open doors. Nurses and doctors waited inside a casualty tent. When boys went down with injuries, the IDF jeeps backed off and the ambulances raced in, sirens wailing. With casualties off the field, the clash resumed.

The PRCS was highly efficient at treating injuries and kept meticulous records. This was the *shabab* casualty list by three o'clock that afternoon:

- Six injured by steel balls; not life-threatening
- One injured by unidentified shrapnel
- Sixteen injured from tear-gas inhalation; one serious and evacuated to hospital
- One beaten by a rifle butt.

Although I could understand the rite, I found it hard to watch children in T-shirts throwing stones at rifle-packing combat troops in body armor. It was always going to end the same way. I mentioned the repetitive slingshot attacks and steady stream of young casualties to my assistant, who had two small children of his own. "They can't live without it," he said with a thin smile.

The clashes regularly had more serious endings. On the Jerusalem side of Qalandiya checkpoint, boys found tactical advantage on high bluffs and hurled stones at soldiers from relative safety. The problem, which I witnessed several times, was that soldiers fired back in the general direction with live ammunition, and Palestinians waiting at the checkpoint got caught in the crossfire. Many such incidents ended with fatalities.

Aida refugee camp in Bethlehem was a perpetual hot spot. Bandak Street, which runs along one side of the camp and ends at Rachel's Tomb, was used as a patrol road—and a deliberate avenue of provocation—by the Border Police.

The Border Police, not universally known for their sensitivity in dealing with Palestinians, routinely sped up and down Bandak Street and stopped at a junction next to the walled-in playground of the UNRWA girls' school. The school had been heavily damaged by IDF shelling during Operation Defensive Shield and still bore the scars of it. Two years on, the girls were lucky to get through a school day without hearing gunfire or inhaling tear gas during play breaks or through the windows in their classrooms.

"Time to come out and play the stone-throwing game," a Border Police trooper would call in Arabic through his jeep's bullhorn. If that didn't draw boys with fists full of stones, the soldiers jacked up the language, taunting them with sexually charged insults that are deeply offensive in Arab culture. It always worked. Soon stones would bounce off the jeep, and steel balls and tear-gas grenades would fly in the other direction.

"Jeep!" The shout brought corresponding whistles from inside the camp. In less than a minute the street was full of *shabab* primed for action. As they ran pell-mell after the Border Police, a toddler in diapers scooped up pebbles and flung them in the air.

"We try to keep them off the streets, but what can we do?" a mother told me. The camp committee and parents discussed whether boys could be discouraged from challenging armed soldiers. It was a politically sensitive issue and had to do with the appearance of strength: no one wanted to suggest anything that reduced the level of militancy or looked like weakness. A decision was postponed.

Girls mostly left the fighting to the *shabab* and tried to get on with their studies. At the Aida school, I asked a group of seven- and eight-year-old girls, all intifada veterans, what they would say to the soldiers if they had the chance. "Go away from us. What have we done to you?" one said. "Don't come too close, because we need to study without your interruption," her friend said. "Don't steal our Palestinian flag," a third said.

Would they have any advice for boys in the camp? They all raised their hands. "Don't throw stones at the soldiers next to the school, because they will shoot us," one girl said. The others nodded. Young girls saw the logic of consequences in a situation devoid of common sense. I tried to imagine a scene in which these Aida school moppets lectured a lineup of Border Police, who hung their heads in shame and promised to stop.

I found it hard to comprehend why armed soldiers would deliberately provoke a fight with children but witnessed such incidents over and again. Perhaps the boredom of rattling around in an uncomfortable jeep overtook good judgment. With the long-standing adversarial mind-set and the conviction that Palestinian children were either terrorists or future terrorists, it probably wasn't a difficult decision to get a little action going.

One placid afternoon in Ramallah, I watched an army jeep drive back and forth past the entrance to Am'ari Camp, which is home to about nine thousand refugees and is set back from the main road. On the first pass nothing happened. Nor on the return pass. On the third drive-by, a few boys came out of the camp and threw stones at the jeep. The driver gunned the powerful engine, drove up the block, did a U-turn, and came back, now accompanied by a second jeep. This time, more boys and more stones. Soon, more jeeps and an APC.

This continued until there were well over a hundred *shabab* pelting the armored vehicles. It ended, as usual, with soldiers firing plastic-coated steel balls and gas into the crowd. There were no injuries that I knew of. Eventually the soldiers drove off, and the boys melted back into the camp.

Jalazone refugee camp, just north of Ramallah, has two UNRWA schools, on opposite sides of the same street. The schools are at the top of a hill at the camp's farthest reaches and uncomfortably close to a settlement. Jalazone was generally quiet in those days, yet tanks and jeeps regularly drove past the two schools. One tank parked in front of the gates when the street was crowded with pupils, and the driver revved the powerful diesel engine, sending clouds of black exhaust smoke billowing into the school grounds, the girls' head teacher told me. She went out and asked the tank commander to leave; he replied by shutting off the engine. When he finally did leave, he drove the Merkava up and down past the school, and the heavy steel treads screeching on the macadam left girls in their classrooms in tears. Such incidents exceeded simple harassment; they were downright cruel.

In the fall of 2003 and spring of 2004, we received reports that soldiers were parking in front of the Jalazone schools and disturbing the children almost daily. Some children were said to have been beaten. I was sent to investigate, and over several days I talked to students and teachers from both schools. They told me that when school shifts changed, a jeep would stop outside the gates or down the hill leading back into the camp. Among the testimonies I took:

- Three boys and one girl said they had been threatened or slapped by soldiers.
- One boy aged eleven was taken into a jeep and struck on the back of the head with a rifle butt; when the boy was released, he went to a local clinic and had his cut stitched up.
- A soldier slapped a boy in the face and jabbed him in the abdomen with the muzzle of a rifle.
- A soldier grabbed one eight-year-old girl by the shoulder of her dress and roughly dragged her toward the jeep. "You're the one who was cursing me," the soldier said. He kicked her and, once inside the jeep, struck her on the head with the butt of his pistol; the blow did not break the skin.
- Five boys said in separate interviews that soldiers demanded they divulge the names of pupils who threw stones. They were threatened with beatings if stones were thrown again.

When youngsters were injured or UNRWA schools taken over or shot up, I took statements and photographs and gathered as much detail as possible; my reports were forwarded to UN lawyers. I conducted investigations in a matter-of-fact way, but the recurring stories from Jalazone Camp got my dander up. For a couple of days in a row, I stashed the UN jeep inside the school grounds and staked out the road.

As the girls walked home, I photographed an army jeep parked halfway down the hill. Soldiers sat on benches inside the open back door with rifles resting on their knees and pointing outward. There was no military reason for the jeep to be there. When I questioned an officer sitting in the driver's seat, he denied that soldiers harassed the children and said they were merely trying to dissuade them from stoning mechanized patrols in the area.

"Why not just leave them?" I asked. "Stones are no threat to armored vehicles, and you're used to it anyway."

"They must not throw stones," he said.

"But when you stop here every day, you are encouraging them to throw stones and frightening the girls and smaller students," I said. The officer slammed the armored door and drove away. Conflict prevention was not part of his equation.

After I filed my report, the harassment stopped for a while. A formal legal investigation went on for some time, and the army cooperated at the highest level; more than a year later UNRWA lawyers accompanied the Jalazone boys to an IDF investigative panel. The children were unable to positively identify the soldiers.

I investigated several cases of soldiers firing on schools when classes were in session, resulting in minor injuries to children from broken glass or shards of plaster. Once, a bullet passed through a window in the principal's office just as he got up to answer the phone. (Another teacher was calling to say there was shooting outside.) I measured the height of the chair and the height of the bullet hole in the window. Had the teacher remained seated, the bullet would have hit him in the head.

"You were lucky," I said.

"*Inshallah*," the teacher replied, pushing around chips of broken glass on his desk.

The IDF usually had three standard replies to our reports: Someone had opened fire on them from inside that location; they were pursuing a gunman; or they hadn't fired the shots that hit the school. The charges and denials went in predictable circles. I just measured distances and figured trajectories, took photographs, collected bullet casings and spent rounds, and interviewed multiple witnesses.

In Jenin, Palestinian fighters caused a serious problem and endangered Palestinian students when they hid explosives in a length of pipe to ambush jeeps as they passed a school. The IDF got wind of it, a firefight broke out, and more than a hundred rifle bullets struck the school walls and shattered windows while girls lay on the floor under their desks. No one was injured.

I got permission to interview the girls, but none of them wanted to talk; they just looked at the floor, and I left them alone. There had been much shooting around the Jenin boys' and girls' schools all year, and tanks intentionally smashed concrete perimeter walls or the steel gates. The head teacher said her girls were deeply traumatized by the continual violence near the school or around their homes. There was no place where they felt truly safe.

During Operation Defensive Shield soldiers preparing to take over an UNRWA school in Tulkarm demanded that a night watchman hand over the keys to the building. When the watchman and other UN officials refused, soldiers broke the lock on the front gate, blew the school doors open with explosive charges, and used the building as a base for the next three days.

Instead of using the toilets, which functioned properly, soldiers used empty classrooms. They carved the Star of David and the epithet "Death to all Arab [*sic*]" on a wooden desktop and proudly chalked the name of their brigade and childish drawings of soldiers beating people on a blackboard. They also cut up the window curtains to blindfold several hundred adult Palestinians held in the school yard. Children became thoroughly militarized as the intifada wore on, and more so when the army invaded and vandalized their schools.

I enjoyed visiting the schools and, when teachers invited me into the classrooms, had stimulating discussions with the older children. Knowing that I was American, they invariably asked penetrating questions about why the United States unwaveringly supported Israel and whether President George W. Bush really hated Palestinians. The children were intellectually aggressive but never rude, and I seldom missed these opportunities.

But after my first few weeks in the West Bank, I quit asking the *shabab* what they wanted to do when they left school. "Suicide bomber!" and "I want to kill Jews!" were frequent replies. Such responses were common from children under the age of ten, who were absorbing the lessons of the intifada more thoroughly than math or science.

▪▪▪

The martyr posters and a related matter were a perennial headache for UNRWA. Israeli government authorities and lobbyists on both sides of the Atlantic routinely complained that the posters children pasted up in the UN schools (soldiers were in the schools often enough to know what hung on the walls) promoted terrorism. They also charged, at home and abroad, that UNRWA tolerated Palestinian militant activities and even had terrorists on its payroll. UNRWA wearily denied such links but did worry that the Israeli accusations could spook the U.S. Congress and jeopardize funding on which the agency relied.[1]

As a major donor to UNRWA, the United States intently followed Israel's accusations. After some members of Congress demanded that funding be suspended, Washington sent a team from the Government Accountability Office (GAO) to Jerusalem and other UNRWA fields in the Middle East to investigate. My colleagues and I told the commissioners, truthfully, that we had never seen evidence of militant activity inside the schools. If Palestinian kids in UNRWA schools had militant tendencies, I said, it wasn't UNRWA's doing.

To reassure the Congress, our international field teams stepped up a regular schedule of inspections. We trudged up and down the stairs of schools and hundreds of other UNRWA installations, peering into dusty closets, toilet stalls, and under stairwells for signs of anything untoward. I joked that we were weapons inspectors, who, like UN inspectors in prewar Iraq, never found anything. The duty was excruciatingly tedious, but we visited with interesting students and their teachers over countless gallons of coffee and wrote a lot of reports about leaky roofs and broken windows, which needed to be fixed anyway.

Apart from their political and financial implications, however, posters of boys holding weapons were not appropriate in schools, where students were meant to focus on other things. At first we encouraged teachers to keep the walls poster-free. Many teachers tried, but it did not go down well. The dead children were heroes to their classmates, and anyone who removed the pictures was dangerously close to being labeled a collaborator. When a teacher in Deheisheh Camp began scraping posters off the front of the UNRWA boys' school, pupils warned her that if she continued, they would throw battery acid in her face. She stopped.

It was an uphill fight, as nearly every vertical surface in every refugee camp was plastered with the posters or with graffiti encouraging armed revolt. When walls were whitewashed, children got a fresh canvas, and new graffiti appeared overnight.

Some adults regarded injuries sustained by children during the intifada as an unfortunate but acceptable price. "It's like a tax they have to pay for their society," one man said as he stood beaming next to a youngster who had been wounded months before. He said he felt happy when a boy told him that he wanted to be a *shahid*—a martyr.

The kids became experts in low-level urban warfare and had elaborate networks of lookouts and signal relays. Since the prospect of death was not a deterrent, they became increasingly daring. One story that made the rounds and was vaguely confirmed to me by an IDF officer had it that a boy climbed atop a Merkava tank lumbering through Jenin Camp and unbolted and removed the top-mounted machine gun. Later, the army reportedly changed the guns' mounting mechanism. This story, whether apocryphal or true, became part of the folklore of Jenin Camp. (Had soldiers seen a boy performing such an act, they would have shot him; interfering with an IDF vehicle was a red line not to be crossed, and soldiers told me they had orders to shoot to kill.)

Doctors and physiotherapists became accustomed to treating young gunshot victims, too many of whom died.[2] Although it was not part of my job, I tried whenever possible to steer kids away from a fight with a probable lethal outcome.

When I approached an army-occupied house in Kafr Qalil, about twenty boys stood behind a waist-high concrete barricade and prepared to stone soldiers in front of the apartment building. There had been firefights in Nablus that morning, and soldiers were in no mood to be stoned.

My assistant had reversed the car well away from the barricade and did not volunteer to accompany me as I waded into the crowd of boys. I was annoyed, but his view was more realistic than mine. When I tried to explain to the boys that the first rock would draw live ammunition in response, I was jostled and shoved. "We will fight them!" they yelled in English, slapping their chests and thumping mine. I left them, talked to the soldiers, and returned to the car. My assistant, who had accurately judged the boys' temper, coolly remarked, "Their brains are boiling."

I got to know that pumped-up mood well and several times came under a hail of rocks in the UN car. The kids got a peculiar glassy look in their eyes when they wanted to fight, and when the tension meter was really high, they could fail to distinguish a white UN four-by-four from a green army jeep. More than once when we pulled up in front of a school or drove slowly along a camp street, boys would pound the doors with their fists and shout, "George Bush number ten! Osama bin Laden number one!"

Once in a while the youthful heat spilled over into the international arena. A U.S. State Department delegation visited the UNRWA schools in Fawwar Camp, south of Hebron, after much planning and secrecy about the timing. The *shabab* learned the details anyway and were ready. As the American convoy sped into the camp, the armor-plated Chevrolet Suburbans were peppered with stones from the well-concealed students.

While delegation members enjoyed tea, cookies, and speeches in the girls' school, secret service agents went next door to the boys' school to check for possible security threats. One refrigerator-size agent returned straightening his cap and adjusting the heavily laden pockets of his vest.

He had been ambushed by boys hiding behind a wall. "They knocked my hat off," he said with a smile that may have betrayed a hint of professional admiration. As the Chevrolets tactically zigged and zagged out of the camp after the visit, boys stoned the convoy again and ripped the number plate off a UN jeep.

Teachers and parents told me that children who had been well adjusted before the intifada wet their beds and had nightmares and a variety of other physical and psychological symptoms. Their grades fell as they fought among themselves, broke furniture, and hit teachers. "This never happened before," a burly physical-education teacher told me in a Nablus-area village that had been under closure for most of the year. "Kids now have no respect for authority. There is no way to control them."

Teachers confirmed what I already knew: children saw death as normal. When one teacher asked his students to draw pictures, their papers came back crammed with helicopters, tanks, soldiers, and bloody corpses. He tried a different tack and asked a boy to draw a picture of rain. The boy drew clouds raining stones. Fresh graves in the local cemetery were festooned with green Hamas banners. When I paused to look, children begged to be photographed among the gravestones. I declined, but the poses they struck were just like the kids' poses on the martyr posters.

A young psychologist who was enormously popular with children in Ramallah-area schools understood the violence. "The only way [they see] to get something from others is to beat them," said Amal Ghanem, herself a refugee. "They feel they have no options, no future."

Camp kids saw almost every aspect of daily life through the prism of violence. Once, my partner, Zeina, and I were walking through Askar Camp in Nablus trailed by the usual crowd of small children who were pleased to have a diversion. Taut-faced teenage lookouts wearing military-style jackets and rolled-up watch caps kept a sharp eye from street corners and upper windows as we walked through the narrow lanes. I was walking with a cane at the time, and this interested a boy of about nine.

"What's wrong with him?" he asked Zeina, who spoke Arabic.

"He was injured," she said.

"Was he shot?"

"No, just injured, somewhere else."

"Well, if he is injured, he is of no use," the boy said. "He is useless and should be killed." Zeina waited for some hours to relay the exchange to me. After that I still enjoyed the rowdy children in the camps but decided to watch them more closely.

The hostilities were taking a toll everywhere. More than two years into the intifada I sat in on a class of teenage girls in Askar Camp and out of curiosity asked how their families had been affected. In a class of 38,

- 8 said a relative had been killed,
- 12 said either they or a family member had been injured,
- 14 said a relative was in an Israeli prison, and
- 4 said their home had been damaged or destroyed by the IDF.

Casualties were widespread, but the picture was not without bright spots. One just had to look. Some teenagers kept their heads down over their books and stayed out of the confrontations. I met exceptional children who managed to hold the long view. "It is very hard to focus sometimes," a straight-A student who lived a block away from "ground zero" in Jenin Camp told me. "I put pressure on myself. . . . I focus because I want to continue the learning. The best way to fight the Israelis is to study."

NINE

COLLAPSE

The pressure of life in an armed environment was compounded by the state of the economy, which had gone from serious to critical. Thousands of Palestinian men lost their jobs in Israel because Green Line checkpoints were closed to them; those who had jobs inside the West Bank found it difficult or impossible to travel to work. In the winter of 2002 a UN official estimated that 75 percent of adult males in a refugee camp near the Green Line were unemployed. All over the West Bank and in Gaza, families whose balance sheets had been precarious before really felt the pinch.

Children began to go without new clothes or school-lunch money. In January 2002 a teacher in Fawwar Camp told me that the families of half of her students were unemployed. Students began to ask her for donated clothes, a request she had never heard before during her teaching career. After a girl broke a leg in a light fall in the playground, the teacher asked her mother how much milk her children drank; the mother conceded that she could no longer afford to buy milk.

The loss of jobs and the road closures thoroughly disrupted commerce and helped push the economy over the edge. Trucks transporting fruit, vegetables, and basic foodstuffs had to take long detours on bad roads, which necessitated frequent repairs, replacement of tires, and higher fuel consumption. Sometimes local produce such as grapes and lettuce just rotted when trucks weren't allowed out of villages. As a result, the retail cost of vegetables, flour, rice, milk, and other goods rose sharply, and sometimes monthly.

The economic chain reactions worked like this. In one northern village, the price of chicken meat tripled, putting that source of protein out of reach for the poorest families. The local poultry farmers, who now had less income, could no longer afford to feed the birds, and chickens soon vanished from the village altogether. The families of farmers and feed suppliers then joined the growing ranks of Palestinians who couldn't make ends meet.

Teachers in the refugee camps had traditionally found a reliable measure of disposable cash in a fixture of grade-school life: the canteen. But students who had come to school with a few small-denomination coins for potato chips or a candy bar in the past now stayed away from the store; I saw them sitting on school walls during breaks, empty-handed. Canteen income, which was used to finance some UNRWA school repairs, fell by half between 2001 and 2002, teachers in different schools said. This decline had social side effects. It reminded students whose parents had money and whose didn't. "This small amount of money is very important for the children," a man who had been teaching for twenty-eight years said.

A grocer up the street said that before the intifada all his customers paid in cash or ran small tabs, which they paid promptly. That year, his books showed a credit balance of $500 and rising, a large sum for a tiny shop in a refugee camp. Grocers in other towns I visited had raised their prices to try to gain back some of the outlay imposed by higher transport costs.

Extended families accustomed to making do were squeezed in ways seldom seen before. I met a woman whose small stipend from the Palestinian Authority had helped her support eleven grandchildren. The stipend, about $23 a month, could not offset intifada prices, and the woman, who was in her midseventies, resorted to selling snacks by the side of the road.

Social workers who traveled the circuit of towns and villages said the economic decline was causing an increase in depression, sleeplessness, and divorce rates. Men who had been successful breadwinners now stayed home; with no daily routine, they suffered a loss of self-esteem as well as a loss of income. Camp officials and Palestinian police officers told me that violence within the family, a subject discussed with great reluctance, also increased.

The long periods of confinement were particularly hard on children.

School day trips, even modest ones to a town a few kilometers away, were canceled for security reasons and lack of cash. A clutch of children in Askar Camp in Nablus pooled the small coins they got as gifts from their parents one Eid and arranged a trip in a donkey cart. A colleague asked where they planned to go. "Why, around inside the camp," they said. There wasn't anyplace else to go.

Some families began selling household goods and sat on the street with clothing, china, or old appliances spread out on a blanket. Hoarded gold was the last safety net, and selling jewelry was a distressing and embarrassing experience.

Israel's policies of closures and restrictions were widespread, and I never found a town that escaped their effects. Many of the army's operations amounted to collective punishment of the population, which is prohibited by the Fourth Geneva Convention. The Israeli government denied that the closures were collective punishment and said that they were necessary to prevent the movement of terrorists. Although Israel had a legitimate need for security, this was a shaky argument because entire towns were penalized, and the bombers managed to get out anyway.

In the winter of 2003 Silat adh Dhahr, a village on the main highway north of Nablus, looked as though everyone had packed up and moved away all at once. In fact, people hadn't moved; they were staying inside their shuttered homes and small shops during the curfews, which IDF units were imposing at their own discretion.

When boys stoned passing jeeps, the jeeps returned and ordered shops to close for a week, ten days, or a month. Shopkeepers told me this had been going on since the start of the intifada. When I passed through on one occasion, some door grates were open a crack so that they could be quickly closed. I stopped and was quickly ushered inside a small grocery store. The week before, soldiers announced that the stores in Silat adh Dhahr and villages to the north would be closed "indefinitely." Breaking curfew could lead to arrest or damage to the shop, so they complied. We chatted with the shopkeeper and his family for a few minutes and bought the makings for our lunch; we'd been his only customers that morning.

Tel, on a hill south of Silat adh Dhahr, was a microcosm of the intifada-related decline. Visible from Route 60, Tel village was in what used to be called Area A, which was afforded full Palestinian civil and security control under the Oslo accords. Surrounded by several smaller villages, Tel was an agricultural hub that produced market-quality figs, dairy products, and olives and olive oil, most of which used to be sold in Israel.

The village also produced a number of militant fighters. It was a frequent target of the security forces, which kept it under general closure for up to a year and frequently entered it to conduct search-and-arrest operations. For a good part of 2002 and 2003 the only way to get past the cordon was to walk out, usually at night, on dirt paths into Nablus, five kilometers (just over three miles) away.

About 10 percent of Tel's workforce had held jobs in Israel, and the village produced and sold enough of its produce to be nearly self-sufficient. In 1993, the mayor told me, Israel began confiscating village land for a bypass highway. The army barred villagers from tending their olive groves on the other side of the highway, and most olive production ceased. After the intifada got under way, about 70 percent of Tel's lands were off-limits to local farmers.

Tel's thriving dairy industry was crippled in the second year of the uprising. Farmers could neither truck in feed for the animals nor take the milk to market, and one month they dumped more than 150 tons of milk. With a quarter of the village's workforce idle for one reason or another, local businesses saw their income fall by half. Eight smaller villages, whose residents used Tel's school, olive press, and flour mill, were hit hard as the economic ripples spread outward.

Twelve kilometers (seven and a half miles) to the east, the villages of Salem, Izmut, and Deir al Hatab lay amid stunning green valleys and rocky slopes. The three villages were conveniently close to Nablus and uncomfortably close to the militant Jewish settlement of Elon More, which was established in 1979 and had a population of about twelve hundred.

The ninety-one hundred Palestinians in the Salem triangle (I call it that because on the map the three villages form an approximate flattened triangle) had lived in near-total isolation for more than a year when I began looking into their predicament.

The triangle was ringed with bulldozed trenches or earth mounds and felt infinitely remote. "You can get to London before you can get to Nablus," went the local joke. A civil engineer who had been unemployed for the two years since he left university asked me if other villages in the West Bank were as cut off as his. It wasn't a rhetorical question; he had not been out in a long time and wanted to know. The villages, all within walking distance of each other, were subject to repeated IDF search operations and random gunfire in the streets. During a nighttime raid in the spring of 2003, the army evacuated families from a large house, fired antitank rockets into an empty apartment, and then entered and sprayed the rooms with gunfire. Soldiers had the wrong house; they later found and arrested their suspect elsewhere in the village.

Residents were seldom let past the outer checkpoints, and jeep patrols frequently stopped them from moving from one village to another. At armored-vehicle barriers on two sides of the triangle, soldiers subjected people to considerable indignities before making them go home. During several visits I was told that soldiers urinated in front of women and used sexually explicit curse words. One made a Palestinian turn his back and emptied his rifle next to the man's ear. Women told me they tried to sneak out of the village at night through a deep valley, but feared injuring themselves among the limestone potholes and rocks.

The unemployment rate in the Salem triangle was said by a UN social worker to have reached 90 percent that year. Forbidden to leave for long periods, people with no farming experience turned to the rich loam bottomlands, hoping to produce their own food. But, as had happened in Tel, the army declared some fields off-limits. In addition, settlers interfered—as they did all around the Nablus region—with the olive harvest. A number of men and women had held steady jobs with the PA or commercial firms in Nablus, and students attended university there; some did manage to evade the soldiers and get to work and school, but they lost many days. The local economy bottomed out. At the time, the UN World Food Programme and the ICRC provided some aid, but residents said it was not enough to alleviate the shortages. Besides, they fumed, they wanted work, not international charity.

One woman, an unemployed social worker, summed it up: "They prevent us from practicing our simple lives."

▪ ▪ ▪

Olives—the fruit, the oil, and the trees themselves—are a central part of life and culture for Palestinians and Israelis. As in other Mediterranean countries, olives are on every dinner table, and the trees, some of them centuries old, are part of the physical and historical landscape. Olive culture and mythology go back as far as the history of the region itself.

In February 2002 the IDF raided several houses in Halhul, off the Hebron road. The army said that a machine shop was manufacturing weapons and that wanted men were in the area. After a raid on a Palestinian police post the night before, soldiers blew the doors off the shop and wrecked drill presses and other machines. An Apache helicopter gunship strafed one house, a tank fired on another, and foot soldiers shot up and damaged others.

To check on refugees, I drove to Halhul and was given a tour of the machine shop and houses. One house had suffered extensive damage from a tank round, which had cracked walls and set a third-floor food-storage room ablaze. The woman who owned the house took me straight upstairs to the shattered room full of charred rafters and wall studs, melted plastic furniture, and broken jars. Preserved carrots and cucumbers littered the floor. The woman was particularly distraught about one casualty. "The olives! Look, even the olives," she said, surveying hundreds of black and green olives with their sprigs of herbs amid glass shards in pools of water.

The annual olive harvest provides significant income for farm families and benefits for a wider area. Some villages have one or more presses that are kept busy for weeks after the harvest as farmers truck in sacks of olives to be pressed for oil. Even the crushed olive stones are saved as a minor source of fuel; they burn with an aromatic and intense heat, the way some hardwoods do.

Olive trees need regular care through the season. They produce more fruit when branches are pruned and the soil is kept loose around the trees. Cultivation and the harvest provide social events as well as necessary chores. The processes, repeated from year to year, maintain a steadfast connection to the land. Symbolically and practically, olives go to the heart of the conflict. What better target, then, for an enemy?

Israeli settlers maintained an aggressive campaign of terror against Palestinian olive farmers, threatening families who tend the trees, stealing the olives, hacking limbs off trees, or bulldozing entire groves. Although the Palestinians have title to the land and may have worked it for generations, the settlers claim that the Palestinians are trespassing and that the land and trees belong to them. Usually, the settlers do not bother presenting their argument.

Palestinians described the incidents in detail. "Who wants to die now?" one settler reportedly said as he ran a family out of a grove. A settler threatened to amputate the hands of any Palestinian caught picking his olives. Some have been injured and even shot dead as they worked the trees.

Around a village called Mughayir, the harassment happened every season. Farmers' cars were torched, a donkey was killed, and threats were made. When farmers filed a formal complaint with the IDF against the settlers, an officer replied: "Why don't you shoot them?" Ignoring the sarcasm, a man replied with the obvious: the farmers did not carry weapons.

Near Itamar settlement south of Nablus, an army patrol rounded up a family picking olives and drove them to Awarta checkpoint, where they were held for a three-hour ID check. The week before, armed settlers invaded the grove shouting at the family and throwing olives in their faces.

"We work like thieves, as quickly as possible," Mahmoud Kawariq, an eighty-six-year-old farmer with a handshake like a carpenter's vise told me. Nearby, he said, settlers chased Palestinians out of their grove and brought in foreign workers to pick the stolen olives.

The harassment sometimes occurred under the eye of army units. I took reports from Palestinians who said they had been driven away from their trees by armed soldiers, or by settlers while soldiers watched without intervening. When I was seen talking to Palestinians near Itamar settlement, soldiers ordered me to leave. A lieutenant said the road was a "closed military zone" but refused to show me the required printed declaration.

The IDF issued a blizzard of new and changing regulations. Palestinians were allowed to pick olives on certain days of the week, or on trees a hundred meters back (328 feet) from the road. They could not use cars or trucks but must carry the olives in sacks on their backs or on donkeys or bicycles.

The restrictions affected agriculture from the initial fieldwork to the final trucking and marketing. In the vineyards around Bethlehem and Hebron, farmers were prevented from pruning their vines or taking their grapes to market without special permission. If an olive press or other machinery broke down, spare parts were available in a nearby town; although a short distance as the crow flies, the trip could take several days of effort.

Other aspects of Palestinian society came under similar pressures. Israel bombed police stations in Bethlehem, Nablus, and Tulkarm, hoping the air strikes would weaken the Palestinian security forces. The IDF went further, arresting or publicly humiliating Palestinian police officers and forbidding them to carry weapons or wear police uniforms. In Dura, west of Hebron, an officer told me that some of his colleagues had been made to strip to their underwear and walk home, an unimaginable affront. The IDF also methodically destroyed the fleets of police cars. Piles of the flattened blue hulks lay rusting outside police stations in Dura, Hebron, and Qalqilya.

Police officers feared being arrested, so they wore civilian clothes, traveled incognito in taxis, or just stayed home or in their station houses. Police chiefs up and down the West Bank told me that domestic crimes, including assault and robbery, had risen as a direct result. To maintain local law and order, Palestinians fell back on old-style clan councils and committees to settle disputes.

It worked, but only partly. The vacuum was filled by the armed factions, which began to enforce the law as they saw fit. At first some residents approved of this because they saw the factions as less likely than the PA police to demand bribes and more likely to keep criminals in check through rough justice. But others worried about the growing strength of Islamic Jihad, Hamas, and the Tanzim (a Fatah militia) and even the appearance of Mafia-style gangs who had Israeli connections. The refugee camps were awash in weapons and competing militia agendas. It did not bode well for an ordered society.

Israel continued its policy of demolishing Palestinian houses, either because they were built without the required permits or because they had been the homes of suicide bombers or Palestinians who had murdered Israelis by other means. In the Gaza Strip, houses and even whole sections of neighborhoods were leveled when the IDF said it took fire from them. It didn't take much to bring the bulldozers, and thousands of refugees were made homeless in Gaza and the West Bank.

When it came to punishment, the IDF made sure the whole neighborhood got the message. In September 2003 IDF units were pursuing a Hamas gunman near Hebron. The man fled to a house in Dura, where soldiers cornered and killed him in the yard. The dead man was a cousin of a woman who lived in the house but did not live there himself. Soldiers made neighbors drag the body out from behind the building and ordered everyone else outside. In full view of the media, who had learned of the operation, the IDF fired rockets and tank rounds into the house, setting it on fire. Then they brought in bulldozers and flattened the building while it burned. For good measure, they blew up a water well and filled in a second one with a bulldozer. I later watched a video of the operation.

The next morning, thirty-two people—eleven of them children under the age of fifteen—were living in tents put up next to the destroyed houses by the International Committee of the Red Cross. Family members insisted that no one who lived in the house had been involved in militant activities. Laila, a forty-three-year-old widow and mother of three, said her children had always made schoolwork their first priority. Now?

"This will allow hatred to grow inside them against the Israelis," she said. "They are all teenagers, and I am scared for them. It's the time to build character, and this is a dangerous time." Her son Ahmed, a ninth grader who aspired to be a doctor, admitted that his heart was changing. "All my friends in school have houses, and I have not," he said. Razan, his thirteen-year-old sister, could barely speak to me. When I first met her, at the UNRWA school just after the demolition, she sat in a chair staring at the floor and shredding a facial tissue. Weeks later her mother said that she had stopped seeing her friends. This story had the beginnings of a happy ending: over the next year, the family home was rebuilt, and the last time I saw Razan she was smiling and studying again. She plans to be a lawyer and has started to take the long view that some young Palestinians acquired during these violent years.

▪▪▪

Army tanks and bulldozers frequently damaged water mains and electric lines running into villages. It was an effective way of reminding residents of who held the power. Outside the barricaded entrance to Fawwar Camp, water was gushing out of pipes broken earlier by a tank while soldiers looked on from a jeep. Villagers told me they had been forbidden to bring up repair equipment, and soldiers confirmed it. I negotiated a compromise under which the Palestinians were allowed to bring in one tractor and enough hand tools to repair the water main. The water supply was restored; with some urging from the outside, the army had let the Palestinians fix what it had broken.

Palestinian contractors were hard-pressed to keep their businesses going because of road restrictions and Israeli duties on materials such as steel and cement. West Bank firms used to buy sand for concrete from Gaza, crushed stone from Qalqilya, and steel from the Ukraine. This successful business pattern changed.

Commercial trips in the West Bank became scarcely worth the trouble. A Palestinian trucker who had cleared an army checkpoint might be stopped by the police and fined $300 for a broken taillight. Contractors told me that their whole supply chain had been turned upside down. To keep the business going, they started buying raw materials in Israel and transporting them into the West Bank on Israeli trucks. The trucks had an easier time at the checkpoint, but their owners in Israel charged higher haulage fees. Israeli authorities didn't object.

Palestinian apartment-block contractors in East Jerusalem applied for Israeli-issued building permits one floor at a time. A separate permit was required to bring a water line up to a building. Fees were overly expensive, and buildings sat unfinished until the builder found the cash. A contractor who started to build without a permit risked seeing his investment blasted into rubble, and the demolitions occurred regularly.

The extra costs eventually were passed down to families who paid to have the houses built. Everyone ran out of money and construction stopped. It wasn't unusual to see laundry lines hanging on balconies of unfinished apartments with no glass in the windows; the concrete skeletons of such buildings dotted the West Bank. As one veteran builder in East Jerusalem told me, "The Israelis control the market."

▪▪▪

The West Bank was deteriorating in slow motion. Spruce towns like Hebron, Bethlehem, Nablus, and Qalqilya began to crumble. If I had been away from Nablus for a week, the wear and tear was noticeable. Potholes that might have been avoided a month before were deep enough to wreck a car. Curbs and median strips had been ground to gravel by tank treads, light stanchions lay where they had fallen, and sewage and water oozed into the streets from ruptured mains. Rubbish was burned in large street-corner bins because there was nowhere to take it, and acrid fumes from smoldering plastic wafted through the refugee camps. Every surface seemed coated with dust, as though no one had the energy to wash it off anymore.

But when the curfews were lifted, repair crews got to work. I lost count of the number of times pulverized street dividers were rebuilt and given new coats of red and white paint and shrubs were planted in the middle. Even knowing the tanks would do the same thing next time, the people of Bethlehem and Nablus got out their brooms and paint brushes. When a family could scrape up the money, they plastered over the bullet and shell holes. It was a matter of pride.

The wide-scale punishments not only were unnecessary but were ineffective. I understood that Israel was determined to stop the suicide bombings and other murders of its citizens. I also thought that Israel had no good idea of how to dig terrorists out of a radicalized Palestinian population that was either happy to shelter them or had no say in the matter. I understood one more thing: Israel wanted to make as few concessions as possible to the Palestinians over the land.

What I couldn't grasp was the strategy behind the hard line. The punishment and gratuitous brutality took away Palestinians' hope for any solution other than more violence. Did Israeli politicians reason that the security forces could crush the spirit out of people and make them submit? Had they concluded that if they made collective lives so miserable Palestinian society would pressure the militants to lay down their guns? If that's what Israel thought, I thought they were badly mistaken. The heavy hand of the occupation just hardened the Palestinians and made them hate. Perhaps Israel had underestimated *sumud,* the Arabic word for resistance—not armed resistance, but the kind of flexible force a tree presents to a gale. Both types would certainly continue.

The first house demolition I saw came early in my tour, in the fall of 2001. Tanks and APCs rumbled into a small northern village at two in the morning and went straight to an old stone house. It was the family home of a Palestinian who had been killed by Israeli police after he shot three Israelis on a bus in Afula weeks earlier. Asleep inside were the man's mother, wife, children, a brother, and other relatives. Soldiers gave the family ten minutes to gather their things and get out and bulldozed the house. On their way out of the village, the army cut the water mains and phone lines.

When I arrived in midmorning, the elderly mother, wearing the traditional long embroidered Palestinian skirt and blouse, was stooped over in the remains of her house looking for anything salvageable. Sticking out of the stones, steel, and buried furniture were a large, new Palestinian flag and a green Islamic flag emblazoned with verses from the Qur'an. Villagers standing around appeared resigned or cheerful. The bomber's mother, who was in her seventies, was completely unruffled. I had not known the story, and asked her to tell me what had happened. She did, and also commented on her son, who had killed the three Israelis.

"I wish I had ten more sons like him," she said vehemently. The Israelis might have more military strength, I thought, but they probably should be reviewing their multiplication tables.

As the wheel of violence turned and turned again, something else was happening. Israel controlled almost every aspect of Palestinian life, and the humiliations were hard for the most stoic to bear. Under this weight, powerlessness turned to victimhood.

Israel's military bludgeon had worked in tandem with Arafat's corrupt and impotent rule to leave ordinary Palestinians feeling battered, alone, and unrepresented. Every mishap, every indignity, every disaster small or large, was the fault of the Israelis.

Just past Haramiya—"thieves" in Arabic—a wadi beneath ancient eroded limestone cliffs on the way to Nablus, a roadside olive grove burned one summer. A hundred or so trees were badly scorched by the fire, which was fueled by dry grass grown high in the untended orchard. As we passed, my Palestinian colleague, seeing it for the first time, remarked that settlers had burned the orchard and said that I should include it in one of the occasional reports I wrote about settler activities.

"How do you know settlers burned the grove?" I asked.

"They must have," he replied.

I agreed that the destruction of the trees was a shame and that his claim was a possibility. But I pointed out that there was no hard evidence that the fire in this uninhabited spot had been arson. Maybe settlers set the fire, maybe they didn't. A cigarette flicked from the window of a car, any car, could have ignited the matted dry grass.

My colleague would have none of it and was angry that I should harbor the slightest doubt. The fire definitely had been started by Israelis, and there was no need for physical evidence or further discussion. Another colleague had the same reaction when we passed the site a few weeks later. I was seen as being less than sympathetic to the Palestinian cause, even pro-Israeli.

The conviction that everything was someone else's fault was eating away at some essential part of the Palestinian spirit; it provided a handy tool for evading responsibility for action and thought. This was the same reflexive process that prompted a Palestinian to comment after a suicide bombing in Israel, "You see? They provoke us. They *make* us do it."

This was not necessarily a character flaw. It grew partly from Israel's repression and partly from an absence of Palestinian political dialogue. Without meaningful leadership from Yasser Arafat, who offered no vision other than armed struggle, a rational human mechanism collapsed into a vacuum. This oxygen-starved hole smothered critical thought and the ability to seek alternatives to the violence.

Publicly questioning Arafat or his well-cushioned PA coterie could be dangerous, as teachers and others discovered even before the intifada, when any deviation from the party line got them banged up in PA jails. Privately, younger Palestinians referred to Arafat as Ali Baba and the Forty Thieves, although some amended the number of thieves to four hundred to encompass the PA. People knew that Arafat siphoned off sizable chunks of international donor money, and they pointed with disgust at senior PA officials' wedding-cake mansions.

Yet they revered the old man with the revolutionary stubble who reportedly spent an hour each day arranging his black-and-white kaffiyeh into the shape of Palestine and tirelessly demanded the right of return and the creation of a Palestinian state with East Jerusalem as its capital. No Palestinian would disagree with that demand.

Arafat was the only leader the Palestinians had ever had, and there simply wasn't anyone else, which is the way the chairman had constructed the leadership. Arafat's funeral at his destroyed *Mukataa* in Ramallah in 2004 was thronged with distraught mourners, and his picture still hangs in PA government offices and the unadorned living rooms of the refugee camps. But Arafat and his Fatah Party were not the only ones to suffer from myopia. Both sides had restricted vision. Other than inflicting punishment and counterpunishment, neither Palestinians nor Israelis seemed to know how to end the violence.

TEN
ALMONDS

It usually began in late January, and I looked for the signs in a clump of scrub pines between Nablus and Tulkarm. Poking up through a dusting of snow or ice crystals in the early morning were a dozen blood-red anemones. Soon they cropped up everywhere, occasionally with a few white ones, along roadside ditches in the north and then in the thousands mixed with wild mustard in the Jordan Valley.

In Greek mythology the anemone grew from the blood of the slain Adonis. In the West Bank the feathery blooms just meant that the winter rains were ending. Other signs appeared on seasonal cue, welcome distractions from the daily strife.

Among the first flowers were the fragile cyclamens, once nearly extinct, blooming purple and pink out of shaded rock crannies. In the hills where the olive trees had hunkered down through the rains, something changed. It was just a guess at first, but branches on fruit trees looked a bit fuller.

Then, as though someone were turning on a giant bank of lights switch by switch, the almond trees started to bloom. One flared pink by the side of the road just before Huwwara village, and the next day more in a field off to the right. Within a week, if the weather cooperated, the rocky hillsides between Hebron and Bethlehem and the hills and valleys between Ramallah and Nablus would be flecked with pink-blooming almonds, and the white and cream of pear and apple blossoms as those trees joined in.

Over in the Jordan Valley, the canvas was spectacular anytime of year, and the seasonal changes were both subtle and dramatic. If you drove out of Jerusalem in a winter downpour, before you got to Jericho you were in warm desert hills that looked as though they had never seen a drop of water. North of Jericho on Route 90, the first days of spring could be easy to miss. One day the sand hills that had been brown all winter sprouted patches of light green stubble; a week later they were lush green and scattered with lupins and other wildflowers.

The conflict was never far away, no matter where you went. IDF artillery positions overlooking the Jordan Valley blended into the scenery, as did the rusted hulks of tanks and snarls of barbed wire from earlier wars. Other reminders were even harder to ignore. In 2002 large signs went up on Route 90 proclaiming the highway: "Gandi's Road, in memory of the late Rehavam Ze'evi, Minister of Tourism." Ironically, Ze'evi, the former general who was assassinated by the Popular Front for the Liberation of Palestine in 2001, earned the nickname Gandi (a transliteration from the Hebrew of Mohandas Gandhi's name) not from his efforts to make peace with Palestinians, whom he had described as "lice" and "cancer" and whose expulsion, or "transfer," he advocated, but from a time as a young man when he shaved his head and was thought to resemble Gandhi.[1]

Aside from the garish signs, Route 90, which starts below Eilat on the Gulf of Aqaba and runs north through the Jordan Valley, past the Sea of Galilee and up to Metula on Israel's border with Lebanon, is one long scenic postcard. West Bank Palestinians' view of Route 90 probably would be limited to what they could find on the Internet or in tourist brochures; unless they had a special permit, they would not be allowed to drive its length.

Jericho, which bills itself as the world's oldest inhabited city, escaped most of the violence of the intifada and was a tropical oasis. In summer it felt and smelled like southern Africa, its streets lined with palm and flamboyant trees and honeysuckle hedges. Checkpoints outside the city were tight, but there were fewer Israeli incursions, and Palestinian police, barred from active duty by the Israelis, returned to the streets before they did so in other towns. Like Bethlehem, Jericho depended heavily on tourism and suffered a catastrophic loss of business during the intifada. Although many restaurants were shuttered and dusty, it was still possible to find a good meal. From the doorway of an empty restaurant, a waiter would rush out at the sound of an approaching car and furiously wave a menu. Jericho's fruit and vegetable stalls may be the best in the West Bank. For a good part of my time in the West Bank, the historic town was also something of a political oasis; generally quiet and relaxed, with its archaeological excavations and other attractions dusty and unvisited, it made a change from the tension elsewhere.

Driving three hundred kilometers (two hundred miles) a day offered some ersatz tourism, although mostly from the windows of an UNRWA jeep, and I saw something different each time we went out.

Bedouin goat herders were about all that moved in the dry hills of the Jordan Valley other than occasional army patrols. Hiking, amid some of the most varied scenery in the Middle East, was not a prudent activity. I tried it once or twice early on but always felt that I was in someone's gun sight. I probably was.

After a morning's long drive, I pulled off the road between Nablus and Jenin to stretch my legs and watch a hoopoe, or *hud-hud,* as it's called in Arabic, a crested, long-billed bird common in Africa and parts of Europe. The bird's spectacular plumage and dazzling, eccentric flight earned it a place in Greek mythology and Persian poetry. Its call is a haunting *hoop-hoop-hooop* that can raise goose bumps as it echoes in a still forest. I hadn't seen hoopoes in my first year, but in the second year their population exploded in the West Bank. In my book, sighting a hoopoe counted as a successful day.

A thousand meters (three thousand feet) up the road and around a couple of bends from the hoopoe, an army jeep cut me off. "You stopped by the side of the road back there. Why?" the soldier demanded. My explanation of impromptu bird watching triggered many more questions and a thorough ID check. We had not been in his line of sight but certainly had been in someone else's.

The sense of always being observed was not delusional. On a wet winter day I was exploring some back roads with an assistant in his first week on the job, and drove past a disused army training camp and firing range. The camp was littered with a few rusting wrecks, but there was no one around; the country looked interesting, so we drove between a pair of concrete cubes in the road.

As soon as we were through the blocks, the unmistakable roar of a Merkava's main gun focused my attention, and a 120-mm tank round tore past the front of the jeep and slammed into a distant hillside. I stepped on the gas, and my assistant's eyes widened at a second crack from the unseen tank. A couple of kilometers (one and a half miles) on, a jeep squatted crossways in the road. A stern-looking young lieutenant walked over.

"Did you know that a tank was shooting at you back there?" he said.

"Hard not to," I said. "But he obviously didn't intend to hit us."

"It was a warning. This road is part of a military installation and is closed, and you should not have been in there," he said.

I suggested that the army put up some signs to save wasting ammunition in the future. He shrugged and walked away.

"This job is dangerous, isn't it?" my assistant asked. He was a phlegmatic man under fire, and the episode became a staple joke for us later.

There was no shortage of wildlife to look at, and because there was so little traffic, all you had to do was pull off and wait. Gregarious bulbuls flitted everywhere, shrikes perched motionless on wires, and Syrian woodpeckers hammered away at the dead branches of black locust trees. If you waited long enough, a multicolored bee-eater might appear or an iridescent Palestine sunbird would hover while it sucked nectar out of a honeysuckle bloom. Sharp-eyed pied kingfishers were a good bet where there was water, and I never tired of watching them dive like daggers into a pond or river.

For most of the year the olive trees wore camouflage, their dusty pale green crowns and gnarled trunks dotting the hillsides. They were transformed by the first winter rain, which knocked the dry season's dust off the leaves. The brighter green stayed until the rains stopped, and while it was present added another dimension to the hills. As the weather warmed, the groves grew a carpet of tiny pink flowers before the olive leaves turned dusty again.

The travel restrictions made it hard for farmers to get their olives to the oil presses. When they did, an age-old agricultural chapter opened again. A venerable Deutz diesel engine was fired up, and the olives were crushed by massive stones older than the oldest man there. I had been looking for a particular village that had three working presses, and when I thought I was lost, found it by following my nose. The smooth smell of fresh-pressed olive oil drifted over the hills and hung in the valleys, and grew stronger as we descended. Visitors to a press always were given a bottle of the green-gold oil and were doubly lucky if they happened to have some bread in the jeep.

A trip to Tulkarm, if there was no curfew, required a stop at a neighborhood bakery for lunch and a take-home stack of flat breads the size of dinner plates and fresh out of the clay oven. The most popular were those baked with *za'atar*—a spice and herb mixture—or with cheese. At checkpoints on the way home, the smell of the fresh bread often brought a smile from the soldiers.

For a trip north from Jerusalem, one might take as a gift loaves of *ka'ak,* the sesame-covered rolled bread that was eaten with boiled eggs and falafel and was a Jerusalem specialty. The same type of bread is baked elsewhere, but Palestinians from Hebron to Jenin claim they can always recognize Jerusalem *ka'ak.*

Another smell of spring came when the weather was still cold, as soon as fields were dry enough to be plowed. South of Nablus and not far from where settlers terrorized the olive pickers every year, farmers tilled, sowed, and harvested a broad valley in narrow strips of alternating crops on both sides of the road. The strips of grains, sunflowers, and onions—whether growing, plowed, or fallow—changed color several times a year.

Most of the farmers were elderly men and women in peasant dress who lived close to the road and farmed much as their grandparents had. They plowed behind a horse (sometimes on an ancient tractor), bent over to hoe or weed by hand, and used sickles to cut grain and adroitly hand-tie it in sheaves. The first plowing of the season turned over the dark earth and chopped up the volunteer onions from the previous season. The sharp smell of the onions carried for kilometers.

From what I could see, the security forces never bothered the people in their fields. Perhaps they were too old to be considered a risk. I always wanted to stop and talk to them but saw no point in satisfying my curiosity at the cost of attracting a passing army jeep.

Jerusalem's Old City shops sold every type of spice and herb imaginable, but we preferred an up-country place that required some determination to get to. Zawiye was not much more than a crossroads about five kilometers (three miles) inside the West Bank, east of Tel Aviv, in an area called the frontier villages. The only way in from the south was past numerous flying checkpoints, at least one fixed barrier manned by aggressive soldiers, and finally a section of road that challenged even the heaviest truck suspension.

Zawiye's small shop was run by a religious Palestinian who kept in plastic bags, boxes, and jars saffron, cumin, several combinations of curry, oregano, and an impressive collection of dried chili peppers, any one of which required discretion in cooking. He imported the more exotic spices from many countries and enjoyed talking about them.

As Israel's barrier wall and fence went up, beginning in June 2002, residents of Zawiye and villages to the north such as Azun, Hable, and Jayous found themselves even more isolated than before. The once-thriving commercial trade between Israel and the frontier villages was cut, and poor hamlets north and south of Zawiye grew even poorer. Now the traffic was all inside the West Bank.

On the dusty road to Zawiye one day I started to see eggshells. They appeared at regular intervals until I came up behind a long flatbed truck with high sides carrying several hundred square cardboard flats of eggs. The flats were stacked about a dozen deep, and the total egg count must have been in the thousands. The truck was going at a good clip on the bone-rattling road, and each time the front wheels and then the back wheels hit a hole, the eggs launched like Ping-Pong balls out of the top flats and splattered on the road. There were still partly intact flats on the top layer, but most of the damage had been done on the lower levels. A steady flow of scrambled raw eggs ran from under the tailgate and corners of the truck bed.

I couldn't overtake on the bad road and dropped back to keep the egg splatter and clouds of dust from congealing on the windshield. My colleague seemed embarrassed at the destruction the truck driver's haste was causing. "He probably doesn't know what is happening to the eggs," he said. The benefit fell to the crows and sparrows, who waited until the vehicles had passed to tuck into their long roadside omelet.

As the season changed again, flowers and fruits leapfrogged each other. Figs and quince began to show up on family roadside stands and in town markets; people had been talking about the figs for weeks beforehand and snapped up the first ones, despite the price, which dropped later. On our long drives we debated which regions produced the best figs and which types tasted better.

The quince, or *sfargel,* a hard yellow fruit, was starting to go out of fashion in the West Bank because the trees required careful disease prevention and the fruits could be eaten only after long cooking. Palestinians told me they replaced the trees with others that required less work. For us, quince jam justified the hours of cooking, and the tangy perfume, unique among fruits, filled the house.

Grapes were a main crop, particularly in the south, and the vineyards and their owners suffered badly from the road closures. When farmers were prevented from reaching the fields, vines could not be tended and produced less fruit. One year farmers and town officials in Halhul told me that tons of grapes had been lost because the security forces kept the trucks off the roads. The vineyards created their own beauty when the leaves turned several shades of yellow and russet in the fall.

When it came to sheer beauty, the terraced valleys of Battir, near Bethlehem, looked as though they had been filmed for an exotic travel documentary. Nestled between two ridges next to the Green Line, part of Battir village was built into a hill next to a series of Roman aqueducts carved out of solid rock. The springs, which flowed even in the dry season, ran into stepped pools whose channels and sides were coated with moss. Palestinian farmers still could have used the old Roman system of measuring the water they drew to irrigate their valley plots. The Battir UNRWA girls' school, which was also built into the hillside, was a regular stop on our inspection rounds. It was run by Sanaa Abu Ghosh, an energetic woman much loved by her students, who took advantage of the rich soil to keep a school garden going. But Battir's idyllic seclusion was not to last. Located between two major Jewish settlements, the village drew increasing visits from the IDF, and bulldozers began to scrape the land nearby for construction of the West Bank barrier.

Change of focus came unexpectedly. After a chaotic day in Qalqilya during an IDF incursion, we cleared a final contentious checkpoint and headed home. As we turned onto the main highway, a reality of a benign sort filled the car: the heady scent of orange blossoms from roadside groves. Then a fast dissolve back to daily life. Dozens of Palestinian men and children sat forlornly beside boxes of oranges they were trying to sell. There were no customers; the only vehicles that passed were army trucks or Israeli settlers, who no longer made impromptu stops. I never stopped either; although I would have been interested to talk with the grove workers, after a long day in Qalqilya I wanted to get home, and Jerusalem was two hours away.

If the main road between Nablus and Jerusalem was blocked due to an incident, we cut across one of two roads east to the Jordan Valley. The Rimonim and Alon roads ran along the edge of the wild Nakhal Reserve, a series of wind-blasted sand hills and gorges where gazelles the size of large dogs bounded across the road and vultures and raptors cruised the air currents. Crested larks ran along the gravel roadside, tongues out in the heat. These roads had observation points with a vista that included a glimpse of Jordan through a shifting purple haze and high clouds. After a day in the north, we sometimes took these roads just for the view, and it was an outing to look forward to on a day off.

For the first part of my tour I tended to avoid the Rimonim Road, despite its panoramic rock-studded valleys and hills, because of a notoriously difficult checkpoint near some settlements where I had spent many hours stranded in fruitless negotiation. Soldiers stationed there must have earned an advanced degree in rudeness, which they once practiced for more than two hours on UNRWA's then–commissioner general Peter Hansen as we tried to cross.

The checkpoint eventually was moved, and I went back to using the road as a pleasant detour. One afternoon we passed a couple stopped at an intersection with a map spread out on the hood of their Israeli-registered car.

"Lost?" I asked.

"Yeah, I think so," said the man in a wonderfully thick accent I took to be Brooklyn. "Is this the Haifa road?"

It was nowhere near the Haifa road. The couple were on the wrong side of the West Bank mountain ridge and a long way from the seacoast. As we helped them sort out map directions, I asked where they were from.

"Philly," the man said with enthusiasm. "Philadelphia. Been there? My girlfriend is from here, from Israel." I didn't bother mentioning that this was the West Bank. He asked what we did, and I told him that we provided humanitarian aid to Palestinians.

"My God, you don't go into those Ay-rab villages, do you?" he asked.

"Sure," I said. "Every day. In fact we're going to one now. Want to come with us? It would be really interesting for you." (I was teasing him, and would have said so in the unlikely event he accepted the invitation. For him and his girlfriend to go to a Palestinian village in those days might have turned out to be as hazardous to his health as he imagined.) He declined the offer, thanked us, and headed off in search of Haifa, still in the wrong direction.

It wasn't a good idea to stop for sightseeing in some areas, particularly in the eastern sections of the West Bank along the old minefields and double electric fence of the Jordan Valley. In the northeast, where the distance to the Jordan border narrowed, the IDF patrolled intensively between sections of the fence and kept an outer dirt strip raked as perfectly as a Japanese garden for telltale footprints.

A few days after Iain Hook, UNRWA's Jenin reconstruction project manager, was killed in Jenin, we were returning in convoy to Jerusalem through the Jordan Valley when a wheel came off a colleague's jeep. It was later thought that all the lug nuts had been deliberately loosened. Repairs could not be done on the scene, and we radioed for a recovery vehicle from Jerusalem. Our senior security officer and others in the convoy had to continue on to attend a meeting, so my colleague and I waited in two jeeps for the recovery vehicle, a task that, inexplicably, took nearly four hours.

Daylight faded and settlers drove past at speed. We grew concerned. It was getting dark, and if it came to it, there was no place to hide in this flat farmland. An army gun jeep with four crew members passed, turned around, and came back. The crew chief inquired about our situation.

"We're patrolling in the area, but we have time between our regular checks, so we'll stick around and keep an eye on you," he said.

"Thanks, but we should be all right," I said.

"Well, you never know. Some people round here..." He didn't elaborate, but I knew what he meant. I was happy to have their company, particularly as the jeep's mounted light machine guns would deter any antagonism. Every half hour or so the crew would drive off and then return.

After dark, the crew chief got a small gas cooker and tea kettle out of the jeep's side compartment and from his pocket a bag of herbal tea picked from a field. "Special blend," he said. It smelled like a combination of lemongrass and alfalfa. These fellows were well prepared for cold Jordan Valley nights in their open-sided jeep.

Over the brew-up we stood around the jeeps in our flak jackets, chatting and watching lights wink on in villages across the river in Jordan. It was an international miniconvention free of politics: my UN colleague was Irish, the IDF crew chief had been born in the Ukraine, one soldier was an Uzbek, one was Brazilian, and the other had been born in Israel. When our recovery vehicle arrived, the crew chief gave me half the bag of tea, boarded his gun jeep, and drove off.

▪ ▪ ▪

For those who could travel freely, northern Israel offered plenty of places to explore on long weekends. But even there you could find the long trail of the conflict or small simmering resentments over one thing or another. Hiking in the Tel Dan Reserve near the Lebanese border, we found a sign tacked to some trees. It read: "The eucalyptus trees were planted in 1939 by the founder of Kibbutz Dan after they discovered that the original riverbank forests had been destroyed by herds of sheep and cattle belonging to the local Arabs."

Down the road a larger ecological disaster had unfolded in the 1950s when Israelis drained an enormous expanse of wetlands in the Hula Valley to make way for agriculture. The environmental consequences were dire, and the swamplands were partly reflooded by the government at great expense. The valley is now a popular nature reserve and bird sanctuary.

We wound up not far away in the Banyas, standing in front of a composite ruin that was a cross section of regional disputes going back as far as was architecturally possible. The lower wall of the ruin was Roman or Byzantine, from the third to the sixth century; on top of that was a twelfth-century Crusader wall, and above that part of a thirteenth-century Ayyubid tower. Then came some kind of nineteenth-century Ottoman structures. Capping this unlikely conglomeration was a shaky-looking Syrian barracks or other military structure made of concrete blocks and dating from the 1960s. Armed civilian guards led an Israeli school-tour group past the ruin.

After thirty months with UNRWA, I left Israel and Palestine with a seasoned appreciation for the tough natural beauty of the place (and for many of its people), which probably hadn't changed much over the centuries. It seemed likely that the almonds and olives and the stony hills would survive this conflict, and with more visual harmony than that archaeological and political layer cake.

ELEVEN

SUMMER WARS

Outside the Middle East between the summers of 2004 and 2006, I followed the news closely. The West Bank barrier kept going up, settlement expansion continued, and the IDF kept up its targeted killings and periodic incursions into West Bank towns. Palestinian suicide attacks continued—there were nine between February 2005 and April 2006[1]—and Palestinians in Gaza kept firing rockets into Israel, mostly at Ashkelon and the perennially shell-shocked town of Sderot.

Beneath this, something else was happening. Friends in the West Bank and Jerusalem, sensible women and men with no militant connections, were talking about the situation in a different way. I had heard pessimism or resignation before, on both sides of the divide. But now in e-mails and phone calls, I sensed hopelessness. Contrary to what U.S. newspapers reported, they said, movement restrictions were tighter than ever, and Palestinians gradually were being squeezed out of East Jerusalem and into the West Bank.

In the United States, where attention was focused on the more immediate horrors of the war in Iraq, the conflict in the West Bank and Gaza was barely audible, except for the shock in some Western capitals when Hamas rode to power in Palestinian parliamentary elections in 2006. When the daily violence of the intifada diminished, it slipped off the evening-news broadcasts. Routine IDF search-and-arrest raids, house demolitions, and long waits at the checkpoints weren't news. U.S. Secretary of State Condoleeza Rice, Prime Minister Ehud Olmert, and Hamas leaders in Gaza and Damascus dusted off the old scripts. Rice insisted that

Hamas recognize Israel if it wanted to see the sanctions lifted; Hamas kept talking up armed resistance against the Zionist enemy. Rice urged Israel to take steps to ease Palestinians' daily lives, and Olmert soothingly said it would be done as security conditions allowed. Overseas, news consumers changed channels. In the West Bank people whose opinions and analyses I trusted said daily life was a misery and was unlikely to improve. Was it hyperbole?

I returned in the summer of 2006 in the middle of a developing crisis, and the story burst back onto the front pages. In the Gaza Strip in June, eight members of a Palestinian family had died on a beach in an explosion that was blamed on an Israeli artillery shell (Israel denied responsibility and said the blast might have been caused by a buried explosive). The Hamas-led government announced the end of a sixteen-month truce, and the gloves were off again. No one was prepared for the next round.

In late June Hamas-affiliated militiamen from Gaza popped out of a tunnel under the Israeli border and attacked an army post, killing two soldiers and capturing nineteen-year-old Cpl. Gilad Shalit, a fresh-faced Israeli with dual French and Israeli nationality. To obtain Shalit's release, militant groups said, Israel would have to release an estimated four hundred women and children out of the nine thousand Palestinian prisoners it holds. Shalit remained a prisoner.

The brazen and militarily successful attack on an army post smack on the hot Gaza border was a major embarrassment for the IDF, and it plunged Israel into a national emergency. Israeli forces launched Operation Summer Rains, the first full-scale thrust into Gaza since the withdrawal of settlers the year before, knocking out a central power plant, bridges, and other infrastructure. Despite devastating Israeli assaults, Palestinian rockets kept flying into Israel.

Just over two weeks later, on July 12, came another unexpected blow. Hizbollah guerrillas launched a cross-border raid from Lebanon, killing three Israeli soldiers and capturing two others. Israel struck back hard. Warplanes bombed Beirut's airport runways and southern Lebanon, causing great destruction and driving hundreds of thousands of Lebanese onto the roads. But Israel's superior firepower wasn't producing the desired effect. Even under relentless pounding by Israeli air and ground forces, Hizbollah managed to fire about two hundred rockets a day into northern Israeli cities; several Israelis were killed, and thousands of terrified civilians fled their homes. When the fighting ended with a UN resolution thirty-four days later, more than a thousand Lebanese and dozens of Israelis were dead, and a good number of Lebanese villages south of the Litani River and parts of Shiite south Beirut lay in ruins.

Among the Israeli casualties were more than a hundred soldiers killed in action and four hundred wounded. Returning troops told of confusing orders and broken supply lines. The war, in which a well-prepared, Iranian-backed militia attacked and then gave nearly as good as it got from the Middle East's most advanced army, was a short, sharp shock that deeply traumatized the IDF and Israeli society. Angry comparisons were made with 1973, when Israel was caught unprepared for a frontal Arab attack; newspaper commentators taunted the government with the bombastic threat made early on by Defense Minister Amir Peretz that Hizbollah's Hassan Nasrallah "will never forget the name Amir Peretz."

Israel had had a long and unneighborly relationship with Lebanon that began after 1948, when tens of thousands of Palestinian refugees poured north across the border and, gradually over the years, set up what amounted to a state within a state in south Lebanon. From Palestinian rocket attacks on Israel in 1968, a series of provocations, counterprovocations and major military actions over the next three decades produced casualties—dead, wounded, and displaced—in appalling numbers, mostly on the Lebanese side. Yet all the violence failed to solve the conflict between Israel and the Palestine Liberation Organization or, later, Hizbollah.

One after another, Israel code-named its strikes, which it hoped would stop the shelling and root out the base camps inside Lebanon. Operation Litani in 1978, Operation Accountability in 1993, and Operation Grapes of Wrath, the massive air and artillery bombardment in 1996 brought no more than intervals of calm. Even Ariel Sharon's attempted geopolitical engineering to install a sympathetic Maronite Christian government in Beirut failed.

The overarching war, which Israel called Operation Peace of the Galilee, lasted from 1982 to 2000 and became a quagmire that was compared then and now with America's disastrous entanglement in Vietnam. The misadventure saw the IDF occupation of Beirut in 1982, the withdrawal to its self-proclaimed "security zone" in the south, and, finally, the pullout in 2000. The PLO eventually was removed from southern Lebanon and Beirut. But Hizbollah remained and, as the years went by, continued to strengthen its social movement—and its military apparatus —in the Shiite community.

Hizbollah's 2006 attack from Lebanon increased friction between Israelis and Palestinians at home. Israelis saw themselves threatened by two Islamic movements with proven anti-Israel platforms. Ordinary Palestinians probably cared less about the external political dimensions than the fact that a well-organized militia was giving Israel a bloody nose.

A two-front war with an unpredictable course meant that Israel put most of the West Bank under closure. To reorient myself after two years away, I hired a taxi and drove north out of Jerusalem. The road through Ram, a once-bustling and hectic village between Jerusalem and Qalandiya checkpoint, was split lengthwise by the wall. An unbroken stretch of concrete slabs blocked the midafternoon sun and cast long shadows over a near-deserted high street. Only a few shops were open; steel-shuttered businesses presented blank facades to the wall, and trash blew down the street. The few passersby shrugged and made palms-up gestures.

Past Ram the wall curved around to the east, and there was no trace of the old Qalandiya checkpoint, where I had spent so many hours. Farther along, at the new crossing into Ramallah, sandbag-topped concrete cubes had been replaced by an imposing gray-steel border post that looked like the old Checkpoint Charlie crossing between West and East Berlin. It was all high metal fences and turnstiles and soldiers safely inside bulletproof-glass booths. There was no delay walking into Ramallah that day, but later when I walked through the turnstiles in the other direction I slid my passport through a slot that snapped shut when I withdrew my hand, and a female military police officer shouted questions at me through a tinny loudspeaker. That was as close as I got to a soldier, and that was the point of it.

Driving around and back toward Jerusalem from Ram, the road where I had sweated through a three-hour traffic jam was no more. Sanitized sections of electric fence and a military patrol road ran along part of it, and I didn't recognize anything except the parched rocky fields. At the Jerusalem end and just before the final checkpoint stood another partly completed terminal meant mostly, I was told, to clear settlers coming in from the northern West Bank. A large yellow sign announced in Hebrew, Arabic, and English: "PRCS [Palestinian Red Crescent Society] and all ambulances have first priority and are allowed to pass the line." It was more a nod to international public relations than useful instructions, since everyone knew the rules and how things worked in practice. In Hebrew, someone had painted a sarcastic addition on the sign: "Priority to terrorists in ambulances."

It was all getting very orderly and formal and, for the Palestinians, very exclusionary. Of the twelve official routes into Jerusalem, Palestinians were barred by military order from using eight of them, according to the UN. As I made the rounds in coming weeks, I got to know the new-style entry points to the holy city. Israel was closing the gaps one by one.

"This is a classic example of ad hoc [reaction to the intifada]," Dror Etkes, a veteran Israeli campaigner with Peace Now, told me. "Nobody [Israeli planners] thought five or six years ago about this. This whole issue of cutting Jerusalem, of reinventing the borders of Jerusalem, and doing it mainly based on demographic priciples . . . to separate the fact of Jerusalem from the rest of the West Bank, this is a new concept."

Palestinians whose families had lived in East Jerusalem for generations struggled to keep their Jerusalem-resident status. One family who owned a second house in Ramallah learned that Israeli inspectors had been asking their Jerusalem neighbors if they really lived there. Jerusalemites mounted urgent court cases to keep from being reclassified as West Bankers.

For years Jewish settlers had tried to buy Palestinian homes in East Jerusalem neighborhoods such as upscale Sheikh Jarrah, and sometimes they broke into the homes when the families were out and squatted until they were evicted by police, often after a lengthy legal process. Now Israelis told Palestinians who owned property in the Arab quarter of the Old City that they could name their price, take the money, and, for the time being, stay put. "We won't take it now," they said, "but in the future. Just so we know it's ours." Financially strapped Palestinians sometimes found it hard to refuse such an offer. But accepting one could—and sometimes did—amount to a death sentence from militants who regarded such a sale an act of treason.

Israel was in the process of cementing its grip on the West Bank and had divided it into three sectors: north, central, and south. Inside the sectors, separate enclaves were further isolated. Access to the roads across the sectors and out of them was highly restricted. The fragmentation (some called it the "salami tactic") wasn't new but a tactical refinement of what had gone before. The movement of Palestinians anywhere was simply going to be managed, and loopholes would be shut. The government said the controls were solely to prevent attacks on Israelis, and that a reduction in attacks proved that the measures were working.

The humanitarian and economic consequences of the closures remained serious, according to the UN and the World Bank. A UN World Food Programme official told me that in 2006, 46 percent of the population of the West Bank and Gaza was "food insecure" or vulnerable, meaning that people there "faced challenges in meeting their food needs." In Gaza the figure jumped to 58 percent. In the two territories more than 600,000 people were receiving UN food aid, up from 480,000 in September 2005, she said.

Road closures were up by 40 percent over the year before, and Israel was establishing a kind of two-tier highway system: settlers and other Israelis could use designated through roads, and Palestinians in some areas, to pass from one part of their land to another, were made to use secondary roads and tunnels that ran perpendicular underneath, particularly in the enclaves around Qalqilya. The road-control strategy had begun in 2003 and 2004 and now was becoming clearer. Israeli planners called it the Everything Flows plan. The tunnels and gates, more of which were in the works, were opened by soldiers three times a day for a half hour at a time, and kept locked when there were security incidents or threats of incidents. Farmers thus continued to be denied unrestricted access to their lands and internal markets.

Palestinians in isolated rural regions thought twice before going to the doctor. Construction of the barrier since 2002, reported one international organization, "has steadily added another layer of obstacles isolating, fragmenting and thus deteriorating the Palestinian health care system."[2]

In Qalqilya and the enclaves, which were encircled by the wall or gated fences, patients wanting to get out for treatment elsewhere or medical personnel wanting to get in required an Israeli permit. Doctors who lived in one place and practiced in another never knew if they would make it to work and were as stressed as their patients.

At the Qalqilya district office of the Palestinian Medical Relief Society (PMRS), Dr. Mohammed Aboushi chain-smoked as he laid out the figures: The UNRWA hospital in Qalqilya served official refugees and sometimes others, but Dr. Aboushi's district, which took in Qalqilya and Tulkarm, had something like ninety thousand Palestinians. Eleven of the sixty-four villages in the district had no health-care facilities, and patients had to travel for the most basic treatment. Apart from the UNRWA hospital, which had a specific mandate, only primary care was available; patients for radiology, endocrinology, orthopedics, dialysis, and other specialties were referred to Nablus, Ramallah, or Jerusalem. Because of the difficulty of travel, Palestinians, particularly the elderly, postponed visits and suffered accordingly.

Over the past few years Dr. Aboushi's staff has seen a marked increase in stress complaints, anemia, and malnutrition and in chronic diseases such as hypertension and osteoarthritis. The health-care system was in a double bind, he said, because half of the total budget came from taxes collected by Israel on behalf of the Palestinian Authority and now being withheld. Dr. Aboushi lit another cigarette and drained his coffee cup.

Israel countered reports of denial of access and said that humanitarian cases were allowed to pass. In reality, some did and some didn't. UN agencies and international and local NGOs collected stories from hundreds of Palestinians who had been delayed or refused over a period of years.

Economic pressures were easy to see, from the restricted fishing zones in Gaza to the network of roadblocks that hindered agricultural transportation. Aid workers related the well-documented story of farmers in the northern West Bank who used to truck their produce out to Route 90, up the Jordan Valley, and out to markets in Israel. In 2006 they were kept out of the Jordan Valley unless they had special permits and had to truck their goods west and north to Jalame crossing; fresh produce often failed to survive the journey. The detours and inevitable delays imposed a corollary punishment: a six- to sevenfold increase in transportation costs on some routes in the West Bank.[3] That Green Line crossing out of the Jordan Valley into Israel was conditionally opened again in 2007.

The World Bank reported that Palestinian incomes were "considerably lower" than before the intifada, and that real GDP per capita in 2005 was about 31 percent lower than in 1999.[4] The forecast was not bright, another World Bank report said: "Looking forward, economic prospects remain grim and highly dependent on political outcomes. . . . The current political deadlock has significantly worsened the economic outlook."[5]

Olive farmers were hit particularly hard by the closures and by ongoing interference from settlers. The estimated nine million trees in the West Bank and Gaza could produce about forty-three thousand metric tons of oil each year. In 2003 about ten thousand metric tons went unsold, and the price dropped below cost.[6]

There was another phenomenon, which I had observed before, when restrictions compelled Palestinian contractors to buy Israeli supplies and rely on Israeli trucks. A senior humanitarian-aid official told me that Israeli businessmen exploited the economic crisis by buying Palestinian olive oil at rock-bottom prices and then reselling it as Israeli oil. He described the practice as "colonial trading."

Farm families did not suffer alone. The Palestinian Authority's vast bureaucracy had nearly ground to a halt under the sanctions. PA salaries, which supported about one million dependents, went unpaid for months at a time. This was why some middle-class Palestinians were selling their belongings on the street.

Although I am no conspiracy theorist, a question that had nagged at me throughout my tour with UNRWA lingered: was Israel trying to crush the Palestinian economy, either to encourage people to leave or to keep them under complete control? As cynical as the question was, much of what I had seen, and was seeing again, had nothing to do with protecting Israelis from terrorists. It was direct pressure on Palestinian economic veins and arteries and solely within the West Bank, not just between the West Bank and Israel.

It was no secret that Palestinians were being punished for voting in Hamas. The theory was that people could be pressured into reconsidering having a government that called for the elimination of Israel. After Israel impounded tens of millions of dollars in urgently needed Palestinian tax receipts, Dov Weissglas, an adviser to the prime minister, joked: "It's like a meeting with a dietician. We have to make them much thinner, but not enough to die."[7] Or maybe it wasn't a joke. It was a question I would return to in discussions with Israelis and international aid workers. Palestinians, who were feeling quite thin enough, were not in doubt about Israel's intentions.

Paying for the occupation and the settlement enterprise also was eating away at Israel's economy. "Israel has suffered greatly—social disintegration, poverty, [a decline in the quality of] education ... [even] increased road deaths because road maintenance is collapsing," the respected Israeli leftist and peace campaigner Peretz Kidron told me.

"The money is going into the territories. One and a half million Israelis are living below the poverty line. One in three children is living in a household below the poverty line. I don't have to look forward. The present is bad enough. And there is a huge brain drain. Do you know how many Israelis are living in California? They don't want to live in this militarist atmosphere. The cost of the settlements ... all at the expense of Israeli children." Kidron, who was born in Vienna in 1933 and fled after the Nazi Anschluss of 1938, had plenty to say about the occupation, and about Palestinians and Israelis.

I rediscovered that without the quasi-diplomatic protection of a UN vehicle, travel in the West Bank was difficult. Renting a car in Jerusalem was not the answer because soldiers would not let an Israeli-registered vehicle into Palestinian towns such as Nablus and Jenin. These were the realities in the summer and fall of 2006, and I eventually found other means.

One way was to ride with UNRWA again, this time as a journalist. The agency let me tag along with an old colleague and friend, Gustav Nordstrom, who is also an officer in the Finnish army reserves and a veteran of several UN peacekeeping missions in the Middle East and Africa. Nordstrom, as I had learned in 2002, was the most unflappable person I could imagine under fire, and a good man to travel with.

Heading west from Huwwara and up toward Tulkarm felt like coming home. Dried Queen Anne's lace and thistles lined the roads, summer heat haze shimmered over the hills, and a hoopoe flapped its way across the road like a windup stroboscopic toy. A tourist could maintain, for a while, the illusion that this was simply a beautiful place.

At Anabta checkpoint south of Tulkarm I recognized a soldier's Quebecois-accented English. He was a Canadian Israeli born in Côte Saint-Luc, outside Montreal. "A lot of Canadians come here to visit, to see Israel," he said, wiping sweat from his face. He was pleasant enough and prepared to wave us through, so there was no point in getting into distinctions between Israel and the West Bank. Coming out of Anabta weeks later, there would be no friendly chat with another group of soldiers.

As we entered Tulkarm, Nordstrom was diverted back to Nablus to investigate damage allegedly done to an UNRWA school. At the Beit Iba barrier into Nablus, the tourist bubble popped. The checkpoint was a dusty, bad-tempered welter of hooting cars and taxis, sweating luggage porters, shouting soldiers, and several hundred pedestrians who weren't being allowed in or out.

The UNRWA girls' school presented a familiar picture, with broken glass on classroom floors and smashed door locks. During a three-day army sweep through Nablus in pursuit of Palestinian gunmen, troops had broken into the school after hours and—in a new twist—were attacked by Palestinian boys outside the school who threw rocks through the windows at them. Nordstrom's assistant pointed out broken pots of poster paint on the floor and letters of the Hebrew alphabet that soldiers had daubed on a wall. *Small boys against big boys,* I thought again.

Sebastia village, up the road and on our way to Jenin, retained some of its ancient grace but had seen better days. The site, rebuilt by King Herod the Great before the birth of Christ, became a powerful symbol for Jewish settlers two millennia later, after the Yom Kippur War. Led by Gush

Emunim and with personal on-the-ground encouragement from Ariel Sharon, they tried with furious energy to found a settlement at Sebastia in 1975. The effort triggered a political crisis and ultimately failed in the face of opposition from Yitzhak Rabin's government. The frustrated settlers moved on and founded Elon Moreh, just east of Nablus. Over the years, Sebastia-area Palestinian farmers were displaced as other settlements went up.

Now the flags of Hamas and the Popular Front for the Liberation of Palestine flew from village lampposts, and Sebastia was home to a few hundred Palestinians in what amounts to a sprawling outdoor museum. Were it not for Israeli military controls, tourists could poke around the weed-grown ruins of the Ottoman-era train station and an amphitheater from Herod's time. Chunks of intricately carved marble columns lay scattered about between two Palestinian tourist shops; judging by the dust and cobwebs lacing the steel doors, the stalls had been closed for some time. The Ottoman and Roman ruins looked as though they could survive this period in history, too.

North of Sebastia, Route 60 was a surprise. What had been a bone-jarring moonscape of a road now was a properly pitched macadam highway with white stripes and cat's-eye reflectors in the middle, paid for with funds from the U.S. Agency for International Development.

On a straight stretch a soldier in combat gear stepped away from his Humvee on the shoulder and waved us to a stop. He looked to be about eighteen.

"Move your car over there," he barked, gesturing to a spot behind the Hummer.

"Why?" Nordstrom asked.

"Because I said so," the soldier said.

"But we have an agreement: United Nations Privileges and Immunities."

"You move your car over here," the soldier replied, gesturing more impatiently and raising his voice.

"We have an agreement," Nordstrom said in his unvarying UN-neutral voice.

The soldier shrugged and rolled his eyes, and another one walked over.

"How you doing? May I see your IDs, please?" he said with a smile and a quick glance. "Okay, go ahead, and have a nice day." The back of the soldier's flak vest was decorated with an oil painting of a landscape, and he had a jet-black tattoo of an ankh, the Egyptian symbol of life, on his neck.

As we drove off, Nordstrom, a firm believer in the economy of words, smiled and said: "I'll bet you feel like you've only been gone for a week." It really was good to be back.

There were no more checkpoints, and the slick new highway ran past the pine-studded Jenin park with its weird and wonderful concrete-over-wire sculptures of fantastic birds and animals. The last time I had been here, the echo of tank rounds boomed through the hills, APC gunners kept fingers on triggers of their machine guns, and the road was torn up. The sculptures had looked the worse for wear.

Now Jenin—both the town and the refugee camp—looked great. The town was busy again, the bulldozed scab at "ground zero" had sprouted new houses, many of them designed by Hidaya and her colleagues, and the bullet and shell holes had been plastered over. The government hospital looked like any hospital in small-town Israel or America, and there were no martyr posters on the corridor walls.

Most of the battle debris had been cleared away, except for what had gone into the horse. On a neatly painted roundabout just outside the hospital stood the camp's first tourist attraction since foreign dignitaries snapped photos in the shattered streets four years earlier. The Jenin Horse was a five-meter-high (sixteen-foot) sculpture by German artist Thomas Kilpper and a dozen Palestinian teenagers, and it was dedicated to hope and the freedom of movement. The horse's "skeleton" was fashioned from the steel and wreckage of homes, and its "skin" from the hulls of destroyed cars and an ambulance in which a doctor had been shot. Children played in the streets after school and either smiled or ignored us. They looked normal enough, and I wondered if what a psychologist in Belfast once told me was true: that children recover with surprising speed from the traumas of war. Palestinian children did talk about the continuous violence, but only if asked. However, the traumas never really went away, and the adults always wanted to talk, wanted someone from the outside world to listen to their stories. "He's nearly mad now, you know. His one son is in jail, and they killed his other two sons, shot one of them in his car." We were sitting in an UNRWA office over glasses of tea, and the UNRWA man was talking about his neighbor. "Then they blew out the walls of his home, which had been rebuilt after his first home was destroyed during the battle for Jenin." Everyone nodded.

"I also have a neighbor whose three sons were killed, all three of them," another man added. "If you like, we can go see him too."

We declined the offer but on the way out passed one of the homes. Explosive charges had buckled all the corner support pillars and knocked down the walls, and a pile of broken concrete lay in the empty living room. The son's car had been towed back and parked in the yard, where it still sat covered in dust and with a dozen bullet holes in the windshield.

We stopped to see Hidaya and her three children, who had just returned from visiting relatives in Jordan. What should have been a two-hour trip to Jenin from the Allenby Bridge across the Jordan River had taken nearly thirteen hours, she said. "The female Border Police officers at the bridge were shouting and cursing Palestinians, even the women," she said. I arranged to come back when we had more time to talk.

The Jalame vehicle crossing out of Jenin sat on the Green Line and near the wall, and its principal feature was the bright yellow industrial-size gate strung with electrified wire, razor wire, and sensors. Soldiers in a watchtower phoned others in a small base up the road, and twenty minutes later they walked down and opened the gate.

Crossing from spare and gritty Jenin into Israel's irrigated valleys required a brief visual adjustment. And a cappuccino at the Café Segafredo at ha-Shita junction. We walked in to grins from the young women behind the coffee bar that I hadn't seen for two years. But as we put in our orders and I kept watching, I saw two levels of reaction. Nordstrom and I got relaxed, welcoming smiles that included their eyes. Nordstrom's Palestinian assistant got something else, and before he had uttered a word. Not open hostility, not rudeness, and still a smile, just a bit more formal and not from the eyes. The Segafredo staff we knew lived in nearby kibbutzim and tended to have liberal political views, or at least to regard all customers in a uniformly friendly way. What was behind the looks?

The body language might have been working in both directions.

Nordstrom's assistant, a tall, muscular man, carried himself—probably unintentionally—with just a hint of swagger, an almost imperceptible chip on the shoulder. He was with two internationals in an Israeli restaurant, and he was a Palestinian.

And that day the staff may have seen him as more than a Palestinian. Israeli soldiers were having a hard slog against Hizbollah in Lebanon, and I heard later that some from local kibbutzim were killed. Nothing in this long clash of peoples and land was ever disconnected from anything else for very long.

On the way home I asked him how it felt to sit in an Israeli café, not in Jerusalem but in northern Israel. He chose his words carefully. "I've lived in Jerusalem all my life, so it feels normal to me," he said. "But..." He paused before continuing. "But there are some things you cannot just throw away." He meant Palestinian feelings toward Israelis. "And there are some things you just feel from them." He fell quiet, and we continued south to Jerusalem.

Over the sixty-five kilometers (forty miles) between the Green Line and Jericho, we counted seventeen Merkava tanks on flatbed transporters heading north for Lebanon. There were more behind them, coming up from bases in the Negev. The Lebanon war was less than two weeks old, and the fighting in Gaza was entering its second month.

TWELVE

"THE BULLETS WERE ZIPPING PAST MY LEGS"

The almond and apple trees would have been in bloom that early spring day in 1948 when the well-armed Jewish fighters came pouring into the valley. Working in one of his fields, Ibrahim Abu Tahoun knew big trouble was coming, but he was also watching the skies and hoping to get his crop of wheat in before it rained again. The turmoil of war was engulfing Palestine, but until then had skirted the valley. When the shouts went up, Abu Tahoun grabbed his old rifle and hurried to the rendezvous point. He was thirty-five years old and had had one day of firearms training.

"About fifty men went to the edge of the village, and I was standing and shooting," he said. "I didn't see any Jews, but I was told to shoot anyway. Then the Jews' bullets were zipping past my legs. It's good that I'm still alive!" The village defense team scattered, and the soldiers kept moving east.

That chapter of the story—and that's all there is—ended with a smile as Abu Tahoun, now ninety-three, leaned forward on his cane and Safiya, his wife, lifted her palms and praised Allah. Safiya, in her late seventies, was just a teenager when the war started. Originally from Jaffa, her family farmed nearby, and she was fifteen when she married Ibrahim.

The village was Miska, about eight kilometers (five miles) east of the Mediterranean coast road. Abdullah, one of Ibrahim and Safiya's sons, tapped a white space on the map just north of today's Israeli cities of Ra'anana and Kfar Sava. All that remains of Miska, he said, is a corner of the mosque.

The Abu Tahouns had met foreigners before 1948: Jewish immigrants first, and then the British. During the Arab revolt, a decade before the *Nakba,* two of Ibrahim's father's cousins who belonged to the armed resistance were hanged by the British. The brutalities of the rebellion years fractured economic cooperation between Jews and Arabs, but in rural areas such as Miska, people still lived alongside each other and got on with farming. During our conversation Safiya returned several times to the once-friendly relations between them and their neighbors, whom she called Palestinian Jews.

Miska, with a population of about fifteen hundred, produced "more food than income," and with regular crops of fruit, barley, sesame, and wheat on five hundred dunams (124 acres), Ibrahim and Safiya were nearly self-sufficient. Ibrahim had said many times that the happiest days of his life were spent harvesting the huge watermelons that did so well in that fertile earth.

Safiya was eighteen when they were, in her words, deported from Miska. Leaflets circulated, and Jewish neighbors came with a warning. "You have a choice: you can leave or you can die. The Haganah [the Zionist movement's paramilitary arm] will come and kill you. We will not protect you from the Haganah." Their days as landowners and independent farmers were over.

"We left the wheat in the rain unharvested. We left everything," Ibrahim said, looking at the floor. "We were the biggest farmers in the area. It had been my father's land, and my grandfather's before that." Taking the horse and their three infant children, they fled to Tira, eight kilometers (five miles) to the northeast. "We spent a month there, and then the Jews attacked Tira and we had to flee again. Jewish groups were killing Arabs at night. Many of them." With no idea where to go, they joined streams of panicked Arabs heading north.

"There were many days living in the mountains. We tried to build tents from branches and nylon," Ibrahim said. "It is very hard to describe. Many people were ill; there was no food, no medicine." After two years of living rough, Tulkarm Camp opened in 1950 and they got canvas tents from UNRWA, in its first days of providing aid to tens of thousands of desperate refugees. "The tents would collapse in the wind and the rain, and everyone's clothes were torn and dirty. Many people died that first winter in the tents," Ibrahim said.

Over the years the tents were replaced by one-room, one-family cinder-block huts with a floor space of nine square meters (ninety-seven square feet), no matter the size of the family. The huts had one door and a single small window and were lined up back to back in rows.

Ibrahim and Safiya's four-room house today sits on the exact spot where the tents were, and they use two original huts as a summer kitchen and storage area. Sitting in the shade of a gnarled old fig tree in the courtyard, they can still picture the tents in the cold rainy winters of more than half a century ago. And they still have their Miska land-ownership documents, issued by both Ottoman and British Mandate authorities.

The house is sparely but comfortably furnished, and on the walls hang a photo of Ibrahim as a handsome young man in trimmed mustache and white kaffiyeh and framed verses from the Qur'an. One verse reads, "With all difficulties there are solutions." The private courtyard has a minuscule garden around its edges, efficiently filled by two small lemon trees, trellised grapevines, a lemon geranium, and ornamental pine and palm trees. The house has another advantage: it is set back off the camp's busy main street and not directly vulnerable to small-arms fire. That street has seen much violence and many casualties, including Safiya, who was wounded in one clash, and other family members.

Safiya served a bowl of fresh figs, and Ibrahim talked, reluctantly, about the *Nakba.* He described the next decades as ones of basic survival, scratching out a living by repairing brass space heaters and using his horse to plow local farmers' fields.

The succession of wars and regional crises of 1956, 1967, and 1973 disrupted UNRWA's supply lines and assistance programs across Gaza, the West Bank, Syria, Lebanon, and Jordan and all aspects of refugees' lives. Safiya and Ibrahim's older children found work in Jordan, and Ibrahim worked in factories and construction, first in Israel and then for seventeen years in Saudi Arabia, returning home in the summers. Through it all, Safiya stayed in Tulkarm and raised the children. Ibrahim, a gracious man, looked for a positive way to describe those years.

"It was a time to sit aside from the struggle," he said. "They gave us time to work in Israel and to forget." The Israelis hoped they would forget Palestine, he meant.

"We did *not* forget," Safiya interjected. "They used us to work in our own country, and we did not forget! One time we went to our land, and we cried like children. There were Jews living there. They had acquired gold."

As the shock of 1948 turned into years of Israeli control and constant military operations, Palestinians lost patience. When the first intifada erupted in 1987, Safiya was among the women who took to the streets. The protests and retribution grew more violent, and Palestinians attempted to physically wrestle detainees away from soldiers.

"The soldiers were beating a sixteen-year-old girl, and they split her head open. I wanted to get her away and to the hospital. She was covered in blood," Safiya said, leaning forward in her chair. "I started to shout, 'Allahu Akbar!' [God is Great], and they chased us." Safiya, then well into middle age and recovering from recent surgery, was lightly wounded in the abdomen, one hand, and both legs by plastic-coated steel balls.

Did she or her friends have weapons? "No. But if I had, I would've shot him," she said in a likely detour into hyperbole. Before she had a chance to seek treatment for her wounds, a senior IDF officer drove through the camp's streets telling Palestinians to go home. "I started shouting back: 'Who are *you*? I will beat *you*.'" One soldier, struck by a rock, was bleeding from a head wound, and another leveled his rifle at Safiya and the growing crowd. Safiya pushed past the soldiers and tried, unsuccessfully, to drag an arrested man from the back of a jeep. The clash ended with no further injuries.

Women and children of the West Bank and Gaza played a major role in the first intifada and confronted the soldiers daily. By the second uprising in 2000, Safiya figured street fighting was best left to younger people, and in any case she drew a sharp line between the style of the two revolts. Guns had replaced rocks and bottles, and soldiers used much deadlier tactics, with even less regard for the safety of noncombatants.

Much of the second intifada has been waged in the refugee camps, including the two in Tulkarm. Ibrahim and Safiya's home is across from the

UNRWA girls' school, which the IDF has shot up and used as a detention center on several occasions. Safiya pointed to the plastered-over bullet holes in her living room, a reminder of the times when soldiers scaled the garden wall, ordered everyone out, and shot at the walls. During one incursion in the winter of 2005, when the army was searching house to house for a wanted militant, Fatima, one of Safiya's grown daughters, asked to be allowed to get a blanket for her mother, who stood shivering in the courtyard. The soldier refused.

Conversations with Ibrahim and Safiya—I've had many over the years—are punctuated with talk of the land and God. As personally devastating as the loss of their land was, they treat the events of the occupation the way all farmers respond to floods and crop failures: fix what you can and endure the rest. Although they understand the clash of two peoples over the land, the soldiers' behavior disturbs and puzzles them. I asked if they have ever been able to see soldiers as individuals.

"I think he is my enemy, because if he is thinking as a human being, his job is to protect civilians, not attack them. They should refuse such orders," Ibrahim said.

"There is no mind to think," Safiya added caustically, tapping the side of her head. "During the British time, the [British] soldiers respected women and children. They behaved totally different from the Israelis. Yes, they helped build the Israeli state, but they did not do that."

But do they ever see the Israeli soldiers as individual people? I asked again.

"I used to see it, but now mostly not," Ibrahim said.

"Totally not. Absolutely not," Safiya said, wagging a finger.

As we sat in the courtyard, I thought of how far apart Palestinians and Israelis are and remembered the soldier who refused a hot drink on a freezing day because "I don't take tea from Arabs." Safiya's view was colored by the fact that she had been beaten twice and shot. "They beat everybody, kill people, uproot the trees, confiscate the land. If someone confiscates the land, do you love them?" she said. I asked if they would ever be prepared to forgive Israelis. "If we go back to our homeland, we can forgive them. But if not, there is no need to forgive," Ibrahim said.

What still bothers the couple as much as the loss of the land is the loss of neighborliness and common courtesy. "My father offered figs to the Jews," Safiya said, holding her two index fingers together in parallel fashion, a gesture she made many times in that day-long conversation. The reference points usually had to do with sharing what the land produced. When trade between the two sides was forbidden during the Mandate, her father continued to sell goats to their neighbors, and once, when he left in a hurry to avoid being caught by British soldiers, he forgot his wallet. "The Jew chased after him and returned it," Safiya said. "We had those links. Why did we lose that?"

"Yes." Ibrahim nodded. "We were eating together, we were Palestinians together. We liked them. We had mutual visits, we felt we had that brotherhood."

It was only with the Zionist immigration, which displaced the Arabs, that the neighborliness ended. Ibrahim told a story of meeting some Polish Jewish immigrants when he was working in Israel. They asked Ibrahim where he was from, and he told them about Miska. "We talked, and the Pole said his son was in the IDF and had been killed somewhere. I said, 'Why did you come here—to lose your son?' The Pole said, 'We won't go back, we are building a state here.' And I told him, that is the price you paid, losing your son."

A few days later, I sat in the Jerusalem office of Dror Etkes, who heads the Settlement Watch program for Peace Now and has spent years arguing that the settlement movement is wrong and a disaster, for Israel as well as for the Palestinians. I mentioned Ibrahim and Safiya's touch of nostalgia for the cooperation between Arabs and Jews. He found the notion worthy but outmoded

> because in the present sense of identities, this is not doable. That was relevant to a prenational, premodern society where Jews really were of the Arab world, were one minority within the Arab world, together with the Christians. They were tolerated...integrated in the Levant within the Arab societies here. Once the Zionist movement came in and...became a main player in this game, the whole cycle of identities changed. Suddenly denomination and religious affiliation became equal to national affiliation and to national identity.

I still hewed to if not the premodern era then some aspects of that time that could be woven into a more just future, like steel rods in a concrete building that would be more stable than the current dangerous edifice. Such illusions were hard to maintain. Even in the week I visited Tulkarm, army troops cruised through the camp late at night, singing and swearing through the jeep's loudspeaker. I would hear more about such IDF tactics in the coming weeks.

I left the Abu Tahoun courtyard reluctantly. Premodern or not, a morning under the fig tree with Ibrahim and Safiya always restored my faith. In what, I was not certain, but it restored it anyway.

I had hitched a ride to Tulkarm that day in a PMRS ambulance, which was ready to make the return trip. When we skirted the queue at Anabta checkpoint, two Ethiopian Israeli soldiers confiscated our IDs, turned their backs, and refused to talk with the driver. We didn't do much better at the second set of blocks. It was a scorching-hot afternoon, and the soldiers were flushed, their uniform shirts soaked with sweat. The discussion was getting nowhere in Arabic or Hebrew, and the driver suggested that I try my hand. The sergeant, who was about nineteen, delivered a condescending lecture on logic and international law-enforcement customs. "If you were in the United States and came up to a checkpoint, would you be allowed to jump the queue? What do you think would happen if you did that? Would you be allowed to go?"

"We don't have military checkpoints in the United States," I said, trying to leave irony out of my tone. The soldiers were as overheated as the Palestinians they had backed up behind the blocks and were not interested in negotiation. Mentioning that our vehicle was an ambulance had no effect because we were not transporting a patient. There was a bit of irritated give and take, and the sergeant eventually handed us our papers with a final injunction: "Don't do it again, okay?" Back in Jerusalem I learned that one soldier and two Palestinians had been shot dead in separate incidents in other parts of the West Bank that day. The afternoon closure was the sort of knock-on punishment—the IDF called it antiterror precautions—I knew well.

Two kilometers up the road we passed a Humvee across the road with no delay but got a blast from a Palestinian. He approached the ambulance driver and in an angry but quiet voice said, "Why do you go around? We've been waiting here for hours. Don't you respect us?" The ambulance driver apologized.

I caught a final vignette through the side windows. A boy of about ten and a man who looked like his father were walking around the long line of pedestrians, jumping the queue. The man stopped to explain something to the boy, who had one arm in a plaster cast and sling but looked cheerful enough. As they started walking toward the soldiers again, the man put his arm around the child's shoulder, and the boy's facial expression changed abruptly. He now wore the most mournful, pitiable look I had ever seen. It didn't work. When they got to the Humvee, the soldiers started shouting at them.

Our driver kept the pedal down and the speedometer at around 140 kilometers (87 miles) an hour most of the way back. A Qur'an lay on the dashboard, and a stethoscope hung from the rearview mirror—all that faith and medicine required, I supposed. At that speed the ambulance swayed from side to side, making me feel carsick. When the driver came up behind a settler's car, he turned on the siren; the settler ignored the challenge and refused to give way.

In Ramallah I hopped a taxi to Qalandiya crossing and joined the queue of sweaty men and women with bags of figs and lemons, all wriggling one by one through the narrow turnstile. Chattering girl students got their book bags stuck in the bars and had to back out and start over as military police shouted commands. On the Jerusalem side, a sign said "Have a safe and pleasant stay."

I still wanted to see the checkpoints from the Israeli side of the blocks, to listen to what the soldiers had to say, whether they believed it made sense to control an entire population to this degree in order to stop suicide attacks. And I wanted to know what the occupation was doing to them, the young men and women who made up the occupying force.

THIRTEEN

"THEY MUST FEAR US"

The IDF ignored my repeated requests to spend time with soldiers. They didn't refuse, they just never returned my calls. But there were different ways to get behind the checkpoints, and one presented itself over coffee with a former IDF unit commander who knew that I had spent much time at Huwwara checkpoint during my UN service. He slid a DVD across the table. "Huwwara," he said.

The video had been produced in 2004 by the IDF for the IDF, as a training film after years of complaints about the soldiers' behavior and human rights abuses. The filmmakers, from the army's Education Corps, may have gotten more than they had planned on; several months later the DVD was leaked to the media.

In the video, it's winter, and the Palestinians waiting to cross Huwwara into and out of Nablus are bundled up against the cold; soldiers' chins are tucked down into winter uniforms and ponchos. Everything is winter gray, army olive drab: sky, road, and concrete cubes, the uniforms, the dull sheen of the weapons, the hard-set faces. I was watching on a computer screen, but I wanted to pull a scarf tight against the Huwwara chill. The DVD probably had been copied many times, and the quality was poor. Sequences were jerky, and, judging by the sky, may have been filmed on different days. Soldiers were not identified by name.

The video opens with a shot of a Palestinian man holding a baby in a white knitted cap. He's arguing with a soldier, whose M-16 rests on a sandbag atop a concrete cube. The soldier tunes out and looks away, down the line of Palestinians and beyond them.

"They have to fear us, otherwise all hell will break loose here," a soldier says to the camera.

"My wife's ill, I'm taking her to the doctor," a balding Palestinian says. An ambulance waits behind him, its roof light flashing.

"You got a permit?" the soldier asks.

"Me? No, I don't."

"No permit?"

"If someone's ill, how can he get a permit?" the man asks.

"You don't treat them normally, you have to suspect everyone here," says a clean-shaven young soldier in glasses, with a slight smile. Without the helmet and combat gear, he might be a student.

Another soldier speaks to a man in a baseball cap holding an infant.

"Anyway, he's not sick. It's his tummy. Sorry, it's not urgent," the soldier says in Hebrew, handing back the man's ID. "Go get a note from Huwwara hospital."

"Is there a hospital in Huwwara?" the man asks in Hebrew. The soldier nods. (The Palestinian, if not the soldier, would have known that there is no hospital in Huwwara village.)

"Go back home, go on, *yallah*!" another soldier yells at the crush of women and men between the concrete barriers as he turns away a man holding a child's hand. "Shut up! What's your problem?" he says, leaning over a barrier. "Go on! *Yallah!* Go back!" The Palestinians are just standing there, tightly packed into the concrete passageway, and aren't backing up. Frustration builds in the soldier's voice. A small girl looks up at him. "Go on! Get back." He pushes a man. The soldiers are in control, but barely. This is how the bad incidents start.

"Everyone get back!" one shouts into a bullhorn. He's holding a fistful of Palestinian ID cards in green plastic wallets.

"Think about it. Saturday, there's hundreds of them and four soldiers," one says to the camera, gesturing over the crowd. "If they don't fear us, they'll attack, do whatever they want."

"Go on, you're registered as single. Think I'm an idiot?" a soldier says to a Palestinian man a head taller, who is arguing with him. The man's wife, a fashionably dressed young woman, tries to convince the soldier that the man is her husband. It's unclear what difference their marital status would have made.

"Go on, get out of here," the soldier says, waving them away.

"You don't believe me?" the woman says. An arm thrusts into the frame, and the soldier mechanically takes the ID card without looking at it as he tries to get rid of the persistent couple.

"Go stand over there; where's your ID?" he orders the man, who has been trying for some minutes to hand it over.

"Sometimes there's no choice; you've got to raise your voice, be aggressive," the soldier explains to the camera. "Throw your weight around, keep them in line. So they'll be forced to behave. It's up to us. If they see us sitting here, not bothering with them, they'll come up to us all the way. If they realize we're aggressive, and I don't mean physically, but alert, then they'll do what they're supposed to. Stand where they're supposed to, keep this place sterile. Safe distance, see? It all depends on us. If there's pressure, you get more aggressive. Make your presence felt more, so they'll realize who's boss."

A soldier behind a concrete cube glances at the sheet of paper an arm shoves at him. "What are you showing me? A groceries receipt?" he says with a grin. "Go home. 'Bye. 'Bye. 'Bye." The Palestinian takes back the sheet but makes a hand motion of stamping a document. He's pushing his luck. "You have no permit, you can't get through. Get back," the soldier says. The man walks away.

"Hey, I said no, right? I told you not to pass," one says across the blocks as another soldier talks into his radio.

"It's closed!" The young soldier in glasses is in a shouting match with a middle-aged woman, who points over his shoulder, the direction she wants to go. The soldier leans forward into her face. She doesn't budge. It's the immutable force against the immovable object, the physics of human personalities.

"You get into such a spin," a voice says. "You must prove to yourself at some point that you're human." He's on camera now, smiling. "That's also something. A process in itself.... Eventually some guys finish this tour of duty really fucked up."

"Eighteen-year-old soldiers are given incredible power," the one in glasses says. "After all, whatever happens with the locals is in our hands." He doesn't finish; a scuffle breaks out and the camera shifts. A teenage girl in a *hijab* is shouting, and a soldier wades into the crowd. A man has his arm around a woman's shoulder, trying to quiet her.

"Everybody back! Get back!" Women and girls are yelling; the camera pans again but can't cover the simultaneous outbreaks.

"Jerusalem's not here. What are you talking about?" a soldier says to two men. One says "Al Quds"—Jerusalem—and points over the soldier's shoulder. "Go get a permit and come back. 'Bye."

The second man keeps trying. "'Bye," the soldier says. "What's the problem?" the Palestinian asks.

"I said go home! Don't you understand Arabic? I said go home!" the soldier shouts.

On the other side of the channel a woman approaches a soldier. He walks briskly toward her, and she turns around. "Get back, we'll check you when your turn comes. Go on!" She comes forward again, backs off again. She stops a third time and gets a third rebuff. "Move it! Go on, get back, then wait, then we'll let you through," the soldier says again, as patient as she is persistent. It's risky. How far can you push without setting the soldier off? As a woman, she is less likely to be beaten than a man, but she is not immune to humiliation or arrest.

Another woman quickly leads away a boy of about five. He's carrying a toy AK-47 rifle and looks back at the soldiers as his mother pulls him along. Why has she let the child take a toy weapon to Huwwara checkpoint?

More arguments. How tense can this get before someone goes off the edge? A man tries to talk his way into Nablus. "Just one hour," he pleads. "There's someone waiting for me. Keep my ID and I'll be back in an hour." "*La! La!* [No]," the soldier says in Arabic, fed up. "Quiet! Don't get on my nerves!" He waves the man away.

Another scuffle. A soldier leans over the waist-high block and punches a man. The man slaps back. Soldiers pile on.

"Look at him! Look what's he's done!" a soldier yells. A woman gasps.

"He's hitting me!" The soldier again.

"Leave him alone," the woman yells.

Two troopers put the man in a hammerlock and wrestle him against the barrier.

"He's assaulted a soldier; better restrain him. Get me some cuffs." The soldier's making a bit of a show. He knows the camera's running. The man struggles but is handcuffed and dragged away by the scruff of his neck and his jacket. A dozen young boys watch from the sidelines.

"He wanted to hit me!" the soldier says, sounding surprised.

"But you approached him?" the cameraman, or maybe an officer with the camera team, asks.

"Biff, bam," the soldier demonstrates, flailing his arms. "I approached him, said 'Come here,' he started hitting me. Why?"

"Why did you approach him?" the voice asks, questioning the soldier's judgment. The soldier's on the defensive now.

"He's been here four times. I tell him to go home and get a permit. He goes like this, as if he wants to pass. What do I know? Maybe he's a terrorist." The camera shifts.

"Everyone without a permit says he's going to the hospital. Fucking with us." It's the young soldier who turned away the persistent woman. "You don't have a permit—go home."

Palestinians press forward a foot at a time, and he pushes them back. "Get back! No one gets to cross. No one!" A woman rests her head on her husband's shoulder. A soldier talking to several Palestinians at once says something to her. He's rattled.

"Nobody gets through! This checkpoint is closed," the sergeant shouts. The Palestinians in the lane aren't doing anything, but they're not going away. For the soldiers, this isn't working according to the manual. They're trying to clap a lid on an already-boiling pot instead of turning the fire down.

"Believe me, when we're here you can't believe what goes on," a soldier tells the camera. "When I get home, I don't know... my dad says, 'What do you do in the army? Why are you so stressed?' "

The soldier spreads something on a piece of bread and eats it, smiling and talking. He's on the spot and knows it. "But I didn't want to hit him. What, I hit him?" he asks, playing coy and licking his fingers.

"Punched him in the face," the voice says.

"What?"

"You punched him."

"By mistake." He licks the sandwich spread off his fingers.

"Really?"

"Yes." The smile is gone. "Some things we did are really forbidden. But he raised his hand. Never mind what I did. It's good I let him go. We would have gotten hell for this."

The next sequence happens quickly, with no indication of what went before.

A staff sergeant, the senior NCO at the checkpoint, walks fast through the blocks and up to a Palestinian man in his thirties in a denim jacket standing with his wife and two small children, who both wear glasses. He lays into the man without warning, punches him once in the chest, then again, hard, and kicks him in the groin or chest. It's filmed from behind the sergeant's back, so it's hard to tell where the last blows land.

"*La! La!* That's enough!" his wife shouts, putting a hand out to restrain the soldier. He throws another punch, and a second soldier jabs the Palestinian with the muzzle of his rifle. The man, holding two large pink shopping bags, staggers but holds his ground. He does not punch back. The smaller of the two children clings to the shopping bags, and the woman keeps trying to put herself between the soldier and her husband. The older son watches from a few feet away, motionless. The two soldiers roughly drag the man away, but the little boy hangs on to the bags like a terrier. When the sergeant realizes he's got the boy in tow, he reaches down and pries his hand loose. The sergeant slaps the man on the side of the head, lightly this time, and hauls him into an armored guard box that flies the Israeli flag. You can't see what happens inside. One boy repeatedly asks his mother something in a plaintive voice. His words are indistinct, but the meaning seems clear. The mother stands there, watching the guard box, touching one son on the head and the other on the shoulder. Neither boy has cried; they seem oddly detached. The younger one keeps turning around something in his hands, something shiny and tightly wrapped in clear cellophane, keen to unwrap it. I wondered what it was. Plastic flowers? The man is let out of the steel box, but the sergeant isn't quite finished. He follows the man, right behind him, and watches, hands on hips as the family sort out their parcels.

As the family regroup, there's this exchange between the camera crew officer and the sergeant: "Think you were wrong about this guy? Think you'd treat him differently now? No pressure, everything calmer." It's the voice of a man older than the sergeant.

"Yes, we'd do it differently. But we have people to check here. If I don't solve this in two minutes, I'll be sitting on it for fifteen minutes." The camera cuts to a quick shot of the family off to the side. The boys are unwrapping something, and the man, tall and dignified, is looking at the soldiers. Like all Palestinians at checkpoints, his expression is deadpan. Now, though, his control almost slips. Anger burns behind his eyes, but he holds it back.

The sergeant goes on: "I ask him again and again, and he's a threat. If he crowds me, so will everyone. There's a limit. A red line. Look: no one gets close here now. Why? Because that guy got hit. They all learn. No one dares fuck with us now. Look at him sitting over there. That's using my judgment. The guy seems okay to you, but he aroused my suspicion. Something in his face."

When the sergeant gestures for his questioner to look, the camera pans to where the family is sitting on some large stones. The man is looking out over the open field, the woman is looking at her husband, and their sons have undone the cellophane parcels. That's when I figure out what week of the 2004 winter it probably is, and close to what day. Eid al-Adha, the Feast of the Sacrifice, fell on the first of February that year, and the rolled-up things the kids have been fiddling with are party hats, their Eid gifts. They wear them now, tall, conical, red and green things covered with spangles, two little gnomes in eyeglasses sitting on the rocks with their parents by the checkpoint. The picture is one of utter desolation. Or that's how it looked to me. To the mother and father, it might have been different. They might have been hoisting the small, supple flag of *sumud*, that powerful resistance that said: "Guess what? You can do that to us, but you cannot spoil Eid. You can beat us, but you cannot crush us." If it was that, the Huwwara soldiers did not get it.

"It bothers me, hitting an older man like that," the sergeant continues. "I try not to do it in front of the others. So I took him off to the side, and no one knows what I did with him. You know, they don't mind the actual beating, but the loss of face in public. In front of his wife and kids. That's why I took him away. I talk to them, they don't understand, so I take them away. Then they understand. Come back quietly. They don't like to be humiliated." Behind him, Palestinian women and men still wait behind the blocks.

"Sometimes it's just nerves. Because you don't see your soldiers, they're exposed, unprotected. You feel threatened, people crowd you in, you can't do a thing. If you set limits, everything works out."

"So that's using your judgment?" the voice asks.

"Both that and nerves. If I'd not hit anyone, they'd all come and demand their IDs back. Now that they know I'm nervous, and they know I'm in charge, no one comes close."

"So you're educating them?"

"Not really educating them, but..."

The video has a denouement, maybe filmed on a different day. The sergeant is forcing a Palestinian man backward over one of the waist-high barriers. Another soldier stands by. An Israeli flag and a paratroop battalion banner flap in the background. A baby starts to wail. The man, in his twenties, straightens up fast, but he can't fight what's coming. He puts his hands behind his back to be cuffed, over the sleeves of his sweater. The sergeant gets a good grip on the loose end of the plastic restraint and yanks hard, tightening the cuffs. He pushes the man against the concrete, slaps him hard across the face, jabs a finger toward his face for emphasis, and slaps him across the other cheek. The man stands up straight and tilts his chin forward as the camera pans to a woman holding the crying baby. They lead the man into a tent, and the sergeant lowers a flap over the plastic window. Nothing further can be seen.

In the next shot, the sergeant, carrying a bullhorn, smiles and confidently strides down the row of barriers. "Look now, when I hit someone everyone waits in line!"

"Why are they disciplined?" another soldier says. "Because they're scared. Wouldn't you be?"

For beating two unarmed Palestinians, one of them handcuffed, the twenty-three-year-old sergeant was court-martialed, jailed for six months, and demoted to private. A signboard at the end of my copy of the fifteen-minute video says this: "Over sixty soldiers from his unit signed and published a petition stating that he is used as a patsy by the military system and high-ranking officers [who] knew that this was the daily routine [at] these checkpoints and did nothing."

FOURTEEN

"EDUCATING THE INDIANS"

Every once in a while a real-time metaphor unfolded that revealed how Israelis and Palestinians saw each other—and themselves. Standing on Atara Bridge early one morning in the summer of 2006, I watched a yellow minibus taxi approach the checkpoint from the Ramallah side.

Atara checkpoint, run jointly that day by the army and the Border Police, controlled Palestinian traffic from tiny Atara village north of a graceful arched bridge over highway 465, and in and out of Ramallah and outlying villages. During Operation Defensive Shield, my colleagues and I had spent frustrating days negotiating to transfer medical supplies across an earth mound here.

The commander, a young sergeant, whirled around as the taxi crept into the middle of the intersection instead of stopping at the outer cubes. The driver would have known the hazards of proceeding unbidden. With a theatrical grimace conveying exasperation and mock pain, the soldier switched his rifle to his left hand and, with his right, made an elaborate gesture instructing the driver to reverse. Seconds passed. The taxi driver reversed a few feet. The soldier twirled his fingers again, a minuscule movement of unmistakable intent: No, not there. *There.* The driver paused and reversed again. Ramrod straight, the soldier executed a series of precise and elegant gestures with his right arm. He looked as though he was standing on the conductor's box in an orchestra pit. To each gesture, the driver responded in corresponding increments, exercising maximum stubbornness and as much panache as is possible in a stationary vehicle. His face, with a graying mustache, hung over the steering wheel, and he kept his eyes on the soldier. Rifles were not pointed, tempers did not blow, and the only language was a mute sarcasm on one side and the pretense of incomprehension on the other. The duel had become a pantomime of epic proportions across ten meters (thirty-two feet) of pavement. I scanned the faces of the soldier, the taxi driver, and his passengers for traces of emotion. There were none. As stylish as it may have appeared, the performance had a theme: fingertip control versus minimum compliance. One more precise flourish, a final few feet of macadam, and the taxi was back at the cube. With a last thrust of his outstretched arm and a downward chop with the heel of his hand, the sergeant nodded briskly, did a parade-ground pivot, and walked away. The driver would have a bit of a wait.

Atara Bridge was the first stop that morning on the way to Huwwara with Machsom Watch (Checkpoint Watch), a group of half a dozen of the two hundred or so Israeli women who have been doggedly monitoring soldiers' behavior and human rights abuses at West Bank roadblocks since 2001. Many of the women are retired or semiretired professionals who watch checkpoints on their days off; most are secular, and some call themselves Zionists. One of their functions in assisting Palestinians is to observe the checkpoints at the busiest crossing times in a manner they describe as "quiet but assertive."[1] They are assertive in spades, pointing out to soldiers in unequivocal language what is allowed and what is not, and telling them that blocking the travel of Palestinians inside Palestinian areas is legally and morally wrong and strategically unsound. Another two hundred group members help Palestinians apply for and collect Israeli permits and other documents.

By standing at the barriers with cameras and notebooks, they inject into the occupation a touch of what Peretz Kidron called the "Jewish mother syndrome." I also saw elements of basic peacekeeping. The women don't exactly bully but are not above lecturing. Soldiers, particularly the younger ones, regard them with emotions ranging from annoyance to mild relief. While a soldier will not tolerate being told what to do by a civilian, he can find it difficult to be harsh with Palestinians under the stern gaze of an Israeli woman older than his mother. Even in the presence of officers, who are far less glad to see them, the Machsom Watch women are not easily brushed off. They leave when ordered to but make their case first and file detailed reports on their observations. They pester senior officers in the Civil Administration, the Ministry of Defense branch that deals with civilian matters in the West Bank, and demand that Palestinians be allowed to move about; they get a mixed response, often condescending or hostile.

That day, drivers of the taxis and cars backed up on all three sides of Atara had been waiting for more than an hour. A taxi driver broke out of the line and explained that he was taking a man with a stomach ailment to a Ramallah hospital. Soldiers made him go to the back and confiscated his keys. Then, perhaps because the Machsom Watch women were taking notes, they returned the keys.

I talked with a soldier in his early twenties who had done his regular service and was back as a reservist. He had a wispy mustache, and longish hair curled from under his helmet. I asked him what checkpoint duty was like.

"It's not the most pleasant thing," he said with a smile. "I've been bombed and shot—I say shot, the bullet just missed me, but I still say shot—and my sergeant took a bullet past his ear." He demonstrates how close to his helmet. "I'm wearing all this stuff"—he tapped the ammunition pouches on his chest—"this black [flak] vest and standing here, and I'm boiling hot."

His commander, who had conducted the taxi duel, walked over, and the conversation ended. "It's a busy morning here, and your presence is making it more so. Please stand over there, by the blocks," he said. Our presence was having no visible effect on the checkpoint but was adding an unwanted element, particularly as Vivi, a Baghdad-born Israeli who was one of the Machsom Watch monitors, kept snapping photos of the soldiers at close range, making a point of irritating them. I asked the commander if we could chat some more. "Maybe later," he said.

As the women watched, I watched them. Five years at the checkpoints were taking their toll; they were discouraged and angry. A Border Police trooper stood in the middle of the intersection, legs apart and the stock of his rifle resting on one hip.

"Look at the way he stands! He has the gun, the uniform, he's eighteen years old, he has all the power. What's to talk about with him?" Hanna Barag, a lively woman of seventy, spat the words out.

Varda, another Machsom Watch veteran observer and a prominent Israeli doctor, asked that I not print her last name. Her thoughts that morning were more with her three sons, all in the army and all on combat duty in Lebanon. That increasingly devastating war was in its third week and, for Israel, was not going according to the book.

"I'm confused today," Varda reflected as she watched the Border Police deal with the Palestinians. "It's more complicated. It's not all white and all black. They're also afraid. They're eighteen." I asked what her sons thought of her role with Machsom Watch. "My sons agree with me," she said. "They are very proud of me."

Two soldiers took off pell-mell down the hill, and others assumed covering positions. We moved closer to some blocks, just in case. It was over in a minute, and the soldiers walked back up, out of breath. They had spotted a Palestinian running down the hill, automatic grounds for suspicion.

"It is very important for us to be monitoring all Palestinians going into Ramallah, particularly from the north, to prevent them from smuggling weapons," the commander told me a few minutes later. "And, the next guy in the queue could pull the trigger. I'm a student. I'm twenty-four, I have my whole life to live, and it is very scary, especially here. This is the most dangerous roadblock in the sector."

He went on to say that several members of his family were Holocaust survivors. "What's that got to do with anything?" one of the women snapped when I repeated the story to her later.

He was a bright young man, and I wanted to have a more substantive conversation. But IDF regulations strictly proscribe serving soldiers from talking to journalists, and I never saw him again.

As we prepared to leave, Barag phoned the IDF humanitarian liaison officer to complain about the morning's delays. A captain and two other soldiers soon roared up in a jeep. The captain talked with the sergeant and strode over to Barag. He was not pleased.

"This is your fault," the captain said. "It was going fine until you got here. The Palestinians see you and think they can do anything they want. You don't understand. Don't you know that they caught two dangerous terrorists in Ramallah yesterday? I am here to keep things in order, and you are disturbing it."

"He forgot security for a moment," she said sarcastically. She related a conversation she once had with the army officer then in charge of IDF West Bank operations, a man she described in highly unflattering professional terms. She demanded to know why the Palestinians were stopped at roadblocks inside their own areas.

"Mrs. Barag, why do you think we built the wall?" he replied. "So the Palestinians can pass?"

Palestinians were not particularly grateful for the women's efforts. On an earlier trip to Atara Bridge, the women caught it from both sides. Soldiers were rude and ordered us to leave before we were kidnapped (an Israeli man had been abducted and murdered in Atara village a year or so earlier). On the way down the hill, the women got a few catcalls from Palestinians packed into the sardine-can taxis.

"Are you here to see our suffering?" one said.

"You change nothing for us," a man in the next taxi said acidly.

It was a quiet ride north toward Nablus, past Zatara Junction, where one of Varda's sons had done checkpoint duty. The women have not wavered in their conviction that the occupation is damaging Israeli society as well as oppressing the Palestinians, but they are disillusioned that it continues with no end in sight.

"We are far outside the mainstream of Israeli society," Barag said. "Israelis think we are undermining the government. Security is the magic word in Israel."

From the backseat, Hava, another one of the monitors, agreed. "The government has brainwashed people and exploits fear," she said. They used the word *brainwashing* several times that day, and Hava compared it with what the U.S. administration does with Americans. "They are frightening people over terrorism," she said.

Huwwara had undergone major changes since my last visit. There was no terminal like at Jenin and Bethlehem, but pedestrians were funneled through the lanes and turnstiles.[2] Soldiers used to make male Palestinians lift their shirts to prove they were not wearing explosive vests. They still did that sometimes, but now they were looking for knives and telling Palestinian boys and men to lift their trouser legs. There had been a rash of incidents in which a Palestinian would pull a knife and stab or slash a soldier. And a new phenomenon had begun. Palestinian boys seeking the status badge of time in an Israeli jail were declaring that they had a knife strapped to a leg or would let one fall on the ground; they would be duly arrested. I had heard in Jenin Camp that some mothers did not mind a son being jailed because there at least he would get enough to eat.

When I worked with UNRWA, my conversations with soldiers at Huwwara usually were brief and to the point and sometimes adversarial. Part of the reason I had come back was to meet the men behind the weapons. I wanted to know something about them, what they thought about the Palestinians and themselves in this situation that saw so little change from year to year.

Sgt. Arnon Gavriel was the senior man at Huwwara that day. He was nineteen, from Be'er Sheva, down in the Negev, had been in the army for a year and a half, and was finishing his second month at Huwwara. He wore the standard ceramic-plate flak vest, extra ammunition, backpack radio, and other equipment that weighed, minus his rifle, about fourteen kilograms (thirty-one pounds). When I introduced myself he was perfectly polite but said he could not talk to a reporter. Then Varda walked up. She smiled and leaned an elbow on the concrete cube and started chatting in Hebrew. Then he said he didn't mind talking, in general terms, about checkpoint duty. Varda translated. Palestinians walking north into Nablus were passing in a steady stream with no security checks; outbound, an estimated four thousand men, women, and children a day were checked, searched, or interviewed before passing the final turnstile.

"It's uncomfortable, and I'm sorry I have to do it, but it is my duty and I have to," he said. "How do I say it? Without doubt it is difficult, but even if it is, I have to check each person as if he's the first person I've seen that day, and I have to be patient and polite."

He thought that the system of lanes and turnstiles was, for everyone, safer than before. "But it is still very slow, and people suffer as they stand and wait. We could make it more efficient. I feel very bad when I see so many people in the checkpoint, so I push my soldiers to help," he said, more to Varda than to me. "I suffer when I see them suffer, but..."

As we talked, the weight of his military equipment seemed to lift, and he became more Arnon than sergeant. He was a large young man with a large face, and his adolescent spotty complexion had not yet cleared. The conversation between Arnon and Varda might have been happening across a backyard fence. He said something that surprised me, and I started to see the kid behind the rifle, or someone who was between kid and soldier.

"Sometimes I feel that I need someone to supervise me, because I feel I may be being too soft on the Palestinians. But if I'm nervous or too rough, I also need someone to tell me that."

Does he ever see Palestinians as individuals or just as traffic? "I do my best. Once with a group of five people, all about my age, I explained why I'm here, the protection against terrorism and so on, and at the end we were slapping each other on the back. We [soldiers] talk among ourselves, and we say that we wouldn't want to be in their position, but we don't want them to bomb us. I understand how they feel, but not the way they behave."

Varda had been studying Arnon, who was five years younger than her youngest son. She turned to me. "He says that until he went into the army he was a student. And I'm sure his mother treated him like he was a prince." She reached across the block and touched him lightly on the arm. Arnon smiled and looked down.

I thought again that Palestinians and Israelis rarely saw each other except as a stereotypical group: traffic versus traffic controllers, faceless and mutually antagonistic. I asked Arnon if he had ever had a personal conversation with a Palestinian. Yes, he said, they occasionally tried a bit of small talk as they searched the shopping bags; it was as much a mechanism to relieve stress and boredom as to bridge the human gap.

However, such attempts just slowed things down, Arnon added. What he didn't add, and didn't have to, was that Palestinians, who spend a good portion of their lives trying to get from somewhere to somewhere else, have no interest in polite chatter while waiting to go through a turnstile.

As others had, Arnon described daily checkpoint life as a job. "The work is very difficult. We are so tired after those eight hours. It's not just the physical strain, but the mental strain. Sometimes my soldiers need to be very strong. Because if I let someone do something he shouldn't do [such as jump the queue], then they all come. And if we let someone through and he's a bomber headed for Jerusalem..." I had never heard a soldier deviate from this line.

There was a commotion halfway up the lanes near one of the turnstiles. Vivi, who speaks Arabic and Hebrew, came back with the story. She had been watching a young private tell one Palestinian after another to lift his trouser legs. They complied and passed, without expression or comment, in a continuous stream. For the soldier, it was getting a bit much, and he was desperate to break the tedium.

"Are those shoes comfortable?" he asked a man, who lifted his foot for inspection. It was one Palestinian ankle and one vacant question too many, and when the man had gone through, he exploded in frustrated rage.

"I can't look at them anymore!" he shouted, to no one in particular. "I want to see Jews!"

"I will speak to my soldier and tell him not to make such an outburst again," the sergeant said, looking at the hundreds of Palestinians on the Nablus side.

On the way back to Jerusalem, we pulled up behind a dozen taxis at a flying checkpoint just before Ofra settlement; drivers and passengers were milling about in the road. Barag told her driver to go around. At the Humvee, where a belt of tire spikes lay across the road, two soldiers walked up, angry and aggressive, with rifles leveled on us.

"You go back, and you wait until all the people are back in their cars and the line is nice and straight," one snarled at Barag. If he talked like that to a white-haired Israeli woman, I wondered how he spoke to the taxi drivers. The argument continued for some minutes, then fizzled out, and he waved us on.

" 'Until the line is nice and straight,' " Hava said. "Like he was educating the Indians or something. He feels it is his responsibility to keep everything in order. He must show that he is strong. And then if everyone behaves..."

By the time we got to the Hizma road barrier into Jerusalem, I was keen for anything to disrupt the afternoon's dreary realities. I looked at the Military Police trooper while she leafed through my passport. She was armed and in uniform, but instead of boots she wore flip-flops and her toenails were painted red. I asked if her shoes were comfortable. She just glared and handed back my passport.

FIFTEEN

"NOT ALLOWED TO SLEEP IN JERUSALEM"

In tandem with the network of physical obstacles, the permit system was Israel's most comprehensive method of controlling where West Bank Palestinians went and how they got there.

There were said to be twelve different types of permits for different professions, activities, travel, or vehicles. Old regulations were frequently amended, and new ones popped up like seasonal plants. In the summer of 2006, Palestinian males between the ages of sixteen and thirty who lived in Nablus, Tulkarm, and Jenin were forbidden to travel south of Nablus without a special IDF permit. As a result, an estimated 105,000 men essentially were confined to the West Bank's northern sector.[1] Constraints remained in force even within the sectors, particularly around Nablus. To reach Nablus's main market, farmers without a permit were allowed to do only truck-to-truck transfers, and only across Awarta checkpoint. Any kind of internal commerce or personal movement in the West Bank was difficult. In November, for instance, the IDF formalized a long-standing travel rule: "Due to repeated attempts (at times successful) by Palestinian terror organizations to exploit Israeli vehicles in order to infiltrate Israeli population centers and carry out terror attacks against Israeli civilians . . . only Palestinians with permits may be driven in vehicles bearing Israeli license plates."

Various types of work and town residence documents, permission to travel to a hospital in another sector, and, of course, permits to enter Jerusalem were another matter. The tattered and much-folded paper documents were being replaced by uniform magnetic-strip cards; loaded with a variety of personal information, everything the Israeli government wanted to know about a person, these cards eventually would be swiped through a reader at crossing terminals. I was surprised that Palestinians didn't need a permit to apply for a permit. In a sense, they did; the hard-to-obtain and precisely worded papers, and particularly the magnetic cards, were links in a closed bureaucratic chain.

There were disagreements within Machsom Watch over what role their members should play in helping Palestinians navigate this dense thicket. Some women said their efforts were vital to giving Palestinians a leg up so they could travel to work; others said that it was cooperating—even collaborating—with the system by collecting the permit fee from a Palestinian and handing it over to the government. Some women had even left Machsom Watch over the internal dispute. However, with the economy in the shape it was, Palestinians had to travel to find work. Machsom Watch helped them do it.

"In the old days, sometimes a Palestinian would ask for mercy at a checkpoint, and sometimes a soldier would say okay," Dr. Yehudit Elkana, a chemist, told me. "Now, it's either you have the right documents or you stay home. If you don't have the right documents, you can wind up in court or in jail."

"The occupation is done not only by guns but by bureaucracy. It is so illogical and so cruel," Barag said. "You can spend your life getting the right permit."

▪▪▪

To explore the arcane intricacies of the permit system, you could talk to just about anyone on the street in the Gaza Strip or the West Bank. It would be a rare Palestinian who did not have a long and convoluted story to tell.

Ahmed M. had spent a good part of his adult life chasing permits, and when we met he was living in Jerusalem in the shadows between legal and illegal. He could work in Jerusalem, but when he went home at night he was in violation of Israeli law. He deeply feared losing whatever freedom of movement he had and the cohesion of his family. His wife was a Jerusalemite, and they rented a home in East Jerusalem. Two of their four children were about to reach the age when they required separate IDs. It made for a nervous life.

During the first intifada, Ahmed was finishing his university studies. With an 84 percent grade-point average, he won a scholarship to study medicine in Moscow. Then he ran into a closed door. Although he had no police record and had not been involved in the uprising, he said, the government wouldn't let him out of the country. After many attempts, he decided that becoming a doctor was out, so he got a nursing degree instead. That career went down the drain because he couldn't find work at a hospital in Jerusalem. He went back to school again and earned a degree in business administration. In the summer of 2006 Ahmed was mopping floors in a large East Jerusalem office block, still hobbled by his West Bank residence permit.

At thirty-six, he was slightly stooped, and his skin and what little hair he had were gray; the first thing he said when we sat down was, "When you look at me, maybe you see an old man." He had made four attempts to obtain either a permit to get him out of Israel to study or one that would get him "into" Israel to live legally with his wife. The problem, he thought, was simply that he was Palestinian, male, and under forty. The first step in applying for an exit visa many years ago had been the mandatory police interview. The police were suspicious. "They see someone who has never had a problem, never been arrested, who has never been politically active, so they think I'm dangerous. The police said, 'What are you doing?' I said, 'Nothing.'" Application denied, no reason given. The security forces do not explain their decisions.

He took an audacious step and went to see an officer in Shin Bet, the internal security service. "I told him that I need to live with my wife and that I need to work. My children need food, and they need to go to school. I said that if he had a black mark against me, he could put me in prison," Ahmed said.

"I don't need you in prison," the Shin Bet officer replied.

"If I'm a dangerous man, put me in prison," Ahmed persisted.

"I won't put you in prison, and I won't give you a permit," the intelligence officer said. The conversation had been man to man and cordial enough. But after four tries, his dream of studying in Moscow was over. "That's what makes me look like an old man," Ahmed said with a rueful smile.

He scraped up enough money to hire a lawyer and took his claim to court. The case ground its way through the system (or never moved at all), and for the next thirteen years he kept doing odd jobs and paying the lawyer. He lay low, not daring to go back to the West Bank to visit his family in case he was barred from reentering Jerusalem. Unlikely as that scenario might have been, he would not risk separation from his wife and children and the collapse of his court case.

During hours of discussions with Ahmed, I could never completely understand his status, and at times I wasn't sure he could either. Although he was a West Banker, he had a permit that allowed him to work in Israel, but only during the daytime. The paper stipulated that he was "not allowed to sleep in Israel," meaning that he had to be back in the West Bank by sundown. So he was illegal only when he went home to his family. Then things got complicated.

The court decreed that because of his ongoing legal case, he must not leave Jerusalem. Now he had two pieces of paper with different stipulations. "The soldiers and police could throw me out because my *tasriya*—my permit—says that I am not allowed to sleep in Israel. But the court says I must sleep in Israel. Some want me to stay, the others want me to leave." Ahmed could see the humor in the Kafkaesque contradictions, but it was a stressful business. His eyes were never still, and he had developed the habit of keeping an eye on the door.

Then came two breaks in the case, a few weeks apart. First the court ruled that he would be allowed to live in Jerusalem with his wife because she held an Israeli ID; for the first time in some years Ahmed would be able to have a legal night's sleep. Then his two older children were granted Jerusalem papers, a good indicator that his would follow. One critical worry that lifted was that as Jerusalemites his children were now eligible for health benefits; the premiums had long been deducted from his paychecks, a useless expenditure until now.

The next time I saw Ahmed, he looked like he had won the lottery. He had a spring in his step and a fresh haircut, and he definitely looked younger. I didn't ask, and he drew out the suspense. After thirteen years and four thousand dollars in legal fees, his provisional Jerusalem ID would be granted, valid for two years. If there were no setbacks, in time he would get a blue-cover wallet with an orange Israeli ID inside, valid for three to five years, and finally the coveted blue ID in a blue cover. *Inshallah*—God willing—was all he said. It was a pleasure to see the way he sauntered down the street.

But even if Ahmed's papers came through on schedule, he would not be exempt from being questioned by the army and Border Police wherever their paths crossed. The normal difficulties of travel, which he still dreaded, were compounded by the gratuitous violence and humiliation.

Ahmed, like many Palestinians, had memorized the long number of his *hawiya*—his Palestinian ID card. The *tasriya* and the *hawiya* must be handed over to any police officer or soldier. "You *must* remember it," he said. "Sometimes they quiz you, and once I was beaten because I could not remember the number. I have also been punched and kicked because I would not speak Hebrew." As a particularly harsh punishment, soldiers will destroy or deface a Palestinian's permit or identification.

Incidents such as these, widely reported by Israeli and other human rights organizations, plunge Machsom Watch women and other peace activists into despair about what is happening to their country and to the Israel Defense Forces.

"For many soldiers, the Green Line doesn't exist," Nava Elyashar said. "They think they're there to save Israel. Many have no idea where they are, just that it's 'Israel.' They begin to hate the Palestinians more and more because they have to deal with them every day."

Hanna Barag agreed, and said the occupation has warped the values of a generation. "The soldiers bring the angry feelings home, then they kill each other over parking spaces. When evil takes these young men, they take the evil back home."

SIXTEEN

SOLDIERS' TALES

"We had taken over three places—the roof of a family home, a closed school, and the top floor of another house," Yehuda Shaul told a group of foreign visitors as he surveyed Hebron's bustling Palestinian market down in the valley. Taxis and cars looked like beetles at that distance, and their constant hooting carried up the hill on the wind. "The Palestinians were shooting every evening, and we had to show who's stronger. The first day, I'm standing in the window, and if the Palestinians shoot, we shoot back. You have an order. You have to. I was shocked. It was mad."

Shaul, a soldier in the Fiftieth Battalion of the Nahal Brigade, was no stranger to violent operations in the West Bank. What shocked him was not so much the order to open fire but that it was not a rifle he was pointing down into the valley.

His specialty weapon was an automatic grenade launcher. Similar in principle to a machine gun, it rapid-fires fragmentation grenades at a range of more than 2 kilometers (1½ miles). Each exploding grenade has a kill radius of 5 meters (16 feet) and will wound anyone within a radius of 15 meters (50 feet). "It is not an accurate weapon," Shaul said with considerable understatement. "A ferocious American weapon," one of Shaul's colleagues added.

"The first day it was tense, the second day less," Shaul said. "And then it became a game. A year and a half before, you were in a [video-game] canyon playing on a screen. Now it's the real stuff. That's all we did every night. Our mission was to return fire."

Now he was ordered to shoot fragmentation grenades toward apartment buildings. Not at advancing infantry or armored vehicles, but at an enemy he could not see. "It's outrageous, it's something that, when you are trained, when you sit down in the desert and you learn about this weapon . . . in your worst dreams you don't shoot it in an urban area."

The nightly routine began to pale. "So you start talking with a sniper. It's a game. 'See that car down there?' " Shaul's eyes traverse the eight hundred meters (874 yards) to where one night's game had led. " 'Think you can take out the rear tire? Five bucks says you can't.' And you open fire." Instead of taking out the rear tire, though, the bullet shattered the car's rear window. If anyone was hurt or killed, no one up on the hill could tell. The sniper lost five bucks.

"You're shooting every night at the Palestinians. But they don't get it, they don't get the message," Shaul said. The unit changed the schedule, not waiting for the Palestinians to open fire. "So every night from five-forty to six-fifteen we shoot at them. Then *they* shoot back." But the Palestinians still weren't getting the message, and kept up their ineffective small-arms fire at Shaul's hilltop post. It was time to escalate. Late one night they got a call-up to mount what's called a "violent patrol." In testimony to Breaking the Silence, the group of army veterans who speak out about their service, another soldier described a "violent patrol":

> We go in two APCs toward Abu Sneineh [a Hebron neighborhood] to make our presence felt, do all sorts of things, just to intimidate them. One is a sharpshooter. We shoot at some houses as we moved through, and all we did was shoot, shoot, shoot. My task was to shatter streetlights. Another soldier shot a grenade into a shop, just to blow up a Palestinian shop. It was so cool —there's nothing like shooting out streetlights just to hear them blow! I remember I had a [big] grin on my face.[1]

Shaul and his fellow platoon members began to ask questions among themselves. They were firing grenades into shops and shooting out streetlights in the midst of a civilian population. Something was wrong. Shaul, eighteen at the time, decided that, given the opportunity to command, he and his soldiers would behave differently; they would be the moral soldiers. Then came the wave of Palestinian suicide bombings and Operation Defensive Shield in 2002. Internal debate ceased.

"That was a feeling of fighting for our own houses, our own homes," he said. "Every night you come back from operations with APCs full of weapons . . . we're fighting terror. Suddenly, no questions anymore." But the doubts didn't go away, and he remained deeply conflicted by what he saw—and did—particularly during the destructive days of 2002 in Ramallah. When he was redeployed back to Hebron, he had been in the army for thirteen months.

Shaul, a religious Jew from what he describes as "an American leftist family" (his mother is American, his father Canadian, and he was born in Jerusalem), saw his own ethical world turn on its head in the army Israelis are taught to revere. Days later, he told me more over lunch. A hefty twenty-three-year-old who wears a ponytail and the religious black kippa, he talked in a rapid but thoughtful monologue, at times with anguish and disgust in his voice.

> My first assignment, I was on a patrol. I was walking through the streets, and there was a checkpoint . . . [at] the bottom of Abu Sneineh. . . . It's a very dangerous place, where a lot of soldiers were wounded. So we said, "Let's go up to secure the post for a couple of minutes." We started climbing up the stairs. Suddenly, I see that the doors are open. And I pushed a bit the doors and . . . I was shocked. It was a Palestinian dentist's clinic. It was destroyed by soldiers. They shit on the floor, they broke all the chairs, the refrigerator . . . everything. . . . And two things happened to me there. One was, I took out a camera, took photographs, and the first weekend I went out [on leave], I distributed [the photos] to all journalists. Of course no one really paid attention. It was the first time that I faced the brutality of occupation. The truth is, it was not the first time. It's the first time I realized what I'm seeing. Because in Ramallah we did worse things. It's the first time that I saw *others* doing it, so I could understand. It wasn't me. It wasn't *my* company. It wasn't *my* people.

The smashed-up dentist's office was Shaul's trigger. Instead of quitting the army, as he had thought of doing, he enrolled in a sergeant's course. Halfway through it, his unit was sent to Bethlehem.

> In June 2002 one of the sergeants in my platoon killed an innocent Palestinian—not innocent, he threw stones, but he killed him. And that's only one example of what happened there in three weeks. And of course there was no investigation, no one really asked questions, no one really cared. To kill a sixteen-year-old Palestinian with a rubber bullet from ten meters [thirty-two feet] because he threw stones, it's something that he deserves, you know, it's nothing to question. A deputy platoon officer used to play with his radio guy. He used to compete who can shoot gas grenades through a window into a house from the street. [I remember] driving through the streets of Bethlehem enforcing curfew and seeing two Palestinian kids, one was like three years old, the other was five years old, eating watermelon on their balcony, and the deputy platoon officer just [throws] the gas grenade on the balcony. And you ask him, "Why?" He said, "They shouldn't observe us and collect information and intelligence."

These weren't isolated incidents. Something was badly wrong inside "the most moral army in the world."

> We have a briefing and then walk out on patrol in Hebron's Casbah. There's a parcel on the street. There are three ways to check it: one, you shoot it and maybe, if it's a bomb, it explodes. Two, you call a bomb engineer, and that would seem a reasonable thing to do, and you wait. Or, three, you grab the first Palestinian on the street and make him pick it up, and if it's a bomb, it explodes. So what do you think we do? That's the procedure. Using Palestinians as human shields is so common. If the road is blocked, you use Palestinians to clean the road. In military terms, it makes sense.

On most days, Shaul said, soldiers had only limited contact with the enemy.

> I was in Deheisheh refugee camp, and we were imposing curfew. We drove two or three APCs and two tanks, driving through Bethlehem. And on one of the streets a group of children were throwing stones. If you're in an APC or in a tank, you don't feel the stones. But our company commander decided it's

> time, you know, to bring justice. So we stopped the vehicles and ran out and started running after them shooting rubber bullets, throwing gas grenades, shock grenades. After like ten minutes we captured the enemy. Ten-year-old boy, bare feet. Blindfolded and handcuffed him, took him through all the garbage and water in the middle of the streets. . . . I was covering the back, so I came last. . . . The Palestinian kid is [inside] on the floor [of the APC], and I hear . . . one of the soldiers screaming at the kid, "You don't think you have to mature, to grow up? People your age are already blowing [up] buses. . . . [Why] are you dirtying yourself throwing stones, man?" . . . Like, I don't think that kid understood Hebrew. It's the mind-set of the soldiers, and all the squad starts laughing, and then I came and I said, "Hey guys, what's the carnival here?" And my squad commander comes to me. . . . Immediately everyone starts, "Hey, shut up, you leftist. . . ." He comes to me, says, "Yehuda, do you have mercy for him? If we don't treat him this way, he will grow up and be a suicide bomber." You know, I believed just the opposite, but I shut up because I want to graduate [from the sergeant's course], I want to be a commander. I don't care about anything [else]. So we enter the APC, and we throw him in the corner. I'm just thinking to myself, *Oh, God, the safety rule is that no one is allowed to ride in an APC without a helmet, right?* In our battalion, when we used to arrest a Palestinian and take him in the APC, we would put a helmet on him because that's the safety rule! You know, if you turn over, a guy can die if he doesn't have a helmet, right? What's going on there? Occupation, we call it.

I asked if any other particular incidents had stayed with him. He paused and hummed along with a Hebrew pop song on the radio, his foot jiggling under the table. "When you look backward you start to remember all the stores that were broken [into] . . . all the cars that were smashed . . . the national radio, the Palestinian National Radio in Ramallah [where] we destroyed all the computers. . . . When you look at it, it's not one incident, it's one big lie. It's full of 'one incidents.' It's a big puzzle. Every piece is one story. My story is one big puzzle. Full of all these."

What about the army's Rules of Engagement, the formal list of procedures that regulates how and when deadly force is used?

> In the first intifada, there always was an investigation after an innocent Palestinian was killed. And each soldier got a booklet with the Rules of Engagement in it. Now the Rules of Engagement are classified and are not handed out in written form to soldiers. They say it's because the dynamic on the ground changes daily.

In other army units, and not for the first time, soldiers were starting to look at their own actions and the big picture and say, "This is something other than war." As Shaul put it, "You can't act nice, or morally, in a corrupt situation."

Avichay Sharon, who joined Breaking the Silence after his service ended, comes from a home he describes as Zionist, patriotic, liberal, and left-wing. His father was wounded in the Yom Kippur War; his grandparents were Hungarian Jews who survived the Holocaust. Before joining the army, Sharon worked for four years as an instructor and guide in the Israeli youth movement. The year the second intifada began, Sharon was in a Special Forces unit of the Golani Brigade, best known for its role in the rescue of Jewish hostages from a hijacked Air France airliner in Entebbe, Uganda, in 1976. Sharon's section conducted search-and-arrest operations, some in Gaza, but most in Nablus and Jenin. As we talked in a West Jerusalem coffee shop, I remembered the graffiti Golani soldiers had carved in children's desktops in a Tulkarm school.

Sharon talked openly, as Shaul had done, about one violent operation after another and said the days and nights of violent patrols and searches all blended together. But as he talked, I kept hearing nonspecific references to six-year-olds and asked if one incident had involved a child of that age.

> Yeah. I remember it very well. It was an arrest operation in Jenin, one of the villages. When you take over a home, you tell everyone to get out of the house. The first person who comes out, you tell them to open up all the doors, get everybody outside, and you check IDs. And then you send the first squad to check there are no weapons hidden inside the house. And then everyone comes in, and you start searching the place. You can imagine what it means

when fifteen people search an apartment. It includes a lot of destruction. A lot of destruction. Usually you take the family and put them in one room. A guard on them. The idea is you have them under supervision, and they don't go around in the house. The second thing is, that way they don't see what you're doing. But this time it was a very small home . . . and when we were searching their room, the kids were kind of in a corner outside, and they were seeing everything. I remember this incident even though it was common, something that happens every night. But for some reason I remember this one very, very well.

He's ready to move on. "But why do you remember this one kid?" I ask. He pauses and continues.

Me and a friend of mine, while we were tossing the room, at some point I'm taking his school knapsack, and, you know, tossing it, everything outside, to see what he had there. All his crayons and notebooks and things. And suddenly I see him staring at me. Very scared. It's two o'clock in the morning, we just arrested his father in front of his eyes, and he's totally, you know, traumatized, scared, crying. And for that one second, we just . . . our eyes kind of connected and, uh, . . . he looked at me, I looked at him, and of course I just turned right away and continued to do what I'm doing, 'cause you can't look at a six-year-old and do what you have to do. Kids are always . . . very hard to deal [with] . . . it's very trivial. I mean it's not. But there was nothing . . . different from any other night. I remember myself thinking, *What the hell am I doing here? I mean, it's a school knapsack, what the hell am I doing here?* There were families . . . we invaded their homes, and sometimes we stayed for days, sometimes for weeks. . . . Now just think about that: the idea of your home becoming your own jail. Where you need to ask permission from a nineteen-year-old [soldier] to take a piss in your own home. It's not something that's happening far away, it's not Foreign Legionnaires who are doing this, it's not mercenaries, it's *us*!

Duty in the occupied territories began to feel like a free-for-all. Soldiers, or their immediate commanders, were given a lot of leeway, and after-action reports, if taken at all, were often exaggerated. Stone throwers became armed terrorists who had attacked soldiers. Sharon told me another story.

> We were in Nablus, and a fourteen-year-old kid was shot by one of my colleagues . . . because they were throwing stones. We didn't have anything but our lethal ammunition and weapons, grenades and our M-16s, and they were given orders to shoot in the air, and you know what happens when you shoot in the air—they run away and come back and run away and come back. Eventually they were told to shoot at their legs, and he shot at their legs and he hit his chest, and a fourteen-year-old kid died, was killed! Why? Because no one cared! And even after he was killed nothing changed; there wasn't even any questions about it! There wasn't even any debriefing about the incident.

Apart from the Rules of Engagement, which were seldom clear, soldiers found themselves inflicting punishment devoid of military necessity. Sharon told me another story from Nablus, which occurred months after Operation Defensive Shield had ended.

> It was winter, the end of 2002 or beginning of 2003, very cold, middle of the night, raining. . . . We were supposed to arrest someone from a very big apartment building. . . . The process was to evacuate everyone. So it took a lot of time. This apartment was full of families, children, and they were all taken outside to stand in the street, and the guy who we were supposed to arrest, he stayed inside the apartment and he announced he's not going to surrender. He had a handgun and he's not gonna surrender. Now the process was to start to shoot at the building with machine guns and tanks and whatever. Shooting, just tearing the whole apartment building [apart], and we were there for the whole night and until the next morning and then some.

Sharon stuttered, stopped, and backed up.

> Think about this scene. Dozens of families and children and innocent people standing in the street with only their pajamas because they were thrown out

> of their apartment; some of the kids are still barefoot. Freezing cold. For eight, ten hours. After the guy was caught, we asked permission from the commander of our unit to [let] the families into one of the apartments, and he refused. There were a few women who really had to go to the bathroom. It's freezing cold, they're there for eight hours already with their kids and everything. They had to pee, you know? And he refused. He didn't let us take them in into one of the apartments to the bathroom. It's just being cruel. It's embarrassing, it's humiliating, it's abusive. This did not have to happen.

These stories—and worse—came out in a cold, controlled torrent. When several dozen soldiers founded Breaking the Silence, they put together an exhibit in Tel Aviv. One display featured about a hundred car keys that had been confiscated from Palestinians at a single checkpoint. After a newspaper reporter wrote about it, the IDF blamed it on a "rotten apple" from some unit and said that confiscation of car keys was not an approved procedure.

"We said: how many car keys do you need? How many rotten apples do you need until you will admit that this is the procedure?" Sharon said. "A hundred is not enough for you? Five hundred? We'll give you five hundred car keys . . . a thousand car keys. . . . Just say the number. When will you admit finally the truth?" The IDF eventually announced that taking Palestinians' car keys was an approved procedure.

> They said, "Oh, don't worry, we legalized it, now it's okay." . . . For me the process as a soldier was total denial . . . not to hear, not to see. I never hit someone, I never beat someone intentionally. I didn't want to see, didn't want to hear. . . . Things go right by you. . . . It's being blind and deaf. It was every day. . . . It's not about the shooting and the battles that we had. When a six-year-old looks at you and you are a monster in his eyes, that is the hard core. When you humiliate a father in front of his kids, that is the hard core. It's an inevitable process. The same person that was standing at that checkpoint, going like this [he crooks an index finger] at a line of six hundred people . . . it's all about different methods of control . . . punishment . . . humiliation. But eventually it's all the same. The operations that we were told, okay, now go in and

> just roam this city and make noise . . . it's two o'clock in the morning . . . we're gonna show them who's boss. Now when I tell this to you it sounds so stupid, so idiotic. I mean you have to be retarded to think about going into a city and just starting a violent patrol just for the fun of it. . . . But in that reality of power and control . . . it sounded so smart. It was very clear to us why we were doing this, because in that crazy reality, crazy things become very rational. And that craziness comes back with us, because its patterns of behavior grow on you, and you become used to them and you embrace them . . . even unconsciously. It's not only about individuals who freak out at the checkpoint. In a corrupt reality the actors are corrupt. You become totally apathetic to human life, to families. . . . Value doesn't count.

Soldiers saw their personalities change during the violent patrols and particularly at the checkpoints, where they exercised total control. One soldier said:

> You start playing with them, like a computer game. You come here, you go there, like this. You barely move, you make them obey the tip of your finger. It's a mighty feeling. It's something you don't experience elsewhere. . . . It's addictive. When I realized this I checked in with myself to see what had happened to me. I thought I was immune . . . a thinking, articulate, ethical, moral man. . . . I thought of myself as such. Suddenly I notice that I'm getting addicted to controlling people.[2]

Sharon (and others) told me stories of soldiers posing for photographs with corpses. "With two dead Palestinians. You know, kind of victory pictures. We killed them. It's not like we thought of them as some kind of animals or less [than] human beings, or some kind of disgusting creatures. . . . We didn't *think* of them."

I had asked Yehuda Shaul over lunch how he had seen Palestinians at the time. Did he ever see them as individuals?

"I don't know," he said.

"Did you just see them as a group?" I asked. He hummed along with the radio, and his foot jiggled under the table.

"You don't see them. You don't see them."

Israelis grow up believing what they've been taught: that the IDF is defending them against terrorists. The violent patrols and black (or covert) operations are unknown outside of the military (and the Palestinian towns, of course) or not talked about. *No wonder these stories stay buried,* I thought.

"We're not accountable for anything," Sharon had said. "We know that none of the reporters will ask us what happened. Nobody will [talk] about a soldier [receiving] orders to shoot and kill anyone walking down the street between one and three a.m."

I interrupted. I had heard this story from another soldier and still found it hard to believe. Commanders gave orders to shoot dead anyone walking on the street between one and three o'clock in the morning? During curfew? It was said to have happened in 2003.

> Not even during curfew... yeah, yeah, an order to shoot and kill anyone walking on the street between one and three a.m., and later on between two and four a.m., on different nights. A man walked down the street and they opened fire, they shot and killed him, they verified his death with grenades and shooting his body.[3] Turns out he was a baker. He had pita bread in his bag! He was on his way to work! I know his name, his age, where he worked. You know what the IDF statement was, that same morning? That the IDF shot an armed terrorist suicide bomber that was on his way to explode on the IDF forces. Did anyone ask a question? No. Did anyone go and check who was killed and why? No. That is not about war. That is about a society that doesn't want to face the truth. That's about a society that sends their best sons and daughters to oppress, to kill, to violate, to humiliate, to abuse and doesn't want to know about it.

"If things are that clear cut," I asked Yehuda Shaul one day, "why is the occupation still going on?"

"I don't think it's the right question," he replied. "It's very obvious why it's going on. Why not? Because on one side you have people who do it, who live this life. You have a lot of people who benefit from it. And the majority is silent."

Avichay Sharon put it this way: "The problem is not the sergeant who slapped a Palestinian around at the checkpoint: It's the sergeant *standing* at the checkpoint. There's a sort of pathology with the Jewish people, especially Israelis, a people who have been persecuted for a long time. It's a paradox that we, as the powerful, don't see ourselves as the oppressor."

As they wrestled with the nearly unlimited power they had over the Palestinian population, Yehuda Shaul and his comrades skirmished on another front: with the Jewish settlers in Hebron.

SEVENTEEN

"I'M GOING TO BUY A POPSICLE, THEN I'M GOING TO KILL SOME ARABS"

Hebron was the crucible. In political and religious terms and even topographically, partly situated in a natural basin encased by hills, the town felt like the point where long-standing animosities fused. Shaul, who spent two of his three army years here, described Hebron as "the microcosm of everything." For the young soldiers, it became a disturbing personal story, and sometimes a turning point in their lives.

Judaism, Islam, and Christianity intersect here, with the Tomb of the Patriarchs—al-Haram al-Ibrahimi, the Ibrahimi Mosque—among the holiest of religious sites as the burial place of the patriarch Abraham, Sarah, Isaac, Jacob, and Leah. Although Hebron Jews and Muslims have managed to live in peace for periods, each community has tended to regard the sites with a sense of propriety.

Two twentieth-century events continue to rub Jewish and Palestinian wounds. A Palestinian building reveals the historical layers of one. Beneath an Israeli flag and a camouflage-draped army observation tower on the roof hang two huge signs, in Hebrew and English, which read, in part: "This land was stolen by Arabs following the murder of 67 Hebron Jews in 1929. We demand justice! Return our property to us!"

The 1929 massacre of the Hebron Jews and others in Jerusalem was an explosion in the long-simmering dispute during the Mandate over access to Jerusalem's holy sites; the British police forces were too small to stop the slaughter. The murders remain a potent symbol of what some Jews see as latent Arab treachery. "If you ask any Jew on the street, he will say, 'Palestinians are Palestinians, and they will stab you in the back,' " Shaul said.

Hebron was under Jordanian jurisdiction after the 1948 war, and the town's Jewish quarter was ransacked. After Israel took control of Hebron in 1967, Jewish fundamentalists founded the settlement of Kiryat Arba east of the town, and a decade later settlers moved into the Hebron neighborhoods of Avraham Avinu and Tel Rumeida. Since then, the IDF has protected about six hundred settlers in the two enclaves, making Hebron the only Palestinian city with a Jewish settlement in the middle of it.

In the winter of 1994, the Jewish religious holiday of Purim coincided with the Muslim holy month of Ramadan. Before dawn on February 25, Baruch Goldstein, a Brooklyn-born Israeli settler, entered the Ibrahimi Mosque in his army uniform during the first Muslim prayers of the day and opened fire with an assault rifle. Twenty-nine Palestinians died and more than a hundred were wounded before he was beaten to death. Goldstein, a doctor who had refused to treat Arabs during his army service, became a martyr for messianic Jews.

Two days after the massacre, posters went up in parts of West Jerusalem praising Goldstein and lamenting the fact that the death toll had not been higher, according to Israel Shahak and Norton Mezvinsky, who monitored the Hebrew press. For months afterward settlers' children wore buttons that read "Dr. Goldstein cured Israel's ills."[1] The funeral arrangements and continuing uproar over the grave site triggered another government crisis that wound up in the courts.

The aftershocks reverberate today. Goldstein's fanatical attempt to block the 1990s peace process partly succeeded. "His plan also used the brutal logic of terror—atrocity causes escalation, thus enlisting new supporters. Hamas responded to the massacre by initiating a campaign of suicide bombings in Israeli cities, which in turn intensified opposition in Israel to the Oslo process," historian Gershom Gorenberg wrote.[2] The wheel turned again.

Since the U.S.-supervised Hebron Protocol of 1997, the city has been divided into two zones: H1, in theory under Palestinian security control, and H2, under Israeli military control. During the second intifada Palestinian Hebron reportedly spent more days under curfew than any other West Bank town, and more than two thousand Palestinian shops were said to have been closed by military warrant.

To explain the situation in H2 and the power of the settlers, Breaking the Silence conducts foreign dignitaries, development workers, and journalists on regular bus tours to some of the town's more uncomfortable sites. Joining one of these trips was a good opportunity to see Hebron from another angle. We entered from the east, my first pass through Kiryat Arba. Figuring that a political clash was not out of the question, I was surprised that the submachine-gun-toting private security guard opened the settlement gate. Hebron's mythology was close at hand, and the bus slowed as we passed Goldstein's grave. This is the inscription on the stone slab: "Here lies the saint, Dr. Baruch Kappel Goldstein, blessed be the memory of the righteous and holy man, may the Lord avenge his blood, who devoted his soul to the Jews, Jewish religion and Jewish land. His hands are innocent and his heart is pure. He was killed as a martyr of God on the 14th of Adar, Purim, in the year 5754 (1994)."

We stopped at a small park, where several on the bus decided to use the public toilet. Before they could walk up the stairs, a settler barged through and slammed and bolted the steel gate. "It's closed," he said. Shaul brushed past him and unbolted it. "Welcome to the mind-set of the Hebron settlers," he said with a smile.

H2 is not for the claustrophobic. On that warm day, the town felt as though all the air had been sucked out of it. Shaul led the group through the deserted weed-grown streets and around the Casbah, now a closed military zone and officially off-limits to Israelis, its stone portals crudely sealed with scrap metal. Mythology also was on display in these overheated streets. Spray-painted in Hebrew on the door of one Palestinian shop was the slogan "This is the boundary of the ghetto—no entry to Jews." Settlers are enraged, Shaul explained, that they cannot enter the Old City. "The worst thing that could happen is that a Jewish government, inside a Jewish state, inside Israel, would prevent Jews from walking wherever they wanted, to get back their properties. That's the meaning of 'the ghetto,' " he said.

To keep Palestinians out of their own shops, and to keep settlers from occupying them, the IDF welded the doors shut. Settlers responded by spray-painting doors with the Star of David and graffiti such as "Arabs to the gas chambers." A few have managed to wrench loose some doors and now live inside. The squatters create another headache for Israeli authorities: eviction is a complex and lengthy legal process.

With its streets of shuttered businesses, Hebron H2 is often described as a ghost town; the portrayal is accurate. Dozens of Palestinian houses are occupied by the army, and others are deserted, firebombed shells. Many Palestinians have succumbed to the intense pressures and left, which is what the settlers intended. Those who stayed have been allowed more freedom of movement in the past year, but the army still calls the streets a "sterilized zone," another term for a closed military area, and few people move about.

The old meat market, shut down after the 1994 massacre and the violence that followed, is a rubble of burned-out shops and smashed stalls. As Shaul gathered his "tourists" in a circle, a police van pulled up and an officer armed with an M-16 kept watch on a group of armed settlers who had appeared behind a low wall of the Avraham Avinu settlement, just above the rubbish-strewn lot. Insults in Hebrew spattered down, directed mostly at Shaul.

"You must have lots of money to buy pig meat!" yelled one armed settler with a beard and long side curls.

"You look like a pig!" another shouted.

"Take off your kippa—you're a pig Jew! You're not one of us!"

Shaul, whose colleague once got a broken nose when their patrol was attacked by the settlers, has a thick skin for such tirades. "Our relationship wasn't so good," he said with a wry smile. "We didn't exactly love each other."

More police arrived and hustled us out of the market area. "It is very tense," one said. Shaul agreed. As we walked around the corner in the stifling morning heat, settlers drove by leaning on their horns and shouting, "Traitor!"

If Hebron's H2 is the crucible, Tel Rumeida is its hottest point and its most poisonous. On this hill with a spectacular view over the Casbah, a dozen or so Palestinian families—there once were several hundred—live under what Israeli journalist Gideon Levy called "a reign of terror imposed by the settlers." Scathingly referring to the settlers as "these violent lords of the land," Levy in 2005 recommended that all Israeli students be taken on a field trip to Tel Rumeida.

> Here is where Israeli schoolchildren should be shown the dark side of their country, their state's violent and law-flouting backyard. A military barracks under whose cover exists the purest evil that the settlers inflict on their neighbors. There is no other neighborhood like this one. Not a day passes without violence, not an hour passes without the throwing of stones, garbage and feces at the frightened neighbors cowering in their barricaded houses, afraid even to peek out the window. Neighbors whose way home is always a path of torment and anxiety. All this is happening right under the noses of the soldiers and police, representatives of the legal authorities, who merely stand by.[3]

With our protection detail beefed up by a squad of heavily armed and flak-jacketed Border Police, we clambered up the steep rocky hill to the back porch of Hashem Azzeh's old stone home. Azzeh and his family welcomed us into their living room with orange juice and an invitation to gather around the television set. When everyone was seated, Azzeh, a lanky man in his forties, pushed the play button and a secretly shot video of a settler attack on a Palestinian doctor's clinic unfolded; as soldiers watched, a mob of settlers broke in and smashed up the place, including the doctor's medical equipment. In another segment, Israeli girls, who look to be about twelve to fifteen years old, block the footpath and pummel young Palestinian girls on their way to school. "Kill all the Arabs!" the Israeli girls shout. "This is Israel, not Palestine." The Palestinian girls duck the blows and keep moving. It's a hard video to watch.

Settler violence, including assaults by children, is endemic in H2, particularly in Tel Rumeida. Soldiers assigned to Hebron have described the mental turmoil they experience in a place where they are required to stand aside and watch the settlers beat Palestinians, unchecked by the law. One soldier, a teacher in civilian life, said:

> The thing that gets to you more than anything else is the total indifference it instills in you. It's hard to describe the enormous sea of indifference you're

> swimming in while you're there.... One story is about a little kid, a boy of about six, who passed by me at my post. He said to me, "Soldier, listen, don't get annoyed, don't try and stop me, I'm going out to kill some Arabs." I look at the kid and don't quite understand exactly what I'm supposed to do. So he says, "First, I'm going to buy a Popsicle at Gotnik's"—that's their grocery store—"then, I'm going to kill some Arabs." I had nothing to say to him. Nothing. I went completely blank. And that's not such a simple thing... [for a person] who was an educator... who believed in education, who believed in talking to people, even if their opinions were different. But I had nothing to say to a kid like that.[4]

Many of the worst attacks come on Saturdays, the Jewish Sabbath and the first day of the Palestinian school week. I asked Shaul why Jews would permit their children to beat up other children on Shabbat. "Some things are more important than Shabbat" was his curt reply.

Someone asked Azzeh, whose own terrified children have been caught in the ambushes, if he ever considered moving away. "Why should I?" he replied. "Three generations of my family have lived here." However, he recently moved his father, who had had a stroke, to a safer location. Had he ever talked with the settlers? Yes, he had approached the ones upstairs on several occasions. The least abusive of the conversations went like this:

"Can we talk?" Azzeh had asked.

"No."

"We live here, and are willing to be neighbors with you," Azzeh said. "Can we be neighbors?"

"No. This land was promised by God to me. You can go to Egypt, you can go to Jordan, you can go to Iraq."

Back at the bottom of the hill, Border Police and soldiers hurried us toward the bus. They did not want an international incident (there had been a few); the longer we walked the streets with Shaul, whom the extremist settlers despised, the greater the probability of one. When the bus door closed, the soldiers went off in another direction and the Azzehs were left alone with their violent neighbors.

"Hebron is the test case for lack of law enforcement in the occupied Palestinian territories," Shaul said. "It is a Wild West by definition; if you're a Jew, you can do what you want here. I don't think there is one paragraph of international law that is not violated in Hebron."

We left the way we went in, through Kiryat Arba. The tour bus had Israeli plates, and this was the only "Israeli" way out of Hebron. This time the armed security guard refused to open the gate and demanded that he be allowed to check the bus passengers. "They might be terrorists!" he said. Shaul, well acquainted with the routine, speed-dialed the police on his mobile phone. When they arrived and ordered the guard to let us through, he refused again and told the bus driver to move in order to uncork the traffic jam that had built behind us. The bus driver stayed put, Shaul folded his arms, and the guard blew his top.

"Go to Hizbollah! You're a traitor! Your father's Hizbollah!" he roared, expanding his insults to include Shaul's more distant ancestors while we photographed the scene through the windows.

As the din of hooting horns and shouts increased, the guard stabbed the button and the gate slid open on greased steel wheels.

EIGHTEEN
THE ESSENCE OF VICTORY

Since its founding in 1948, Israel has lurched from one crisis to another with the Palestinians and its Arab neighbors, but always in the same general direction. Successive Israeli governments have held paramount the need to protect the Jewish state from "existential threats" because, as the well-worn cliché goes, "it's a tough neighborhood." Palestinians see Israel's strategy and tactics more as "maximum land, minimum Palestinians."

The seeds of Israel's policies go back further than 1948, to a paper written in 1923 by Ze'ev Jabotinsky, the founder of Revisionist Zionism. In his excellent and aptly titled book *The Iron Wall: Israel and the Arab World*, historian Avi Shlaim points to Jabotinsky's treatise as the focal point of Israel's outlook ever since. Jabotinsky well knew how Palestine Arabs would react to Jews seizing the land and said the choices were stark: "We must either suspend our settlement efforts or continue them without paying attention to the mood of the natives. Settlement can thus develop under the protection of a force that is not dependent on the local population, behind an iron wall which they will be powerless to break down," Jabotinsky wrote.

> As long as the Arabs preserve a gleam of hope that they will succeed in getting rid of us, nothing in the world can cause them to relinquish this hope, precisely because they are not a rabble but a living people. And a living people will be ready to yield on such fateful issues only when they have given up all hope of getting rid of the alien settlers. . . .

> It is my hope and belief that we will then offer them guarantees that will satisfy them and that both peoples will live in peace as good neighbors. But the sole way to such an agreement is through the iron wall, that is to say, the establishment in Palestine of a force that will in no way be influenced by Arab pressure. In other words, the only way to achieve a settlement in the future is total avoidance of all attempts to arrive at a settlement in the present.[1]

In 1936, thirteen years after Jabotinsky's article and twelve years before the founding of Israel, David Ben-Gurion, then the chairman of the Jewish Agency Executive, elucidated his philosophy—it might be dubbed "peace later"—in language that was very close to Jabotinsky's and is only slightly reworded by modern Israeli politicians. It was at the start of the violent Arab rebellion against the burgeoning Jewish population during the British Mandate.

"A comprehensive agreement is undoubtedly out of the question now," Ben-Gurion wrote, practically quoting Jabotinsky. "For only after total despair on the part of the Arabs, despair that will come not only from the failure of the disturbances and the attempt at rebellion, but also as a consequence of our growth in the country, may the Arabs possibly acquiesce in a Jewish Eretz Israel [Land of Israel]."[2]

From Ben-Gurion onward, several prime ministers, defense ministers, and generals, some more hard line than others, have held a fervent belief that Israel is destined to live in, or on the edge of, a state of perpetual war in order to survive, and that the only thing Arabs understand is the language of the sword. After the 1967 war, Moshe Dayan, Israel's flamboyant and eccentric defense minister, argued for the imposition of an enlightened, or benign, occupation. In a memo to fellow government ministers, he wrote, "We should see our presence in the territories as permanent. We must consolidate our hold so that over time we will succeed in 'digesting' Judea and Samaria and merging them with 'little' Israel."[3]

Dayan envisioned that social services would be developed in the West Bank and Arabs would be allowed to work in Israel. But in essence they would be ruled. Gershom Gorenberg wrote: "They would not be citizens; they would not even be allowed to live in Israeli cities in the West Bank. Dayan wanted the West Bank as a benevolently run colony, one so close to home you could go there for lunch... and be home for dinner."[4] It was Zionism combined with colonialism.

"The Zionist movement was not a veggie movement," Dror Etkes of Peace Now told me. "It was an evangelical movement, a national movement which understood quite early that their plans to colonize Palestine eventually will necessarily collide with the Palestinian interests. And we have to make sure we are stronger then them. They understood very well ... that their success depend[ed] on their ability to reduce the number of Palestinians on the land. And to take as much of the land as possible."

In 2007 Prime Minister Ehud Olmert was following a well-trodden historical path, Etkes said. "This government, just like most past Israeli governments, doesn't have and will not come up with clear policies and vision regarding the future of the Territories and settlements, and even less so regarding the Palestinian population [of 2.5 million] residing there." The government appears to have made its choice between continued settlement construction and peace, he said.[5]

The fundamentalist settlers have always been fast on their feet and adept at taking advantage of any government vacillation or division. Since 1967 a changing blend of government support, hands-off attitude, and an unwillingness to make hard decisions has allowed them to create extralegal and deep-rooted "facts on the ground."

Although the Israeli security forces—institutionally and as individuals—have remained largely indifferent to assaults by Jewish settlers on Palestinians, a few have opposed the violence and warned that the settler movement is destabilizing Israeli society.

High-ranking soldiers who have tried to keep the settlers within the bounds of Israeli law have been thwarted. The former senior army officer in the Civil Administration in the West Bank, Brigadier General Ilan Paz, had his own run-ins with settlers, who tried to ruin his army career. When he retired in 2005 after twenty-seven years in uniform, he told *Ha'aretz* that although the violent extremists may number only a few hundred, they are a law unto themselves.

> In their settlements, we have a hard time enforcing the building laws. An inspector or a policeman who goes there is under threat of violence. There were

> cases in which the entry of our people to settlements was prevented, under verbal threats. For years there has been restraint in the face of the settlers' violence. All the enforcement agencies, from the junior police officer to the senior judge, share in this.... Think about what happens to soldiers and police under attack by extremists in Hebron. It's terrible. The judicial system hasn't found the way to deal with the violence of children under the age of twelve in Hebron. When they are arrested, they refuse to state their names and their parents refuse to come to release them from custody. And in the face of that you are an eighteen-year-old soldier who has to cope.... The settlers have learned how to exploit that wonderfully. They have learned how to threaten a policeman, what is permitted and what is forbidden. The IDF cannot feel proud in the face of what is happening in Hebron.[6]

Some Israelis, military and civilian, say the fundamentalist settlers know perfectly the reach of their power. "Israel is beholden to a small bunch of messianic Jews who have friends in high places, both in Israel and in the U.S.—and other countries too—and they feel they can do what they want," Susan Laurenco, of Machsom Watch in Tel Aviv, told me.

Peretz Kidron, who translated Yitzhak Rabin's memoirs into English, said Israelis concerned about the future of their country should be worried:

> Certainly Jewish fundamentalism, like its Muslim and Christian cousins, is recognized as a great menace and is a cause of great concern among liberals and progressives here, and much discussed. The fundamentalists are everywhere in evidence, the most obvious cases being the settler movement (particularly its more extremist wing) and Yigal Amir, who assassinated [Prime Minister Yitzhak] Rabin [in 1995]. Apart from its generally ambiguous attitude towards the settlers, the Israeli establishment is simply scared stiff of them!

Forty years of settlement growth and related violence have hardened into an amalgam of hatred and retribution that will be difficult to break. One veteran aid worker told me that in thirty years of working in the world's war zones he has not seen such intense hatred between combatants.

Ami Ayalon, a former head of Shin Bet and a retired career naval officer, is now a peace campaigner and member of the Knesset for the Labor Party. In 2007 he was asked if he stood by his oft-quoted remark that the Palestinians and Israelis hate each other. "I cannot say that *I* hate Palestinians, but I think, as a nation, as a society, yes, most Israelis hate Palestinians and most Palestinians hate Israelis," he said. "We do not trust each other and both sides feel that the language of the other side is only the language of violence and power. So the question for us is how to create a different dictionary, in which societies and states will understand a different language—the language of diplomacy and negotiation." He conceded that the People's Voice, the peace group he founded along with Al Quds University president Sari Nusseibeh to promote a two-state solution, hasn't made much headway. Ayalon gave an example of the visceral antagonism from his post–Shin Bet days when he was part of behind-the-scenes peace moves.

> I had a very interesting meeting in London... during the intifada. A Palestinian friend approached me [and said], "Ami, we won. We Palestinians won." ... I asked him, "Are you crazy? What do you mean 'We won'? You are losing so many people... and we are losing so many people. What is the whole essence of victory?" He said, "Ami, you don't understand us. Victory for us is to see you suffer. This is all we want. Finally, after so many years, we are not the only ones who suffer in the Middle East."

When he thought about it, Ayalon saw the vindictiveness as a double-edged sword. "In a way it is the same for us. We suffer, we lost many people, and [at] a certain point we were looking for revenge. And we forgot what is the whole idea of victory."[7]

I had seen it myself, in the West Bank and in other conflicts. The spy chief's tale reminded me of a Croatian woman I knew in Zagreb during the wars in the former Yugoslavia. The woman, who had been described as "pleasant, motherly, kindly, articulate, well read and well traveled," was sharing a brandy with a friend when the conversation turned to reports that Croatian irregular forces had murdered elderly Serb women in the Serb Krajina region. With a sweet smile and no change in inflection, the woman said, "Nothing gives me more pleasure than the thought of Serbian grandmothers being burned in their beds."

Many Israelis regard Palestinians, and Arabs in general, with deep distrust, or even fear. An erudite and thoughtful West Jerusalem doctor who describes himself as center-left on the political spectrum pointed to the Jordanian bullet holes from 1948 that still scar the front of his apartment building; he insisted that the occupation of the West Bank (he prefers *disputed* to the word *occupied*) cannot end just yet. When I asked him what would happen if Israel withdrew the army, he drew his finger slowly across his throat. "They would kill us all. We pulled out of Gaza, and they brought the Katyushas (rockets) up. I don't believe pulling out of the West Bank would bring us peace." Yet, this doctor, like many Israelis, said he "intensely dislikes" the West Bank settlers and regards the settlement enterprise as "bad policy."

Dror Etkes described the standoff between Israelis and Palestinians as having a "tragic symmetry."

> You see it very clearly on the Israeli side, around the issue of settlements. [They have been] building settlements for forty-something years. And then one day you wake up and you're surprised that everybody's calling you the new South Africa. That everybody's blaming you for holding a crude and nondemocratic, racist, semi-apartheid system in the West Bank. I mean . . . what is the whole idea behind settlements? And to our surprise, the Palestinians are rioting against it and taking violent steps against it. On the Israeli side, [there's a] total inability . . . to assume responsibility for our collective decisions.

Nor have the Palestinians taken responsibility for their actions. Lacking good leadership, or even charismatic politicians with bold forward vision, they have not helped themselves. The suicide bombings left Palestinians isolated when they most needed allies and interlocutors at home and abroad. It was just too easy for outside observers, with America chief among them, to think of Palestinians as aligned with al-Qaeda, even though for some years Palestinians had eschewed international terrorism.

"This whole issue of suicide bombing," Etkes said with some exasperation. "I mean . . . you guys . . . you're killing hundreds of citizens in the streets [during the intifada]. What do you think? That your cities are not going to be destroyed? You're building and establishing and nourishing [a] death culture. What do you think we're going to do to you? This inability to see that your collective decision, or your decision to behave in a certain way has an impact on you . . ."

Palestinian society, at least what I saw of it as a non-Arabic speaker and reader, tended to be less introspective and self-critical than Israeli society. There was limited debate about the value of the suicide bombings, but more at the academic level than on the streets. Open dissent was not practiced.

Palestinian politicians and Fatah spokesmen frequently opposed the suicide bombings as "counterproductive" or "not helpful" to the cause of an independent state. It was a sterile and incomplete analysis, itself counterproductive. I never heard a Palestinian condemn the grisly attacks on civilians as immoral or a violation of international law. Some may have thought or said so, but in their isolation Palestinians seemed to feel that unity and resistance were the only sovereignty they possessed. And besides, someone almost always said, "Look what *they* are doing to *us.*" But as detached as the argument was, it had an element of truth. Targeting Israeli civilians *was* counterproductive; it ensured that international support remained beyond Palestinians' reach.

I kept returning to questions of strategy, and mainly on the Israeli side because Israel is the stronger party. Israel has an imperative requirement to protect its citizens and cities against attacks, but the legitimate security concerns are conveniently used as a front for political agendas, many said.

"The concept of security is magic," said Susan Laurenco of Machsom Watch. "Even the High Court buckles under when they hear the word. The security excuse allows Israel to [expropriate] more land, to create more facts on the ground that have absolutely nothing to do with security—except in the mind-set of the majority of the population." Inflated security concerns bond naturally to the legend of the ethical army and its need to project deterrent power. In a nation forged on the battlefield, the legend has been easy enough to sustain, even when Arab neighbors made clear (and proved, in the case of Jordan and Egypt) they wanted lasting peace. With its carefully nourished reputation for invincibility (excepting strenuous public criticism after the costly 1973 and 2006 wars, when the armed forces were seen not to be invincible), the IDF over decades acquired a strong political role and great influence in national policy making. Ariel Sharon's provocative and aggressive moves of entering Lebanon and pushing north to Beirut in 1982 are one example. The strength of Hamas, the plethora of militias in Gaza and the West Bank, and regional threats, such as Hizbollah in Lebanon and a hostile and potentially nuclear-armed Iran, have made it easier for the IDF and hard-line politicians to still the dissent of Israel's left.

But the IDF's activist stance and often-accepted sway over civilian governments during forty years of occupation has earned the army a reputation in some quarters of Israeli society as—in Peretz Kidron's phrase—a "gang of thugs."

"The army is now much more militarist and aggressive," said Kidron, who did his military service inside Israel but refused to serve in the territories. "There is almost nobody left who took part in the 1973 war. All their experience for the past thirty years has been fighting guerrillas. It's the style of gang warfare."

Israelis have bought into the national myth, he said. "It doesn't work. There's no Plan B. It's Plan A all the way, and it's the club. These dream scenarios: 'We will beat them into submission.' 'They hate democracy'—that's [George W.] Bush. 'They hate Jews'—that's us. That's what the army of occupation is—to subjugate and terrorize the population."

Palestinian historian and political scientist Mahdi Abdul Hadi offered a parallel metaphor for the IDF. "This big, blind elephant which is the army, blind and angry, rampages. The elephant says, 'Who is this under my foot? How dare you do this to me?' " Abdul Hadi said, referring to army operations in the West Bank, Gaza, and Lebanon and making the motion of crushing an object under his heel.

Military and political myths intertwine and function together, leaving little room for diplomatic maneuver. Kidron said that one strand of the legend is refusing to talk with the enemy, as Hamas is considered today.

"You talk to them, or you have the myth 'there's nobody to talk to.' ... They couldn't talk to Nasser because ... they couldn't talk to Sadat because ... they couldn't talk to Arafat because he was a terrorist. [You have] an ideological refusal to talk to the Arabs on the basis of equality."

Retired major general Herzl Shafir, who began his army career as a teenage soldier in the 1948 war and headed Israel's Ceasefire and Disengagement delegation after the 1973 war, remains, with a group of other senior retired officers, close to government policymakers. He told me that Israel had made a mistake by refusing to talk with Hamas after it came to power, even though Hamas has been deservedly described as a terrorist group. "There is no place in the world where anyone fought terrorism by fighting an organization, because terrorist organizations are based on people," said Shafir, who would not describe himself as a pacifist. "My idea was, don't try to change the results [of the election]. Society decided, and it was a democratic election. Any change we tried in the past failed. Another mistake is that we insisted Hamas declares it recognizes Israel. Who needs their recognition?" What he meant was, watch and see what they do.

Shafir, who has photos of himself as a smiling and confident young combat officer in his study, is measured, yet sometimes contradictory, in his evaluation of the effects of the occupation. If necessary, Israel can withstand the costs for another generation, he said, but it is unhealthy for Israelis as well as Palestinians. "It's not good for morale, and it disturbs people. It disturbs the possibility of Israel to develop stronger and quicker. It also disturbs society because quite a lot of people [the settlers and their supporters] think we don't have to leave the territories." He added that most Palestinians alive today know only life under occupation, and it has frayed the fabric of their society.

Forty years later, the occupation showed no signs of ending, and no plausible exit strategy appeared on the political horizon. The settlers seemed stronger than ever and faced no government pressure that would threaten the enterprise. Several Israelis described the state's strategy to me as a kind of political *parve,* the Jewish dietary prohibition of cooking meat and milk products together; it's a neither-nor measure that indefinitely postpones political solution.

But on the ground are Israel's policies designed, as I'd wondered after observing the West Bank for nearly three years, to squeeze the Palestinians until they buckle under pressure and emigrate? "An effective short-term strategy is Israel's desire and ability to strangle the Palestinian economy," Laurenco told me. "That's real."

Gen. Shafir vehemently disputed the assertion, except for what he called "local stuff," pressure on Palestinians from individual soldiers at checkpoints. "I have never heard of it. It is not policy or strategy," he told me. "There is no reason for it." If such a policy did exist and was enacted, he emphasized, it would only serve to strengthen terrorists.

Etkes, however, believes that such a policy does exist, even if unofficially. "The answer is yes, and it's very often being hidden not only from the world [but] also from the soldiers themselves, and very, very often being camouflaged or being excused or being explained by security reasons," he said. "I would say there [have been] two main attitudes. I think one is: choke them, kill the Palestinian economy so they will leave. And the other one... the opposite: allow them to prosper as much as possible and they will be quiet."

When I raised the question with Dr. Abdul Hadi in his Jerusalem office, he shrugged. "This has been one of the pillars of Zionism: evacuate, immigrate, clean the land [of] the Palestinians," he said. The pressure, he added, is having a disastrous impact, particularly on the Palestinian middle class.

> With the wall... the continuous closure of... every town... they will not have farms, they will not have factories, they will not have business, they will not have cultural centers. And [so] they move from Qalqilya to Nablus. And the same thing in Nablus; they have to move from Nablus to the Jordan Valley; from the Jordan Valley they have to move to Amman.... Shopkeepers, barbers, professionals, those who facilitate your daily life, middle-class peo-

> ple [who] don't have wealth, [who] don't have property, they live on a daily basis. Their work is crippled continuously. And the only alternative is to find a way to survive and maintain what's left of their identity. They are fleeing to Amman and to Egypt. And they will not return, for sure.

Israel is currently writing the law simply because it can, Abdul Hadi said. "This is the law of might. It's the law of the conqueror, the law of the gun. It's not the law of values and principles and human rights and international law."

With UNRWA and international NGOs providing a good measure of education, food aid, and other assistance to Palestinians in the occupied West Bank—the duty of the occupying power, according to the Fourth Geneva Convention—I wondered if Israel wanted to fashion Palestine into a wholly dependent, humanitarian client state. "We already are one," Abdul Hadi said.

Abdul Hadi and Peretz Kidron, in separate interviews, said the same thing: the idea is to wall the Palestinians off where they can't attack Israelis and are out of sight. People in Tel Aviv and Haifa simply don't want to know about Palestinians or the West Bank.

"The main motive is that we don't want to see them, don't want to hear them. We just want to pretend they're not there," Kidron told me at his home in the picture-postcard town of Ein Kerem, said to be the birthplace of John the Baptist.

> Many Israelis want a two-state solution out of enmity—"We don't want to live with the dirty, stinking Arabs." Basically Israel is going back to the Bantustan concept, the reservation. Basically Israel doesn't want a Palestinian democracy, it wants a *mukhtar* [a local government leader or official], where if there is a problem you send someone in and explain, and if things get bad, you send in a couple of tanks. The Israeli establishment would be very happy with that scenario. Of course, no Palestinian would have [such a thing], but Israel would like a [Palestinian] dictator who would be corrupt.

The government, then, makes only a token effort at finding a real political solution, he said. "All the polls show that most Israelis believe in an end to the occupation. But the Israeli political system . . . you have a half-dozen people [who come up with a plan and say to the Palestinians], 'Sign on the dotted line, and you have no further claims.' Like an insurance policy."

The problem, Israelis and Palestinians told me, is that the obsolete concept of absorbing and controlling the West Bank, as Dayan and others envisioned it, has given Israel a bad case of heartburn.

Dror Etkes found the metaphor when he was walking along a beach thronged with seabirds in Denmark a few years ago. "I saw a bird lying on the sand, dying. She had a huge fish stuck in her beak and was not able to swallow it. My image was immediately Israel. Trying to swallow something bigger than what you can. You're trying to digest or to swallow something which is indigestible."

If the metaphor is accurate, why does Israel continue the occupation? It was the same question I had put to Yehuda Shaul. "Israeli society is very conservative and very nationalist," Etkes said. "Israeli society is also very passive. Most Israelis tend to see things as happening to them, being inflicted on them. . . . Taking responsibility means also being politically active, it means also to go to the street. To take steps which in a democratic [country] are allowed, in order to change policy. [This is] something most Israelis do not do. You have here [a] very well-organized and very motivated [political] Right. The only street movement in Israel today, in Israeli politics, is the Right."

At the height of the bloodshed in 2002, I asked an Israeli friend, a retired army officer, for his views on the Palestinian suicide bombings. In a wide-ranging discussion about war and politics, he insisted that Israelis should look to their future. "Never mind, for a moment, what is happening now," he said. "This is not a Palestinian problem. It is our problem. We must decide what kind of country we want to be."

▪ ▪ ▪

In the middle of September 2003, three years after the second intifada began, the horrific cycle of violence continued unabated. On one day Hamas suicide bombers struck twice. The first explosion killed 7 and wounded more than 50 in the Café Hillel in Jerusalem's German Colony;

the second blast killed 8 soldiers at a bus stop near Rishon Letzion. The next day, the Israeli Air Force tried to assassinate a Hamas leader in Gaza; he and his wife were wounded, and their son was killed. The country was awash in rumors, which Israel didn't bother to deny, that plans were afoot to assassinate Yasser Arafat. And in the first week of October, the eve of Yom Kippur, a twenty-nine-year-old Palestinian woman blew herself up in a Haifa restaurant, killing 20 people, 4 of them children, and maiming 50 others. Hope for change of any kind was at an all-time low.

During September's carnage, an article appeared in the *Guardian* under the headline "The End of Zionism." Its author was Avraham Burg, the outgoing speaker of Israel's Knesset. "The Zionist revolution has always rested on two pillars: a just path and an ethical leadership. Neither of these is operative any longer," Burg's article began. "The Israeli nation today rests on a scaffolding of corruption, and on foundations of oppression and injustice. As such, the end of the Zionist enterprise is already on our doorstep.

"It turns out that the 2,000-year struggle for Jewish survival comes down to a state of settlements, run by an amoral clique of corrupt lawbreakers who are deaf both to their citizens and to their enemies. A state lacking justice cannot survive. The countdown to the end of Israeli society has begun," he thundered in paragraphs that sounded as though they were being handed down from a mountaintop.

> It is very comfortable to be a Zionist in West Bank settlements such as Beit El and Ofra. The biblical landscape is charming. You can gaze through the geraniums and bougainvilleas and not see the occupation. Travelling on the fast highway that skirts barely a half-mile west of the Palestinian roadblocks, it's hard to comprehend the humiliating experience of the despised Arab who must creep for hours along the pocked, blockaded roads assigned to him. One road for the occupier, one road for the occupied.
>
> This cannot work. Even if the Arabs lower their heads and swallow their shame and anger for ever, it won't work. A structure built on human callousness will inevitably collapse in on itself. Note this moment well: Zionism's superstructure is already collapsing like a cheap Jerusalem wedding hall. Only

> madmen continue dancing on the top floor while the pillars below are collapsing.
>
> Israel, having ceased to care about the children of the Palestinians, should not be surprised when they come washed in hatred and blow themselves up in the centres of Israeli escapism. They consign themselves to Allah in our places of recreation, because their own lives are torture. They spill their own blood in our restaurants in order to ruin our appetites, because they have children and parents at home who are hungry and humiliated. We could kill a thousand ringleaders a day and nothing will be solved, because the leaders come up from below—from the wells of hatred and anger, from the "infrastructures" of injustice and moral corruption.[8]

The article raised a commotion in Israel. In the West Bank it felt like a window thrown open in a stuffy room. Three years later, although the stir caused by Burg's angry, eloquent words was gone, the Machsom Watch women reminded me of the article. Dr. Yehudit Elkana boiled it down to one short sentence: "It is a rotten society with no moral standards."

But if so many people held such views, I asked, why didn't the situation change? Nava Elyashar quickly corrected me. "It's not that there are so many of us; it's that there are so few."

NINETEEN

WORLD CUP QUARTER FINAL

The kid looked quite prepared to kill someone. He had an M-16 slung from a shoulder, braces on his teeth, a flourishing case of acne, and a nasty scowl. He and a friend, who also packed an assault rifle, were about sixteen and were walking down a hill to a natural spring off the Alon road east of Ramallah. It was a hot day, and I was playing tourist on my way back from Jenin. I had never found time to sit by the spring, once a popular picnic spot for Palestinians, and hoped it was as cool in the summer as they said it was.

Starting down the hill, the boys looked at me with the kind of disdain peculiar to armed teenagers, and I tried some casual conversation. It was brief.

"Beautiful place," I said.

"*All* of Israel is beautiful," the kid snarled in an American accent. Maybe it was the acne.

The spring was crowded with settlers, many of them armed and none smiling except for a dozen happy youngsters splashing about in the pool. I turned around and went off in search of gazelles.

That evening I sat on my balcony in East Jerusalem watching giant eucalyptus trees sway in the wind as though fanned by deep sea currents. It was a Friday in midsummer, and at sundown the muezzin's call to prayer from the mosque up the street sounded simultaneously with the Shabbat horns from West Jerusalem. The plaintive tones rose and fell, clearly definable at first and then mixed by the breeze into a pleasant religious cacophony. As it grew still and Muslims and Jews went to their observances, I thought back on the past months. At times, particularly evenings with my feet on the railing as I watched the oceanic eucalyptus trees breathe, the place felt as lovely as it ought to be.

I got a lot of advice from Palestinians and, mostly, Israelis about what to put in this book. My doctor, an Israeli man in his eighties, told me to "put in a lot of facts and stay away from conclusions." The retired general suggested that it would be simple or "superficial" to write much about the treatment of Palestinians at checkpoints and other difficult aspects of their lives. I disagreed: there was nothing superficial about people being kept under curfew or subjected to violence and daily humiliation as they tried to go to work. But I knew what he meant: those hardships have been extensively reported, and I should get on to other matters.

I was not embarrassed to record the "superficial." Common events, in aggregate, can be a key to seeing the whole. Here, even the act of buying flowers could assume a partisan edge. In the fall of 2001, when I was still new to the West Bank, I was returning to Jerusalem from Hebron on a Friday afternoon with a Palestinian colleague and stopped at a roadside flower stand near the city limits. Having long bought fresh flowers at street-corner stalls in European cities, it was a reflexive action. But as I was paying, a young settler at the nearby bus stop gave me the finger and made some choice comments about the UN. The flower seller was unfriendly, and when I got back in the car my assistant was clearly uncomfortable. I had not known it, but the stands provided for the Jewish custom of buying flowers on the eve of the Sabbath. After another Friday purchase from a surly roadside vendor, I bought flowers from a Palestinian shop in East Jerusalem or an Israeli shop at Ramat Eshkol on the west side. Both places were friendly, but the flowers on the west side were fresher and more varied; the owner was better off than his Palestinian counterpart and could afford better quality at the wholesale level. For that reason I split my custom. In Beit Hanina, on the east side, a husband and wife put in long hours to make their business succeed; the woman's hands were red and chapped from the work. But in East Jerusalem, the people who could afford tulips were the internationals; Palestinian families spent their money mostly on fresh vegetables and meat. By 2006 the shop had gone and had been replaced by a store selling cheap imported children's clothing.

Food was usually a safe and neutral topic, and long hours in the jeep had been instructively spent discussing hummus or olive oil. I once watched in fascination as my Palestinian colleague ate a large bunch of romaine lettuce, leaf after leaf, between Jenin and Nablus and informed me about its digestive benefits. You couldn't get romaine that good in Bethlehem that year, he said.

But even food could provide a platform for competitive discussion. I had such a conversation in Jerusalem with two women, one Israeli and one Palestinian, about *za'atar*, the tangy herbal condiment prevalent throughout the Mediterranean. I asked the women, who were well read on many subjects, about its main ingredient. Was it oregano, or was it thyme? I won't say which woman was the Israeli and which the Palestinian. The conversation went like this.

"It is oregano and sumac and salt," one said.

"No, it is thyme, not oregano," said the other.

"No, it is definitely oregano."

"No, you are wrong. It is thyme."

"No, you are totally incorrect, it is not thyme." Both women paused and agreed that *za'atar* does contain salt and, usually, olive oil.

"And sumac."

"No, it is not sumac, it is sim-sim."

"No, it is sum-sum, not sim-sim. Sim-sim is sesame."

"But it has sumac in it."

"These are not sesame seeds."

"One variety has, but only that one. The other has sim-sim."

"But doesn't it have sesame seeds?" I asked, having never seen *za'atar* without the seeds.

"No. Sim-sim."

"No, actually. Sum-sum."

"What is the difference between sim-sim and sum-sum?" I asked.

"They are both the same," one woman said. (She was right, I learned later; it's a matter of pronunciation.)

"So *za'atar* contains sim-sim and sum-sum?" I said.

"It depends on the variety of *za'atar*."

"How many varieties are there?" I asked, rather sorry I had started this yet absorbed by the edginess. We were not discussing 1948 or 1967 but a herbal mixture that all three of us agreed was as essential to life as the bread it was served on.

"Two."

"But what about sumac?" I asked.

"They contain sumac also."

"Both?" one woman said.

"Sometimes. Or one or the other," said her colleague.

The women were still smiling, but through slightly clenched teeth, and I changed the subject. The argument followed me out the door. One woman whispered in my ear: "She doesn't know what she is talking about. It really is thyme." That afternoon I went down to Kit Kat Koffee in Salah ad-Din Street with my friend Yousef, who has the definitive word on such things, and bought four large bags of *za'atar* (two varieties, one brown and one green) to take back to the United States. Both contained oregano. But then, I might be wrong.

Rumors circulated in 2003 that *za'atar*—Palestinians also use the name to mean the actual plant (whatever it is) rather than the mixture—had been stranded in the occupation's no-man's-land. Because it is a protected plant, the story went, Israeli soldiers were preventing Palestinians from picking it on the roadside. I never saw evidence of this, but the herb entered the mythology.

Earlier that week, Salah ad-Din, East Jerusalem's vibrant main shopping street, had been an unbroken wall of closed gray and green doors, from the pizza parlor at the bottom up to Herod's Gate into the Old City. Only a taxi company's door was open, and only a crack, with the owner peering out for potential customers. Even the old woman who sat on the sidewalk selling mint and parsley was gone. A strike had been called in sympathy with the Lebanese who had been killed in Israeli bombing raids. When a strike was announced, young men from the militant factions went from shop to shop ordering owners to close. Most did, some objected. Business was bad enough, and no shopkeeper wanted to lose a day's revenue.

"They have no brains! They are foolish!" one Christian Palestinian shopkeeper fumed. Young toughs he described as "Islamists" burned his shop a number of years ago because he sold liquor. Now he closed when the young men told him to. He couldn't afford the possible consequences of refusal.

As a visitor and a Western capitalist by nature, I couldn't see what the strikes accomplished. Closing for the day was unlikely to impress the Israelis and might even please them. So I did an unofficial survey and asked area businesspeople if the closure cost them money.

"Yes, but not much," a drugstore owner said. "It's only for the day, and it's solidarity. It's something we can do. And remember, in 1936 shops were closed for six months."

Al Jazeera and Al Arabiya television networks had been broadcasting nonstop coverage of bodies being pulled from the rubble in south Lebanon. Palestinians deeply felt the tragedy of Lebanese civilians.

When I asked a young Palestinian woman I knew whether she approved of the sympathy strikes, her eyes filled with tears. "At least . . . at least that," she said. The strikes were a sad nod to how little political power the Palestinians had. But they also were a reminder, to themselves and others, of the strength of their national spirit. I got the point.

▪ ▪ ▪

I picked a noisy day for a return trip to Jenin. When I phoned Hidaya from outside the terminal to say I'd be walking across, we heard an explosion. She thought it might have been a stray Hizbollah missile from Lebanon. It turned out to be an Israeli missile, which killed two Islamic Jihad fighters and wounded several other people in Jenin Camp. Later, sitting at a friend's kitchen table, four loud bangs rattled our coffee cups. This time it was several Hizbollah missiles aimed at Israeli cities; they'd gone well off course and exploded in fields just outside town. When I asked what he thought of Hizbollah rockets landing in the West Bank, his eyes widened and he said, "Fine. Let them land right here in the center of Jenin." I took his remark to be a mixture of hyperbole and general frustration: even if the missiles accidentally killed a few Palestinians, what counted was that they were raining down on Israel every day.

The reaction of my elderly friends in Tulkarm had been the same. "Excellent!" the old man beamed. "Great! They have broken Israel," his wife added, punching the air with her fist. "Just to let the Israelis know we have someone defending us," she said. Although she was wrong on those two points, I heard the sentiment repeated across the West Bank during the month-long war: "You are being punished for having punished us for so long."

I had arranged to meet a former IDF soldier, one of the gun crew who had kept us company the night our UNRWA jeep broke down in the Jordan Valley. Uri and his wife, Katerina, secular Jews originally from Eastern Europe, had driven from their home in northern Israel to Jerusalem for a Saturday lunch. West Jerusalem restaurants were closed for Shabbat, and we met in a hotel restaurant on the east side. It was an unintended experiment, and as we placed our orders, in English, I wondered whether the Palestinian waiters would be offended; on the one recent occasion I had seen Israeli guests in this hotel, they had behaved as though they were on a colonial day out during the British Raj.

Although we had different opinions about Israeli-Palestinian relations and the occupation, there were plenty of other things to discuss. We wound up not talking about his army service at all. "I could fit all my army experiences into ten minutes," he said. His days in uniform were well behind him.

Uri and Katerina were relaxed, generally open-minded, and able to keep subjects in separate boxes—a useful skill in wartime. Uri returned to the table after a trip to the washroom and smacked his forehead. "I asked where it was, but I forgot for a minute, and I asked in Hebrew," he said. The waiter had responded politely in Hebrew. The simple exchange went as it should have, but revealed the small across-the-divide concerns that mark most such encounters. It also showed common propriety: Uri hoped he hadn't been inadvertently rude to the waiter by speaking Hebrew.

I was still curious why Uri and his gunners had stopped to provide armed protection for us on that lonely stretch of Route 90. He could have given us the once-over and driven on. He said it was because he didn't have to stay with us that he did. When he drove by the first time, he radioed his headquarters that a UN vehicle had broken down. An officer told him he didn't have to stick around. But as far as Uri was concerned, we were simply two people with a disabled vehicle in a potentially dangerous location. I'd brought some tea from America that was pretty close to what he had given us that night on Route 90, and we agreed to stay in touch; we still had more to talk about.

▪ ▪ ▪

Patches of common ground were still accessible. One such place was the Aroma café at the Hebrew University in Jerusalem. After a bag search by an armed guard, Israeli and Palestinian students mixed easily at tables under the pine trees. It was a popular meeting spot, and many internationals frequented the place because of the atmosphere.

But bad memories stayed fresh. Near there on July 31, 2002, a Palestinian sent by Hamas left a bag in the cafeteria of the Frank Sinatra Student Center on the Mount Scopus campus. The explosion killed 9: 4 Israelis and 5 foreign nationals, including 4 Americans, and wounded nearly 100 others. An Italian friend of mine who was studying Hebrew scripture ate in the cafeteria every day; that Wednesday she had gone somewhere else for lunch. Several of her friends were among the casualties.

Palestinians continued to pay the price for such attacks. In 2006 the IDF and Shin Bet still barred Gaza Palestinians from studying in the West Bank. Terror groups used Gaza students to pass messages, the security services claimed. Young university careers were interrupted, sometimes irreparably.

Despite the advanced polarization, small pleasantries showed up in unexpected places like cyclamens growing out of a rock ledge. As I was getting a haircut at a Palestinian barbershop in an out-of-the-way street, a young Israeli woman with a baby in a stroller stuck her head in the door and asked for directions. It was not an area of East Jerusalem frequented by Israelis, particularly on foot. Mother and baby were both flushed with the heat, and the barber, who spoke Hebrew, invited her in to rest. The barber, his other Palestinian customers, and the woman chatted amiably and unhurriedly, and he called a cab to take her to the East Jerusalem settlement where she lived. When I asked the barber later if he thought the impromptu meeting was unusual, he found my question unusual. She was lost, he said.

Other times it was just rock ledge with no flowers. A Palestinian clerk's smile faded fast when a conversation strayed onto the subject of America's role in the world. "I have no bad feelings toward individual Americans," he said unconvincingly, "but Bush and [British Prime Minister Tony] Blair are the real terrorists." I asked if he ever went over to West Jerusalem, less than a mile from where we stood, to eat or shop. "I haven't been to Jaffa Street in ten years," he said bitterly. "I have no reason to go there. Why should I? Why go and be treated like an animal?" Then he tugged the underlying thread. Jews and Israel control America and control the world, he said, expanding that twisted and tired diatribe common in the West Bank and some other Arab countries; I excused myself and left. I recalled that some years ago I used to clip for Palestinian friends thoughtful columns about the conflict by *International Herald Tribune* columnist Roger Cohen or by Tom Friedman of the *New York Times*. "He's a Jew, isn't he?" was a frequent response. There was no hatred in the question, just an ingrained assumption that a column in an American paper by a Jewish reporter would be biased in favor of Israel; I never got a reaction to any of the articles. This damage was going to take a long time to undo.

As a perpetual asker of questions, I probably provoked such remarks. They were easily avoided, and Palestinians and Israelis often relished the opportunity to change the subject.

Jihad Fararjeh's place in Deheisheh refugee camp was a good place to do that. Working with Jihad at UNRWA, I had never made time for a social visit and had not met his three children, who were now 14, 7, and 5. Fararjeh's parents were 1948 refugees from a small village west of Bethlehem called Zakariya, now the Israeli city of Beit Shemesh. When his parents fled east and were allotted small plots of land in Bethlehem by the UN, Jihad's father chose a spot on top of the hill. Neighbors cautioned him that it was "a jungle up there, with wild animals," and opted for plots closer to the main road. The hill turned out to be a good choice. Jihad and his wife, Aysheh, built their house on the site where the original one-room UNRWA hut stood, and the home has escaped much of the intifada's direct battle damage.

At thirty-four Jihad is a solidly built man with a green thumb and the talent many Palestinians have of applying every shekel to building a home one floor and one tiled veranda at a time. When you walk up the hill and through the gate, the noise of the Bethlehem road subsides, and you enter a world of calm and botanical order.

Great variety flourishes in a small area. Apple, guava, clementine, lemon, and fig trees (five types of fig grafted onto one tree) grow companionably with vegetables and potted flowers, all roofed over with trellised grape vines.

Deheisheh Camp has seen extreme violence, particularly in the forty days of curfew during Operation Defensive Shield, and their children—Basil, Zeinab, and Dudu—have seen things no child should see. A powerful explosion blew out all the windows on one side of the house, and a man was burned to death in a car next door. Other neighbors and friends were killed or wounded, and when heavy gunfire rang through the streets at night, the family would huddle in a safe room with the outside doors unlocked, hoping that soldiers would turn the handle instead of blowing the door off the hinges. "It's one of the things you learn to do in the camps," Jihad said.

In one of those flukes of the intifada, Jihad may have watched the same violent patrol Yehuda Shaul's unit conducted on the Bethlehem road in 2002. He described—exactly as Shaul had—soldiers getting out of APCs, chasing children and dragging one back, slapping him around, and throwing him into the armored vehicle. Although there were dozens of similar incidents, the details of these two, including the date and location, were nearly identical.

The family has also been caught in repercussions of the political crossfire. Aysheh worked for the Palestinian Authority's Education Department, but she hadn't been paid for five months because of the international refusal to fund the PA after Hamas won parliamentary elections. Finances were tight.

Working with UNRWA and crossing the West Bank checkpoints daily, Jihad and the other assistants faced the challenge of having to interact with Israeli soldiers in an apolitical manner.

"When I'm working, I'm not supposed to be thinking as a Palestinian. I'd say to them, I'm neutral when I'm in a UN car. But as a Palestinian, I'm thinking, *Okay, you're in our land and you're not giving us peace. You want me to think about you in a good way?* It's very hard." Jihad also conceded that, unlike during the first intifada, Palestinian armed resistance and attacks on civilians escalated the conflict.

"It'll never be solved this way," he said. "You need strong people to solve it, you need help from outside," he said. "On our side we have strange thinking, and on their side... a strange situation. But if there was a will for peace, I think that in six months they [both sides] could solve everything."

We mostly kept off the topics of politics and war. I got a lesson in fruit-tree grafting as their kids and the smell of roses drifted in and out of the conversation. They were the kind of children any parent would want.

The lack of a clear Palestinian political strategy is difficult for everyone to take, although Palestinians are reluctant to talk about it with outsiders. While all want an end to Israel's occupation, they feel let down by a dysfunctional system that has a Fatah president in Ramallah, a Hamas prime minister in Gaza, and an uncompromising Hamas politburo boss in exile in Damascus.

I wanted to talk to some West Bank settlers and had hoped to find the physics teacher and his wife and daughters I had met a few years ago; but I had lost their phone number. A friend introduced me to a woman who lives in a religious settlement between Jerusalem and Nablus. She agreed to talk, but only, she said, if I agreed not to "twist her words into an anti-Semitic view." An American Israeli who converted from Roman Catholicism to Judaism and who has lived in the West Bank settlement for many years, she works as a traveling nurse and often visits Palestinian communities. She referred to Palestinians as "just Arabs" and in the derogatory way I'd heard from other settlers. One of her sons had been badly wounded by a Palestinian roadside bomb as a child, she said, and two of her other sons were in IDF combat units, positions that made her particularly proud; she mentioned them repeatedly, each time emphasizing the word *combat.* The land was all Israel, she said, and while peaceable Palestinians were welcome to live and work there, there was no reason for them to have their own state.

When I asked if she would allow that some people might consider her views extreme, she narrowed her eyes and suggested that I was anti-Semitic. By my question, she said, I was "talking the talk" of anti-Semitism. Later, when I described the interview to Israelis in the peace movement, they said that such views, while prevalent among messianic Jews and frequently among immigrants, are indeed extreme and not representative of the settlers.

Seventy years after David Ben-Gurion wrote about driving the rebelling Arabs to despair in order to build a Zionist state, some Palestinians seemed to be on the brink of that condition. The day before I left Jerusalem, the manager of my East Jerusalem hotel came out to wish me a pleasant trip. "Write something good about us," he said.

"I'll write true stories, that's about all I can promise," I said.

"Oh, please don't write true stories," he said with a smile. "Then we won't have any hope. Give us something to hope for." It was somewhere between a joke and an appraisal.

I couldn't offer the hope, but others may have been in a position to do so. Ami Ayalon, the former Shin Bet chief, said that the way forward lay, eventually, in a difficult compromise. "The only way to create a better future is for us to give up some of the dreams of our past. This is the only way for us to explain to Jews, to Palestinians, that we have to create something new, something better. We cannot go on killing each other for the next five hundred years." He added a remark from his wife: "We Israelis shall have security and stability when the other side, the Palestinians, shall have hope."[1] Ayalon's wife might have taken it a step further. Hope, like food, is perishable; it is not sufficient for long-term sustenance.

Jihad and Aysheh's kids were roughly the same age as Hidaya and Munther's in Jenin; Yazan was 13, Leen was 10, and Dalia, a curly headed bundle of mischief, was 5. All six children had seen violence of one kind or another: soldiers searching their homes, breathing tear gas on the school bus, listening to abuse at a crossing. They had all learned that even a smile can be hazardous.

"I just want to soften their hearts," Hidaya said about the soldiers. Civility came naturally to her, but she had decided it wasn't worth the effort. "I don't want to trigger the soldiers." When she automatically thanked one who handed back her documents, he shouted, "Don't thank me! Just take your ID and leave!"

Hearts are hard in Jenin or maybe just weary. I had hoped to set up a meeting, either there or in Israel, between Hidaya and some Israeli peace activists, whom she had met on the three-week Partners for Peace tour of the United States in 2004. But Hidaya hadn't the energy for it. She recalled that one Israeli woman, the first Jew she had met as an adult other than soldiers, opened their first conversation by saying: "You're the best-dressed refugee I ever met!" A clumsy compliment meant to break the ice, certainly, but it fell flat.

"You cannot imagine that they see you as an equal," she said. "With so many years of humiliation now, it's just too much for us. I don't think Israel will ever give us a state of our own, violence or no violence." Memories of the U.S. tour were more unsettling than reassuring of international understanding. At a lecture stop in California, a man in the audience told Hidaya he assumed that all Palestinian children carried weapons, and in Chicago a man said it was a shame the Israelis hadn't killed many more Palestinians. "I was frightened," she said. "You can't predict what people's reactions will be if you tell them you are Palestinian or Muslim."

As far apart as Palestinians and Israelis were, I found cause for optimism in the plain sensibility of Jihad and Aysheh and Hidaya and Munther and their particularly sensible children. I found it with the women in Machsom Watch and with former soldiers in Breaking the Silence, Yesh Gvul, Peace Now, and other groups. These people had steel in their backbones, and not the kind of steel that was intended to drive the other side to despair.

I rode in the back seat with Dalia, as consciously glamorous in purple sunglasses as a five-year-old can be, and Munther and Hidaya drove me out to the Jenin terminal. Two taxi drivers chatted in the shade of the dusty eucalyptus trees, but no one was crossing.

Under the surveillance cameras, I walked through four sets of turnstiles, past the bullet-proof sentry booths, through four more doors, and past closed rooms with signs saying "Secondary Inspection Booth." I wondered if there was a tertiary inspection booth. My footsteps echoed in the empty maze, and when I took a wrong turn a voice gave me curt directions over the loudspeaker. At the final inspection booth I slid my passport under the glass and asked the soldier if he had heard the Hizbollah missiles exploding. "They shook the whole building," he said.

There was a final unattended steel gate a few hundred meters up the road, and the wind had blown it partly shut. I got out, opened it, and drove through. When I got out again to shut it behind me (leaving a gate the way I found it was an old country habit that was hard to break), a disembodied voice floated over the wind: "You . . . do . . . not . . . have . . . to . . . close . . . the . . . gate!" I waved back at the loudspeaker and drove on, past the fields where the Hizbollah missiles had landed.

Passing the back-to-back cargo terminal, where every head of lettuce and appliance going in either direction is transferred from one truck to another, I thought how anachronistic and wasteful this war is, two old enemies slugging each other senseless over a piece of land that could be shared equitably—and prosperously. In human and economic costs, the occupation and the violence it generates retard every aspect of development, except that of the usual war profiteers. The conflict also threatened to become another costly anachronism that destabilizes security beyond its borders: a proxy struggle similar to the old ones in Africa, this time between the West and Iran.

Yazan, Leen, and Dalia still have nightmares, particularly when there are army incursions into Jenin; on those nights, Dalia sleeps in bed with her parents. Like most Palestinian children, Yazan and Leen can relate vivid tales, and I had heard several. After saying good-bye to Munther and Hidaya, I thought of two stories they told me at the kitchen table after a lunch of fish stew.

For a kid's perspective on the priorities of daily life, I liked Leen's story.

As the family cleared Beit Iba checkpoint out of Nablus one day, a soldier did the unexpected. He put his hand in the car and shook hands with all three children.

"When I got home, I washed my hands with all the soap in the house," Leen said. I didn't know Leen very well, but figured this self-assured and thoughtful girl was going to say that she was appalled to have been touched by an Israeli soldier. It wouldn't have been an unnatural reaction considering her life experiences to date. So was it that?

"No, no, no," she said, smiling. "Not that. It was because he was dirty from being in that place. His hands were black with dirt, and so was his face." She hadn't been thinking about the soldier as an enemy; she was just a ten-year-old girl with an aversion to grime.

Back in June 2002, when Yazan was nine, armed soldiers surrounded the house, burst in, and began searching the apartments. "There were about thirty of them, and they were all in combat gear and flak jackets, and they were very aggressive," Hidaya said. It was the third or fourth search that year, and Hidaya calmly gathered the children around the television as a distraction.

When the soldiers had finished, four of them flopped down in easy chairs next to Yazan. It was the World Cup quarter final that day, England and Brazil, a nail biter.

"What's the score?" one asked. Yazan told him.

"Who are you for?" the soldier asked.

"Brazil," Yazan said.

"Me too," said the soldier.

Hidaya laughed as she looked back on the incident. "They were sweating all over my chairs and the floor in their dirty uniforms. But for five minutes they had a normal conversation!"

No more normal conversations were recorded in Jenin in the years that followed, only the repetitive cycle of occupation and destruction. In August 2006, the month Yazan and Leen told me their war stories, sixteen Palestinian children were killed in the West Bank and Gaza Strip. But in the middle of the ongoing violence, a quiet trend continued that few people, other than parents, noticed. Many children—such as Yazan, Leen, and Dalia in Jenin and Basil, Zeinab, and Dudu in Bethlehem—found a way to shut it out. They made it to school every day and stayed on top of their grades. As I read the steady diet of dreary news from the West Bank, I remembered what a fifteen-year-old high school student in Jenin refugee camp told me during the most violent days of the intifada: the best way to fight is to study.

ACKNOWLEDGMENTS

I am grateful to the many Palestinians and Israelis who contributed to this book with their views and information and who graciously endured my questions over the years. A tip of the hat to the Palestinian UNRWA assistants who put up with my occasional brusque manner and did the translations.

Thanks to UNRWA for allowing me to contribute to the humanitarian aid effort in the West Bank, and to the staff in the refugee camps and West Bank towns.

Gratitude to David Shearer, Pierre Bessuges, Majed Abu Kubi, Beatrice Metaireau, Juliette Touma, Allegra Pacheco and others at the Jerusalem office of the UN Office for the Coordination of Humanitarian Affairs (OCHA).

Thanks to the stand-up Israelis in Breaking the Silence, B'Tselem, Peace Now, Yesh Gvul, Machsom Watch, and any like-minded groups I may have omitted for their efforts for peace. The people are too numerous to list but know who they are and that I appreciate their help.

Personal thanks to Kimberly Abbott, Abdullah Abu Tahoun, Mahmuda Ali, Bahia Amra, David Balham, Blixt, Scott Custer, Dror Etkes, Hanan Gurel, Peretz Kidron, Gwyn Lewis, Sarit Michaeli, Ori Nir, Gustav Nordstrom, Maria Traficanti, Peter from the U.K., Greta Van Bleek, Tom White, and Yousef with his good humor. An extra thank you to veteran peacekeeper and analyst Corinna Kuhl for the encouragement.

Thanks to Helene Atwan, the director of Beacon Press, for her sharp eye and patience in editing this book, and to all the other staff for their keen attention and hard work.

NOTES

INTRODUCTION

1. The Golan Heights was captured from Syria and is still occupied by Israel. As Syrian territory, the Golan's future will require a settlement between Syria and Israel.
2. The second intifada never officially ended, but wide-scale military exchanges had largely stopped by 2005. B'Tselem, the Israeli human rights group, maintains statistics on casualties and says (www.btselem.org/English/Statistics/Casualties.asp) that 4,057 Palestinians were killed by Israelis and 1,020 Israelis were killed by Palestinians between September 29, 2000, and January 31, 2007. B'Tselem says the figures change from time to time due to ongoing research.

ONE: "GOD GAVE IT TO US"

1. In its annual report for 2006, released in February 2007, Peace Now cited settlement population figures from Israel's Interior Ministry. The report is available at www.peacenow.org.il.
2. This report can also be found on Peace Now's Web site (see n. 1).
3. Israel Shahak and Norton Mezvinsky, *Jewish Fundamentalism in Israel,* new ed. (London: Pluto Press, 2004), 78.
4. Ibid., 159.
5. Gershom Gorenberg, *The Accidental Empire: Israel and the Birth of the Settlements, 1967–1977* (New York: Times Books, Henry Holt, 2006), 367.
6. See www.peacenow.org.il/site/en/peace.asp?pi=57.
7. Geoffrey Aronson, *Sharon's War for the Settlements,* Report on Israeli Settlement in the Occupied Territories, Foundation for Middle East Peace, vol. 12, no. 2 (March–April 2002), citing a figure given by Israeli member of Knesset Avshalom Vilan of Meretz.
8. Peretz Kidron, comp. and ed., *Refusenik! Israel's Soldiers of Conscience* (London: Zed Books, 2004), 93.
9. Yigal Sarna, *Yediot Aharanot,* March 19, 2002, cited by Aronson, *Sharon's War for the Settlements.*
10. The report is available from Peace Now, www.peacenow.org.il/site/en/

peace.asp?pi=58, or from the government of Israel, Ministry of Foreign Affairs, www.mfa.gov.il/MFA/Government/Law/Legal+Issues+and+Rulings/Summary+of+Opinion+Concerning+Unauthorized+Outposts+-+Talya+Sason+Adv.htm.

TWO: CHECKPOINT

1. UNRWA's mandate is to assist registered refugees, that is, Palestinians or their descendants who lost homes or means of livelihood as a result of the 1948 war. The question of whom we could help became murky at times, unless a person was ill or injured, in which case we always provided aid.

THREE: LONG WAY AROUND

1. Tom Segev, *One Palestine, Complete: Jews and Arabs Under the British Mandate* (New York: Henry Holt, 2001), 421–22; first published in Israel as *Yamei Kalaniot* (Jerusalem: Keter Publishers, 1999).

FOUR: CLAMPDOWN

1. Martin Kolinsky, "The Collapse and Restoration of Public Security," in *Britain and the Middle East in the 1930s*, ed. Michael J. Cohen and Martin Kolinsky (London: Macmillan, 1992), 158, as cited in Tom Segev, *One Palestine, Complete: Jews and Arabs Under the British Mandate* (New York: Henry Holt, 2001), 424.

FIVE: TERROR

1. Jerusalem Media and Communication Center, *Palestinian Opinion Pulse* 5, no. 14 (July 2004): 6. The figure of 76 percent included respondents in the West Bank, and in the Gaza Strip, where support usually ran higher. By comparison, in May 1997, only 24 percent of Palestinians supported suicide operations, the poll said. See www.jmcc.org/publicpoll/pop/04/jul/pop14.pdf.
2. Palestinian Center for Policy and Survey Research, Palestinian Public Opinion Poll No. 9, October 7–14, 2003. At the same time, 85 percent of those polled said they supported a mutual halt to the violence.
3. Americans for Peace Now, *Middle East Report* 3, no. 31 (Washington, DC, February 25, 2002). The report cites news stories in *Ma'ariv* on February 20, 2002, and *Ha'aretz* and the *Jerusalem Post* on February 25, 2002. British troops in nineteenth-century colonial Sudan are said to have wrapped the remains of Muslim suicide attackers in pigskin, and it has been done in various conflicts since then.

SIX: OPERATION DEFENSIVE SHIELD

1. The United Nations Development Programme, the United Nations Children's Fund, and the World Food Programme ran substantial assistance missions in the occupied territories at the time.

2. Report of the [United Nations] secretary-general prepared pursuant to General Assembly resolution ES-10/10 adopted on May 7, 2002, section 29. B'Tselem, Human Rights Watch, and Amnesty International also cited testimony from Palestinians who said they were used as human shields; and former soldiers confirmed to me in 2006 that using Palestinians as human shields had been a common practice.
3. Tom Segev, *One Palestine, Complete: Jews and Arabs under the British Mandate* (New York: Henry Holt, 2001), 425.
4. These figures are disputed. Globalsecurity.org, the on-line security and military-information organization, states that the figure of 40,000 square meters (160 meters [525 feet] by 250 meters [820 feet]) damaged by combat is based on its own analysis of IDF imagery. The IDF said the central destroyed area was a quarter of that size; the UN said it was larger.

   Amnesty International said: "About 169 houses with 374 apartment units have been completely destroyed with additional units partially destroyed." It cited UNRWA as the source. (Amnesty International, *Israel and the Occupied Territories Shielded from Scrutiny: IDF Violations in Jenin and Nablus,* November 4, 2002).

   Human Rights Watch said that at least 140 mostly multifamily buildings were completely destroyed and more than 200 others were damaged badly enough that they were uninhabitable or unsafe. (Human Rights Watch, *Jenin: IDF Military Operations,* May 2002).

   Amnesty International and Human Rights Watch both said in their reports that 4,000 persons had been made homeless. Israel says that those numbers are exaggerated.
5. From Gush Shalom, www.gush-shalom.org/archives/kurdi_eng.html#1. The statement first appeared in *Yediot Aharanot* on May 31, 2002, and was translated from the Hebrew and reprinted in English by Gush Shalom.
6. Amnesty Intenational, *Israel and the Occupied Territories.*

SEVEN: REFLECTIONS: ISRAELIS AND PALESTINIANS

1. Israel Radio later reported that Leena had threatened a soldier, who fired warning shots in the air and at her feet, and shot her only after she brandished a knife. A Palestinian who was present at the demonstration denied that Leena pulled a knife but said she carried and waved a Palestinian flag. He said Leena and others fled into an apartment building, where she was found and shot.

EIGHT: "CLOUDS RAINING STONES"

1. To meet the terms of the amended Foreign Assistance Act of 1961, section 301 (c), UNRWA must certify to the U.S. State Department that it is "taking all possible measures to assure that U.S. funds do not benefit terrorists and those receiving military training from guerrilla groups." This requirement

and other aspects of the GAO's investigation are contained in a November 17, 2003, letter to two U.S. senators and two members of the House of Representatives and can be found at www.gao.gov/new.items/d04276r.pdf.

2. According to B'Tselem, from the start of the second intifada through January 31, 2007, in both the occupied territories and Israel, 815 Palestinian minors were killed by Israeli security forces, and 119 Israeli minors were killed by Palestinians. The statistics, which can change as they are updated from time to time, can be found at www.btselem.org/english/Statistics/Casualties.asp.

TEN: ALMONDS

1. The idea of "transfer," or shifting the Palestinians to Jordan by force or by offering a financial incentive, did not originate with Ze'evi but dates back to a strand of early Zionist thinking that has briefly resurfaced from time to time.

ELEVEN: SUMMER WARS

1. "Suicide bombings since Israeli-Palestinian truce," Associated Press, April 17, 2006.
2. Médecins du Monde (MDM)—France, *The Ultimate Barrier: Impact of the Wall on the Palestinian Health Care System,* February 2005. Report available at www.medecinsdumonde.org.
3. World Bank, Technical Team Report, *An Update on Palestinian Movement, Access and Trade in the West Bank and Gaza,* August 15, 2006. The report added: "Internal fragmentation also interferes with governance and the maintenance of public order, and disrupts access to education and health care. The bank estimates that internal closures accounted for approximately half of the decline in real GDP (perhaps some 15 percent) observed between 2000 and 2002. The Separation Barrier adds a particular set of movement and access difficulties, and has been estimated by the Bank to cost the Palestinian economy some 2–3 percentage points of GDP per annum." The report can be found at http://siteresources.worldbank.org/INTWESTBANKGAZA/Resources/M&ASummary+Main+MapAugust31.pdf.
4. World Bank, *West Bank and Gaza: Economic Update and Potential Outlook,* March 15, 2006. The report can be found at http://siteresources.worldbank.org/INTWESTBANKGAZA/Resources/WBGEconomicUpdateandPotentialOutlook.pdf.
5. World Bank, Report No. 36320 WBG, *West Bank and Gaza: Country Economic Memorandum, Growth in West Bank and Gaza; Opportunities and Constraints,* vol. 1, September 2006. The report can be found at http://siteresources.worldbank.org/INTWESTBANKGAZA/Resources/294264-1159361805492/CEMSept25,06.pdf.

6. UN Office for the Coordination of Humanitarian Affairs, *The Olive Harvest in the West Bank and Gaza,* October 2006.
7. International Crisis Group (ICG), *Palestinians, Israel, and the Quartet: Pulling Back from the Brink, Middle East Report N°54—13 June 2006* citing *Ha'aretz,* March 23, 2006, as its source for the quote. The ICG report added: "Similarly, a senior UN official stated that the sentiment in Washington was that Palestinians should 'survive, but not thrive.'" Crisis Group interview, April 2006.

FOURTEEN: "EDUCATING THE INDIANS"

1. See www.machsomwatch.org.
2. The IDF installed the turnstile system at Huwwara after the army training video was made.

FIFTEEN: "NOT ALLOWED TO SLEEP IN JERUSALEM"

1. United Nations Office for the Coordination of Humanitarian Affairs, *OCHA, Humanitarian Update, occupied Palestinian territory,* August 2006.

SIXTEEN: SOLDIERS' TALES

1. The story was read aloud in translation from the Hebrew by another soldier that day. It also appeared, in slightly different wording, in the English-language booklet of testimonies collected by Breaking the Silence, *Soldiers Speak Out about Their Service in Hebron* (Jerusalem, 2004), 25. The group's English-language Web site is www.breakingthesilence.org.il.
2. Ibid., 10–11.
3. Soldiers told me, and Breaking the Silence, that "verifying" or "confirming a kill" was a practice, often by an investigating officer, of throwing grenades or firing several rounds at the body of a Palestinian who had been shot and was believed to be dead.

SEVENTEEN: "I'M GOING TO BUY A POPSICLE, THEN I'M GOING TO KILL SOME ARABS"

1. Israel Shahak and Norton Mezvinsky, *Jewish Fundamentalism in Israel,* new ed. (London: Pluto Press, 2004), 100–101.
2. Gershom Gorenberg, *The Accidental Empire: Israel and the Birth of the Settlements, 1967–1977* (New York: Times Books, Henry Holt, 2006), 370–71.
3. Gideon Levy, "Twilight Zone/Mean Streets," *Ha'aretz,* September 8, 2005.
4. Breaking the Silence, *Soldiers Speak Out about Their Service in Hebron* (Jerusalem, 2004), 17.

EIGHTEEN: THE ESSENCE OF VICTORY

1. Ze'ev Jabotinsky, *Writings: On the Road to Statehood* (in Hebrew) (Jerusalem, 1959), 251–60, quoted in *The Iron Wall: Israel and the Arab World,* by Avi Shlaim (London: Penguin Books, 2000), 13–14.

2. David Ben-Gurion, *My Talks with Arab Leaders* (Jerusalem, 1972), 80, quoted in *The Iron Wall,* by Shlaim, 18–19.
3. Gershom Gorenberg, *The Accidental Empire: Israel and the Birth of the Settlements, 1967–1977* (New York: Times Books, Henry Holt, 2006), 172.
4. Ibid., 173.
5. Dror Etkes, *Peretz's Mixed Message: Defense Minister Talks about Peace but OKs Construction in Isolated Settlement,* in ynet news, www.ynetnews.com/Ext/Comp/ArticleLayout/CdaArticlePrintPreview/1,2506,L-3353607,00.html (January 17, 2007).
6. Amos Harel, "Goodbye, Cruel West Bank," *Ha'aretz,* August 19, 2005.
7. Ami Ayalon, *The Interview,* with Owen Bennett-Jones, BBC World Service radio, January 7, 2007.
8. Avraham Burg, "The End of Zionism," *Guardian,* September 15, 2003. Burg's essay originally appeared in Hebrew in *Yediot Aharanot,* was translated and adapted by *The Forward,* and was reprinted in the *Guardian* with the permission of *The Forward.*

NINETEEN: WORLD CUP QUARTER FINAL

1. Ami Ayalon, *The Interview,* with Owen Bennett-Jones, BBC World Service radio, January 7, 2007.